Judgment and Sensibility

Judgment and Sensibility

Religion and Stratification

E. Digby Baltzell

Edited and with an introduction by

Howard G. Schneiderman

Transaction Publishers
New Brunswick (U.S.A.) and London (U.K.)

Library of Congress Catalog Number: 93-41656
ISBN: 1-56000-048-1
Printed in the United States of America

Library of Congress Cataloging-in-Publication Data
Baltzell, E. Digby (Edward Digby), 1915-
Judgment and sensibility : religion and stratification / E. Digby Baltzell ; edited and with an introduction by Howard G. Schneiderman.
p. cm.
Includes bibliographical references and index.
ISBN 1-56000-048-1
1. Social classes—United States. 2. Upper classes—United States. 3. Elite (Social sciences)—United States. 4. WASPS (Persons)—United States. I. Schneiderman, Howard G. II. Title.
HN90.S6B34 1994
305.5'2'0973—dc20 93-41656
CIP

Among the blessings of my life, I rate my intellectual and personal ties with a small number of former graduate students very near the top. The inner core of these students attended my graduate course in Social Organization at Penn during the academic years of 1970 and 1971, among them Howard Schneiderman who has been one of my closest friends ever since. For his untiring devotion in putting together two volumes of my writings, of which this is the second, I thank him with all my heart and with all my mind.

Contents

Introduction
Thoughts Out of Season: E. Digby Baltzell and the Protestant Establishment

Howard G. Schneiderman

Judgment and Sensibility is the second volume of the collected essays of E. Digby Baltzell, one of the keenest observers and analysts of America's upper classes since Thorstein Veblen. Spanning four decades of writing, these essays cover a wide range of topics, including contemporary politics, democratic elitism, Puritanism, Judaism, higher education, urbanization, and the U.S. Supreme Court, among others. As in *The Protestant Establishment Revisited,*[1] the first volume of Baltzell's papers, these subjects are observed and analyzed through the sociological lenses of class, status, power, and authority.

Underlying many of these essays is the idea that taking the lead, and setting the tone, in America is never easy. What makes the problem of leadership in America so difficult to resolve is that class, status, power, and authority, which are inextricably connected to leadership, tend also to violate the basic egalitarian ethos at the core of American culture. This fundamentally paradoxical relationship between hierarchy and equality is addressed in many different ways in the essays collected here, as it is in all of Baltzell's writings.

Although the Protestant Establishment, about which Baltzell has written both admiringly and critically, is almost invisible in American political and cultural life today, it provided him with a virtual case study of how class and authority are intimately connected. For Baltzell, an open and authoritative establishment is a necessary and desirable part of the process of securing responsible leaders in a democratic society. This theme is woven into the fabric of the essays in this volume with both judgment and sensibility, and accounts for a certain "thoughts out of season" quality to the book because Baltzell's ideas often go head to head against the prevailing academic anti-elitist conventional wisdom of our day.

Judgment and sensibility, however, imply no lack of passion, of which Baltzell has plenty. Witness the following from "Blue-Blood Blues," one of the essays collected in this volume: "Throughout most of this so-called Century of the Common Man," writes Baltzell, "the subject of class in America has had much the same closed-closet status as masturbation and fornication: ladies and gentlemen simply did not talk about such things in mixed company or in public. Since the '60s, however, when every damned thing was dragged out of the closet, and ladylike and gentlemanly manners were dismissed as elitist, everybody has been free to talk about anything, anywhere at anytime, few suspecting that a world without closets might already be well on its way to barbarism. In this new climate of opinion, I should not have been taken by surprise when one of my students at Penn during the '70s came up to me after class and asked: "What's *your* class background professor?" "None of your business, my boy," I replied with a smile. Nor should I have been enraged as I watched Diane Sawyer rudely ask George Bush, in front of millions of TV viewers, to explain why people thought of him as a wimp. Had I been Bush, I would have kicked her, but Bush did his best to answer her patiently and politely."[2]

The passion, and even anger, pouring forth from the above passage would surprise no one who knows Digby Baltzell and his work. A sociologist of the first order, Baltzell earned his Ph.D at Columbia University in 1952 after studying with Robert Merton, Paul Lazarsfeld, Robert Lynd, C. Wright Mills, and Robert MacIver among others during the mid- to late-1940s.[3] But unlike many sociologists of his generation, of whom one is reminded of Nietzsche's stinging critique of academic scholars, in *Thoughts Out of Season:* "What a school of politeness...to take everything objectively, to be angry at nothing, to love nothing, to understand everything—makes one gentle and pliable,"[4] Baltzell has demonstrated again and again in his work that understanding does not come from facts alone, but from a passionate involvement with them. In his private and personal life Baltzell is a kind and charming man, a very polite man, in a word, a gentleman. In his public and professional life as a noted sociologist and historian, however, Baltzell can be the intellectual equivalent of a tough street fighter, as evidenced in many of the essays collected here.

A member of the upper class himself, Baltzell has carved out a reputation as "a WASP with a sting,"[5] for his criticism of the WASP upper class's continuously decreasing contribution to national leadership positions. In a trilogy of classic books—*Philadelphia Gentlemen,*[6] *The Protestant Establishment,*[7] and *Puritan Boston and Quaker Philadelphia*[8]—Baltzell has written what amounts to a fully articulated sociological history of the rise and fall of the American upper class as an authoritative establishment in American history. This theme was also the focus of many of Baltzell's essays collected in *The Protestant Establishment Revisited,* as well as those in this volume. But by the mid-1960s the sun had set on upper-class authority in America, just as it would set on many other traditional sources of authority by the decade's end. Thus, in Baltzell's writings one hears echoes of lament and anger whirling through his thoughts about the decline of authority in American society: "I think the '60s were a tragic disaster," he has written, "and we're still paying for it. It was a great revolt against civilization...."[9] But things were not always as such.

At its height, according to Baltzell, the Protestant Establishment, dominated by a group of wealthy and powerful consanguine families of old-stock, white, Anglo-Saxon Protestants, or as they are now generally called, "WASPs," provided the nation with an authoritative core of important and influential leaders. These old-stock WASP families exercised national authority in the presidency, as well as the cabinet, in diplomatic circles, and in other governmental jobs. They took the lead in legal and juridical roles, and as heads of important corporations, banks, investment houses, and other commercial interests, not to mention churches and colleges throughout America. In short, they set the tone for American political, business, and cultural life. As such, WASPs were less an ethnic group than a high-status group. The Protestant Establishment's power and authority, as well as its social class and status, rather than its ethnicity, were driving forces in American history and contemporary society. Yet it must be said, and I think that Baltzell would agree, that the Protestant Establishment is now all but gone from the American scene; or as Robert C. Christopher, the author of *Crashing the Gates: The De-Wasping of America's Power Elite,* says "relatively few members of the national social aristocracy have made truly major contributions to the political or economic development of the United States in the last four decades."[10]

But what are the cultural and social conditions within which an establishment could effectively operate? Taking the lead, and setting the tone, in a democracy is never easy, neither for individuals nor for a social class. Complex and imperfect, democracy has been called, by no less a judge than Winston Churchill, the worst form of government—except for all the rest. The problem of leadership in America is particularly difficult to resolve because our democracy is beset with two special paradoxes not shared by more hierarchically oriented societies. The first paradox—the paradox of leadership itself—involves the ideal of egalitarianism and the reality of inequality of social class, status, power, and authority. These elements of inequality violate the egalitarian ethos at the core of American culture, while being indispensable to its survival—an uncomfortable fact of democratic life with which we must always live. The second paradox—the paradox of social mobility—also involves the ideals of egalitarianism, which stress the principle of an open class system in which everyone has the opportunity to rise to positions of leadership and success based on merit. But this meritocratic principle of achievement often leads to a very different reality in which ascription, as well as achievement, come to bear on success. After all, successful men and women always want to pass on to their children whatever advantages they themselves have earned, in the form of enhanced and unequal opportunities for education and a leg up in their careers, thus violating the basic premises of our egalitarian values. Both of these paradoxes are always at play in American society, and, as we shall see, they are part of the story of how the Protestant Establishment was able to command deference and to exercise authority in America until about the middle of this century.

Oddly, it was not when the Protestant Establishment was at the height of its authority, a period referred to by Joseph Alsop in his memoirs as the "WASP Ascendancy,"[11] and somewhat earlier by Baltzell and me as the period of "WASP Hegemony,"[12] but only when it was declining, that the acronym WASP came into existence. So much a part of our contemporary language is the term WASP that many readers may find it curious that it was nowhere to be found in the best and most definitive dictionaries before the mid-1960s. This is probably partly due to the fact that like many newly minted words, no standardized usage had been associated with it. The term WASP, however, has been in use since the 1950s, at least among intellectuals, but didn't enter our general usage until the mid-1960s when it was made popular by Baltzell in his widely read book, *The Protestant Establishment,* which chronicled the decline of WASP authority in American society.

While lacking a standardized definition, the term WASP is closely identified with the American upper class, as well as with various elites in the American system of political and social stratification. For instance, *Webster's Third International Dictionary* defines WASP as: "an American of northern European and especially British stock and of Protestant background; especially a member of the dominant and most privileged class of people in the U.S." Expanding on this same theme of stratification, Christopher Hitchens, the author of *Blood, Class, and Nostalgia: Anglo-American Ironies,* citing Baltzell, wrote about WASPs that "somewhere in the subtext of all this is the ticklish question of race and the awkward matter of class. Ethnic hierarchy in America actually confuses the two things in a revealing minor way, since the word WASP, which denotes a racial and religious group, is only ever applied to a certain social layer of it. (George Bush is a WASP. George Wallace may have been a white Protestant of Anglo-Saxon descent, and even rather vocal on all three points, but a WASP he was not.)"[13] To this last point we might add that while presidents such as Theodore Roosevelt, William Howard Taft, Woodrow Wilson, and Franklin Delano Roosevelt were WASPs, Lyndon Johnson, Richard Nixon, Gerald Ford, Jimmy Carter, and William Jefferson Clinton are not; and although after his presidency Ronald Reagan was knighted by Queen Elizabeth, neither was he a WASP despite being wealthy, white Protestant, and of Irish descent. But if only some Americans of Anglo-Saxon heritage are WASPs, how did they become so? How did a relatively small group of families become a national upper class, and how did a relatively small subgroup among these families come to have disproportionate power and authority in America from just after the Civil War to just after the Second World War?

A century and a half ago America was very different than it is today. The vast majority of Americans were white, of Anglo-Saxon origin, and Protestant. They lived in small towns, not large cities, or on farms, not in suburbs. Wealth, status, and power were diffused throughout these small communities in ways that are largely foreign to us now. For instance, Alexis de Tocqueville, the author of *Democracy in America,* and the most prescient observer of American society, could truthfully write in 1835 that "in America there are but few wealthy persons; nearly all Americans have to take a profession."[14] And Tocqueville knew that these professions were sources of prestige and authority in the small communities of which America was composed. Not great wealth, but rather eminence, as a minister in a local church, or as a lawyer or jurist, or merchant, or doctor, commanded deference and authority. Thus, Henry Adams, the brilliant author and historian, born in 1838, and scion of one of America's leading establishment families—son of Charles Francis Adams, the American ambassador to Great Britain, grandson of President John Quincy Adams, and great-grandson of President John Adams—could look back upon his own childhood and remember that "down to 1850, and even later, New England society was still directed by the professions. Lawyers, physicians, professors, merchants were classes, and acted not as individuals, but as though they were clergymen, and each profession were a church."[15] All of this is to say that authority in America until just after the Civil War was highly localized, as was deference, power, and leadership in general.

Great changes were in store for America, however, in the aftermath of the Civil War. Throughout the 1870s and 1880s urbanization and industrialization, coupled with the growth of railroads and large corporations, broke down small town ties of community, and in Richard Hofstadter's terms "transformed the old society and revolutionized the distribution of power and prestige."[16] This status revolution was accompanied by a significant shift in population from rural to urban America. In 1850, for instance, only 15 percent of Americans lived in cities, but by 1880 this percentage had just about doubled, and by 1890 about 35 percent lived in urban areas. The tidal waves of immigration that began during this period helped swell the urban population even further, and by 1920 more than half of all Americans lived in urban areas. The trend toward urbanization has continued to our day. In 1870 only about one in four Americans lived in cities; since 1970 this percentage has been stood on its head, with only one in four Americans not living in cities or their immediate vicinity.

Immigration also changed the ethnic makeup of America. In 1790 over 80 percent of the population was white, and between 60 and 70 percent of the white population was of English ancestry. Of the rest of the white population, about 10 percent was Irish, 8 percent Scotch, and

9 percent German in ancestry. By 1920 over 90 percent of the population was white, but only 44 percent of the white population was of English ancestry (while Americans of Irish ancestry were about 11 percent of the population, the proportion of German Americans had nearly doubled to about 16 percent.) Also, by 1920 other ethnicities—Italian, Polish, Russian, and Spanish, for example—accounted for almost 30 percent of white Americans. By 1990 about 80 percent of the population was white, but only about 25 percent of the white population was of English ancestry; Irish Americans, however, now accounted for about 20 percent of the white population, and German Americans matched those of English ancestry at about 25 percent.

But the great post–Civil War transformation was especially noticeable with respect to wealth. When Tocqueville published the second part of *Democracy in America* in 1840, there were not even twenty millionaires in the entire United States, and he was entirely correct when he wrote that "though there are rich men, the class of rich men does not exist; for these rich individuals have no feelings or purposes, no traditions or hopes, in common; there are individuals, therefore, but no definite class."[17] But the industrialization of America helped change this situation. In the thirty years between 1870 and 1900 the national wealth quadrupled, and the number of millionaires grew enormously. By 1893 it was estimated that there were over four thousand millionaires in the United States, and at least one hundred and twenty men who were worth over $10 million each. In fact, in 1892 the U.S. Census Bureau estimated that about 9 percent of American families accounted for over 70 percent of the nation's wealth. This trend toward accumulating wealth has continued, and in this regard it is notable that according to a recent estimate[18] there are over 3.2 million households in the United States today worth over $1 million. It is also worth noting that among America's seventy-three billionaires listed in *Forbes* "Four Hundred Richest People in America" for 1992, there were a few WASPs such as Henry Lea Hillman, but many more self-made men, such as Henry Ross Perot. And while David Rockefeller, Laurance Spelman Rockefeller, and Paul Mellon represent a few old-money families, John Werner Kluge, Samuel and Donald Newhouse, Ronald Perelman, Ted Arison, Edgar Bronfman, Leslie H. Wexner, Jay and Robert Pritzker, Samuel LeFrak, Kirk Kerkorian, and Milton Petrie, among others, represent the enormous drive and achievement of talented individuals from religious and ethnic groups that have been excluded from the precincts of the Protestant Establishment, but who have succeeded in leaving most old-stock families trailing in the dust.

While today great wealth is scattered among millions of families of all racial, ethnic, and religious backgrounds, during the period of the status revolution it was concentrated in the hands of relatively few. This newly created wealth formed the basis of a new class of rich men, a largely WASP business aristocracy of the sort that Tocqueville had said was absent from American society as late as the 1840s. Writing in 1955, Talcott Parsons described the process by which this business aristocracy had come into existence as follows:

> There is a continuing tendency for earlier economic developments to leave a "precipitate" of upper groups, the positions of whose members are founded in the achievements of their ancestors, in this case relatively recent ones. By historical necessity these groups are strongest in the older parts of the country. Hence the cities of the Eastern seaboard have tended to develop groups that are the closest approach we have... to an aristocracy. They have generally originated in business interests....[19]

Following Parsons, Baltzell, in *Philadelphia Gentlemen,* showed how the newly rich industrialists and their families eventually formed a national upper class, which then drifted apart from local community roots.

This new national upper class was formed in American cities in the latter part of the nineteenth century when successful money-makers—businessmen, merchants, and bankers—many of whom came from low social class backgrounds, founded families whose individual members through marriage, private education, and club membership associated themselves with old-money families. Through these associations, generation after generation, they came to constitute a business aristocracy in which upper-class values, wealth, and power were preserved. This business aristocracy, as Baltzell put it, "too often placed the desire for material comfort and security above the duties of political and intellectual leadership."[20] Nevertheless, up to the Second World War, upper-class WASP families, living in fashionable neighborhoods and listed in the *Social Register,* helped to shape the business and cultural life of cities across the country. They educated their children at private prep schools, such as The Taft School, Groton, Hotchkiss, St. Mark's, St. Paul's, Foxcroft, and Choate, and colleges such as Princeton, Harvard, Yale, Vassar, and Smith among other elite colleges. They belonged to exclusive clubs—there are over two hundred and fifty listed in the *Social Register* today, from the Acorn in Philadelphia and the Algonquin in Boston to the Wilmington Country Club in Delaware and the Yale Club in New York—and helped shape the business and cultural life of cities across the country. At the beginning this WASP upper class was relatively open to new talent, and assimilated newly arrived individuals and their families into its ranks, but within a short time upper-class status appeared to be limited to old-stock Protestant families, which led Baltzell to ask "what is the future function of a predominantly Anglo-Saxon and Protestant upper class in an ethnically and religiously heterogeneous democracy?"[21]

This question invokes the image of declining class authority in America reminiscent of a similar situation described in Tocqueville's *Ancient Regime,*[22] which showed that when new men of talent, wealth, and power were refused membership in the French aristocracy by noblemen who drew a caste line, class authority failed and set the stage for the French Revolution. A similar crisis of leadership in America had developed by the mid-twentieth century because the white, Anglo-Saxon, and Protestant national upper class had, by excluding talented individuals and their families from membership because they were from ethnic and racial minority groups, become a privileged caste rather than an authoritative establishment,

The old local upper classes had been, by and large, based on social considerations of family, rather than on business connections and wealth, and they had been open to newer ethnic groups as well as to old-stock Protestant Americans of Anglo-Saxon heritage. Thus, as late as the 1870s, as Baltzell shows in essays in this volume,[23] Jews were assimilated into the local upper classes of American cities such as Boston, where Louis D. Brandeis, the future justice of the U. S. Supreme Court, could join exclusive patrician clubs. The son of a wealthy Jewish merchant who had immigrated to Louisville, Kentucky, from Prague in 1848, Brandeis entered Harvard Law School in 1875, and immediately rose to the top of his class. He soon became friends with many Boston brahmins, such as Samuel D. Warren, Jr., the son of a rich manufacturer, with whom he founded a law firm after graduation. Brandeis had no difficulty in joining the Union Club, or the Exchange, nor did anyone object to his joining and eventually becoming one of the directors of the Union Boat Club. Brandeis's experience was hardly singular, for before the 1880s and the coming of a new national WASP upper class, wealthy Jews, especially German Jews, were able to assimilate into the local upper classes of most American cities. Thus the Morgenthaus, Ochses, Sulzbergers, Strauses, Lehmans, and Guggenheims—families that are still well-known today—were an integral part of the nineteenth century New York establishment.

The new national upper class that formed in the 1880s was different from the old local upper classes. For one thing it was clearly anti-Semitic. Historians and sociologists have suggested that WASP anti-Semitism was a reaction to the enormous number of immigrants from Eastern Europe, and some, Baltzell included, have tried to distinguish this upper-class bigotry from other types by calling it "genteel," or "social" anti-Semitism; but, from another point of view, differences in degree aside, bigotry is bigotry no matter what it is called. In 1880 there were only about a quarter of a million Jews in America, but by 1920 there were over four million, and over 350,000 cramped into New York City's Lower East Side alone. About 80 percent of the four million American Jews in 1920 were of East European, as opposed to German, extraction. These new immigrants brought with them very different values, languages, and cultures than did the German Jews who were already well established here by the 1880s. Whatever the reasons, the new national upper class now became exclusively white, Anglo-Saxon, and Protestant, and began excluding Jews from the institutions that were associated with it. As Baltzell has shown, "upper class anti-Semitism was perhaps more blatantly displayed in the five decades after 1880 than at any other time in our history."[24]

By the 1890s Jews were being excluded from membership in patrician clubs throughout the country. In 1893, New York's Union League blackballed the son of one of its Civil War era founders, Jesse Seligman, because he was Jewish. And by 1913 President Woodrow Wilson decided against having Louis Brandeis in his Cabinet, after opposition to his appointment was voiced by patrician New Englanders who had invited Brandeis into their social circle in the 1870s and 1880s. Bankers, lawyers, real estate magnates, railroad tycoons, stockbrokers, and others from families such as the Astors, Baldwins, Cuttings, Depews, Elliotts, Fishes, Griswolds, Hewitts, Iselins, Jaffrays, Kanes, Livingstons, Martins, Newbolds, Otises, Posts, Roosevelts, Schuylers, Twombleys, Vanderbilts, and Winthrops were part of the national metropolitan WASP upper class, as were the Harrimans, Rockefellers, Tafts, Cabots, and Lodges. There were no Jews or other ethnic minorities among them.

This national WASP upper class paid more attention to wealth than to family, and was more conscious of ethnicity than the earlier local upper classes throughout America. Excluding all but WASPs, this national upper class gained a profound self-consciousness through a network of exclusive clubs, boarding schools, resorts, and Ivy League colleges that promulgated a subculture of common values and common norms of behavior, that is to say, common morals and manners. The need for commonality can be easily understood. The geographic distribution and larger numbers of the new national upper class required criteria beyond geographical propinquity, face-to-face dealings, and local intermarriages that had prevailed in the preindustrial local upper classes. In spite of its anti-Semitic and anti-ethnic bigotry, however, this new national upper class served an important purpose in America: It provided a pool of national leaders generally committed to liberal democracy. This was of no small value, for as the eminent political scientist V.O. Key, the author of *Southern Politics in State and Nation,* wrote in 1949, "the operation of democracy may depend on competition among conflicting sections of the `better element' for the support of the masses of voters. Hence, the workings of democracy require a considerable degree of disagreement within the upper classes.... In the absence of popular leadership from the 'better element,' the breach may be filled by persons and groups with few scruples and often little ability."[25]

Nothing illustrates Key's point better than Theodore Roosevelt's succession to the presidency in 1901, which marked the beginning of a cycle of presidents of upper-class origins, a cycle that lasted forty-four years, ending with the death of Franklin Delano Roosevelt in 1945. This cycle, which began at the turn of the century, reflected a new national upper class's contribution to the political leadership of the nation. The patrician reformer Theodore Roosevelt, having inherited considerable wealth, had a certain loathing for the self-made millionaires of his day, whom he said "made the till their fatherland." He was followed in office by two other establishment presidents, Taft, a Republican as was Roosevelt, and Wilson, a Democrat.

The election of 1912 shows the remarkable range of the new WASP upper class's interest in politics, and of its capacity to compete for the support of the masses as Key suggested it must. In this election the three patricians who served, or would serve, as president from 1901 through 1921 were all candidates, and represented different political parties and different political platforms. Theodore Roosevelt running as a Progressive outpolled Taft, the incumbent Republican, but lost the election to the Democrat, Woodrow Wilson. Following Wilson's administration, the 1920s were presided over by presidents of upper middle class backgrounds, Harding, Coolidge, and Hoover, thus interrupting, but not ending, the cycle. Franklin Delano Roosevelt and a host of fellow patricians of inherited wealth and privileged backgrounds came to Washington in the 1930s and 1940s, thus keeping the cycle going until at least 1945. Although big government was here to stay by the beginning of the century, the entry of the patrician into national political life infused it with a new sense of noblesse oblige.[26] Establishment figures such as Theodore Roosevelt, Taft, Wilson, and FDR entered political life to see that the huge machinery of government was administered honestly and efficiently.

Not all members of the new upper class, however, contributed to the leadership of the nation. In fact, relatively few did. Many observers actually felt that there was a shameful lack of responsible leaders in this country at the turn of the century. For example, James Bryce, author of *The American Commonwealth,* one of the best books ever written about our country, concluded that the majority of citizens pay so little attention to public affairs that "they willingly leave all but the most important to be dealt with by the few." Attributing this lack of interest to individualistic tendencies, Bryce suggested that an individual's interests and priorities are ordered as follows: "first, the occupation by which he makes his living..., secondly, his domestic concerns, his family and relatives and friends, thirdly,...his religious beliefs or observances, fourthly, his amusements or personal tastes, be they for sensual or for intellectual enjoyments, fifthly, his civic duty to the community."[27] Although Bryce was aware that the order of these interests varies from citizen to citizen, he was certain that civic duty would almost always rank last. As he said in *The American Commonwealth,* "individualism, the love of enterprise, and the pride in personal freedom, have been deemed by Americans not only their choicest, but their peculiar and exclusive possessions."[28] That these very American values born of democracy should be an obstacle to fulfilling the democratic spirit was an irony that Americans would have to deal with.[29] Basic to this complaint was an understanding that, as Bryce later said, "as a rule, that which the mass of any people desires is not to govern itself, but to be well governed."[30]

Also of concern was that the higher-status, better-educated classes from which public leaders were most likely to be drawn were most apt to be affected by the love of money, and that in practice they set the moral standard for all the rest. This, of course, is exactly what Baltzell sees as the function of an establishment. Indeed, early in this century when the Protestant Establishment was in its heyday, William James and others saw the leading political stratum drawn from the upper classes as a "tone-setting" class,[31] because they believed that it is this class that forms the standard not only for those who conduct public business but also to a great extent for the whole community. A tone-setting class, or what Baltzell calls "an establishment" should, according to James or Bryce, set a high standard. If it sets a low standard, tolerates base motives and actions, "it depraves the morality of the community...and politics are defiled and debased, selfishness and trickery are taken to be natural, and public life becomes the favorite hunting ground of unscrupulous and reckless men."[32] Once the moral or civic standard is lowered it is difficult to raise it again.

One of the best examples of the responsible patrician in politics was Theodore Roosevelt, a member of the solidly educated achieving classes willing to take the lead in civic duty, who, as a young man did not consider himself above going into local politics in the lower house of the New York legislature.But Roosevelt, who had served as the police commissioner of New York City from 1895 to 1897—just a few years before becoming president of the United States—was indeed the exception in terms of local politics. And while the WASP upper class contributed men such as Roosevelt to national business and politics, it effectively abandoned local politics, in many cases to the sometimes unscrupulous men of other ethnic backgrounds.

As America grew, there was plenty of room for talented individuals from outside this class to exercise their talents, especially in the cities of America. While a few cities, such as Philadelphia, which did not elect an Irish Catholic mayor until 1964, maintained WASP leadership through most of this century, most, such as Milwaukee, which elected its first Irish Catholic mayor in 1863, or Boston, which followed suit in 1885, were dominated by ethnic elites since the latter part of the nineteenth century. Thus New York City elected its first Irish Catholic mayor, William Grace, in 1881, its second, Hugh Grant, in 1889, followed by Thomas Gilroy, in 1893. With the exception of two WASP mayors, Seth Low and George McClellan, who were in office from 1902 to 1909,

New York had an unbroken string of seven Irish Catholic mayors from 1910, when William Gaynor was elected, through 1934 when an Episcopalian, Fiorello LaGuardia, son of a lapsed middle-class Italian Catholic father and an Austrian Jewish mother, was elected to the office. LaGuardia, who was mayor until 1945, was followed by another Irish Catholic mayor, William O'Dwyer, then by an Italian Catholic, Vincent Impellitteri, an upper-class German Catholic, Robert Wagner, and finally, after a half century of ethnic mayors, by a WASP, John Lindsay, in 1966. Following Lindsay's departure in 1973, New York elected its first Jewish mayor, Abraham Beame, in 1974, and its second Jewish mayor, Edward I. Koch, in 1978. Koch was followed by New York's first black mayor, David Dinkins.

If many of the great American cities were governed by ethnic minorities during the last hundred or so years, what effect did these new power holders have upon the authority of the Protestant Establishment? For one thing, the old-stock establishment based its authority on deference, in much the same way that Walter Bagehot said the English aristocracy had in the nineteenth century. Ironically, this process was at work in the Democratic party, which has been in this century, by and large, the party of immigrants, ethnics, and minorities. In the words of Andrew Hacker, a political scientist, "Ed Flynn might boss the Bronx, but he would defer to Franklin D. Roosevelt (of Harvard); Carmine De Sapio rides behind Averill Harriman (of Yale); and Jake Arvey cleared the way for Adlai Stevenson (of Princeton). The seeming inconsonance of the fact that the party of the immigrant accepted old-stock patricians as its leaders is good evidence of the deference that was paid to the *ancien regime.*"[33] The Protestant Establishment might not have governed the cities of America, but for the first half of this century it set the tone and the atmosphere of culture and politics at the national level.

But, if Baltzell is correct in telling us that the WASP establishment set the tone and atmosphere for the exercise of national authority, how and why had it been able to do so? Asked another way, what is an establishment? Simply put, it is a group of leaders within an elite whose families are part of an upper class. Those few members of any upper class who form an establishment stand in contrast to the majority, who are satisfied to have high status but little or no authority, in other words, to those who form a caste. The American establishment has been made up of WASP families such as the Adamses, Bayards, Breckinridges,

Frelinghuysens, Harrisons, Lees, Livingstons, Lodges, Roosevelts, Stevensons, Tafts, and Washburns, who have followed the aristocratic ethos that emphasizes the duty to lead, rather than the snobbish caste ethos that emphasizes only the right to privilege. Just four families, the Adams, Harrison, Roosevelt, and Taft families, for instance, have not only provided the nation with seven presidents among them (thus accounting for more than one-sixth of all our presidents), but have also contributed eleven governors, ten ambassadors, ten U.S. senators, twenty-seven members of the U.S. House of Representatives, six cabinet officers, and two justices of the U.S. Supreme Court, not to mention five mayors of major cities, and over fifty state and local offices and legislative positions.

These four families are representative of the sort of leadership provided by the Protestant Establishment. In fact, the U.S. presidency, the most visible position of leadership in the nation, has been dominated by establishment figures. Of our forty-one presidents, seventeen—Washington, both Adamses, Jefferson, Madison, Monroe, both Harrisons, Polk, Tyler, Taylor, both Roosevelts, Taft, Wilson, Kennedy, and Bush—have come from clearly upper-class backgrounds. And even though Kennedy was our only Catholic president, he was clearly upper class and educated as a WASP. But aside from the presidency, establishment families have provided more than their share of governors, justices and chief-justices of the U.S. Supreme Court, diplomats, U.S. senators and congressmen, and cabinet officers.

A moral force within the putatively amoral world of politics and power elites, an establishment of leaders drawn from upper-class families can protect freedom in modern democratic societies. Such an establishment of political, business, cultural, religious, and educational leaders succeeds in its moral function when it sets, follows, and enforces rules of fair play in contests of power and opinion. This point was brought home by the German sociologist Ralf Dahrendorf in his brilliant analysis of the post-World War II political elite in Germany. "This elite is a mere sociological category without social reality," he wrote, and "it is my thesis that the German political class has developed from unity without plurality, to plurality without unity, and that both these states are highly detrimental for the constitution of liberty.... Liberal democracy demands an established political class...[and] a democratic elite has to be united in status, and divided in politics."[34] Similarly, in one of his most penetrating insights into the sociological functions of an establishment—indeed, one that Baltzell favors quoting—Tocqueville wrote that "a powerful aristocracy does not merely shape the course of public affairs, it also guides opinion, sets the tone for writers, and lends authority to new ideas."[35] In other words, it has hegemony over society. Whereas Marxists see hegemony as a social evil, Tocqueville, like Dahrendorf, saw it as necessary to the well-being of society. Establishments give coherence to society. They do not eliminate conflict, but prevent it from ripping society apart.

One of the ironies of American history is that while power has been accessible to many, its sources remain hidden from the sight of most. This irony did not escape the eye of Reinhold Niebuhr, a leading theologian and social critic. "The knight of old knew about power. He sat on a horse, the symbol of military power," wrote Niebuhr, "but the power of the modern commercial community is contained in the 'counters' of stocks and bonds which are stored in the vaults of the bank. Such a community creates a culture in which nothing is known about power, however desperate the power struggles within it."[36] Those who have and control power in America are, as Niebuhr well knew, often protected from sight just below the edge of public scrutiny by egalitarian mores and traditions that deny their very existence.

It is this blind edge of the power structure of American society that marks the line between the upper-class authority of the establishment and the power elites. The genius of an establishment lies in its capacity to put moral brakes on power by applying an upper-class code of conduct and responsibility to it. This capacity was at work, for instance, when Joseph Welch, senior partner in the old-stock, patrician Boston law firm of Hale and Dorr, serving gratis as the U.S. Army's special counsel, stood up to Senator Joseph McCarthy and finally brought him down, ending the career of one of the most dangerous demagogues in American history. Nevertheless, McCarthyism marked the beginning of the end of establishment rule in American national politics. After all, it was the establishment itself that McCarthy attacked. Alger Hiss, a patrician from an old-stock Baltimore family, a graduate of Harvard Law School, was associated with other establishment figures, such as U.S. Supreme Court Justice Oliver Wendell Holmes, for whom he clerked, President Franklin Roosevelt, for whom he was a special adviser at Yalta, his friend former Secretary of State Dean Acheson, and the new secretary of state, John Foster Dulles. In 1950 Hiss was convicted of perjury for denying Whittaker Chambers's accusations that he was a Communist. That same year Senator McCarthy began his four-year campaign to rid the government of Communist sympathizers, and his attack on the establishment, especially on patricians such as Dean Acheson, whom McCarthy branded "a pompous diplomat in striped pants, with a phony British accent." Although the Protestant Establishment survived McCarthy's onslaught during one of the most disgraceful, and dangerous, periods in our history, it was already beginning to lose its legitimacy.

During the anarchic 1960s the legitimacy of the Protestant Establishment crumbled as conspiracy theories of history and society came to the fore, fostering the growth of cynicism about all forms of institutional authority in America. Thus in *Cultural Literacy,*[37] a well-known recent book that has been criticized as elitist by some on the academic left, E. D. Hirsch listed "the Establishment" as one of the ideas literate Americans should know. But for all the charges of elitism against him, Hirsch defined "the Establishment" in a cynical manner his critics would applaud. In the *Dictionary of Cultural Literacy,* he described "the Establishment" as follows: "Individuals and institutions that exercise social, economic, and political authority over a society. The term has a pejorative connotation because it suggests that political and economic power is in the hands of the few."[38] Perhaps all sociologists would agree with the first part of this description, but only a few would openly disagree with the pejorative connotation attached to the term.

A deceptive myth in liberal democracies like America is that civil liberties and freedom of expression are valued by most members of society, and most certainly by those at the bottom and middle of the social structure. But as Samuel Stouffer amply demonstrated in his classic study *Communism, Conformity, and Civil Liberties,*[39] and as others have found since, this is not the case. Such freedoms are always most highly valued and protected by the elite few who are better educated, and who believe in the liberal democratic tradition, and the last bulwark of freedom may well be, as Baltzell has suggested, "a unified Establishment from within which the leaders of at least two parties are chosen, who, in turn, compete for the people's votes of confidence, from differing points of view and differing standards of judgement, yet both assuming the absolute necessity of using fair means in accusing their legitimate opponents of fallibility rather than treason."[40] The sociological alternatives to rule by establishments have been, historically, rule by functionaries and bureaucrats or rule by demagogues, neither of which has proven satisfactory in protecting freedoms.

During this last century America has undergone a social revolution in leadership. Whereas the WASP upper class dominated America's political, economic, and intellectual elites up to the late 1940s, thus controlling the nation, today WASPs no longer have that control, nor perhaps does any other group. Thus Peter Schrag ended his cogent book, *The Decline of the WASP* by suggesting that "America is not on the verge of becoming two separate societies, one rich and white, the other poor and black. It is becoming, in all its dreams and anxieties, a nation of outsiders for whom no single style or ethic remains possible."[41] American leadership has for the last half century been increasingly dominated by atomized elites, like those in Germany described by Dahrendorf, rather than by an establishment. The difference is of some consequence, because an establishment is a real group, a *gemeinschaft,* or community, subject to all the forces of social control, that at least potentially can instill and enforce moral standards in its members, if not society at large. An elite, however, is a *gesellschaft,* not a real group, but merely a convenient sociological category not subject to the forces of social control, and not a moral entity.

The castelike exclusivity and bigotry of the Protestant Establishment served to destroy its class authority. Yet America's best democratic traditions might still be best served by having an establishment of some sort to provide moral authority and leadership to the nation. Of course, those traditions dictate that we should choose the most talented available men and women to represent us in positions of moral and political leadership, regardless of their class, religious, ethnic, or racial backgrounds. But we should not be surprised if these individuals try to pass on to their children all the advantages they can, nor if these individuals and their families intermarry with each other and constitute a new establishment—albeit one more open to talented newcomers, and less exclusive than its predecessor.

In this regard it is notable that the most publicized and interesting recent political marriage in America was not between WASPs, and may reflect a new establishment in the making. In June 1990, Andrew Cuomo, the son of New York's Governor Mario Cuomo, married Kerry Kennedy, the daughter of the late Robert Kennedy, who was United States senator from New York, United States attorney general, and candidate for the presidency when he was assassinated in 1968. This very newsworthy marriage brought together two of America's most powerful political families, and Catholic families, no less. The Kennedys, perhaps America's best-known Irish Catholics, are by birth, education, and achievement, one of the few non-WASP families in what remains of the Protestant Establishment. The bride is the great-granddaughter of John Francis Fitzgerald, a mayor of Boston and a United States congressman, the granddaughter of Joseph Patrick Kennedy, a self-made millionaire, and ambassador to Great Britain, the niece of President John F. Kennedy, and Senator Edward Kennedy, the daughter of Senator Robert Kennedy, and the sister of United States Congressman Joseph P. Kennedy II. She has a law degree, and is executive director of the Robert F. Kennedy Memorial Center, a human rights organization. The Cuomos, by contrast, are a newcomer family to America's political elite, an Italian-American family that produced one of the nation's most powerful governors. The groom, a second generation politician who has just been appointed to a post in the Clinton administration, has prepared himself for politics by running a New York City organization that builds transitional housing for the homeless. That Kennedys and Cuomos now stand shoulder to shoulder with Rockefellers, Tafts, Duponts, and other scions of the old Protestant Establishment, hints that the open class principle may be overcoming the tendency to caste.

One comment by Governor Cuomo on the day of the wedding, however, as reported in *The New York Times*, reveals some of the differences between new men of power, such as the governor, and establishment types such as the Kennedys. After having been urged repeatedly by his son, Andrew, to wear morning coat and ascot, the governor finally refused, saying "penguins look good in tails, birds look good in tails. Tails are the ultimate expression of form over substance. Who likes them? Probably three people in the country, and I would neither vote for those people nor appoint them to any office." Perhaps the governor had forgotten just how splendid the bride's uncle, President Kennedy, had looked in tails at his inaugural ball. But then again, the governor, a man of substantial intellect who graduated *summa cum laude* from St. Johns University in 1953, did not have the privileged upbringing of President Kennedy, who graduated from two of the Protestant Establishment's favorite schools, Choate and Harvard, where he learned the morals and manners of the upper class into which he became assimilated. Undoubtedly, the most famous and memorable words ever spoken by President Kennedy were those from his inaugural address: "Ask not what your country can do for you, but what you can do for your country." What most people do not know is that in his welcoming address to the boys in JFK's class at Choate, the headmaster, George St. John, had uttered similar words: "Always remember, it is not what Choate can do for you, but what you can do for Choate." Thus did the future president learn lessons about both form and substance, and later felt as much at home in tails as in the Oval Office. One would expect the governor's son, now part of an establishment family, to learn to feel more at home in tails than his father. If the remnants of the old Protestant Establishment can manage to assimilate new families into its precincts, and inculcate ideals of public service and commitment to liberal democracy, it may yet survive and provide the nation with leadership, as it did earlier in the century. But will it do so this time as a properly open establishment, accepting achievement, rather than ascription, as its basic principle of inclusion? There are reasons to think that it may, as well as that it may not.

If the Protestant Establishment's values of achievement, conscience, industry, antisensuality, and civic-mindedness have become the backbone of American values, as Richard Brookhiser, in *The Way of the WASP,*[42] makes the case that they have, since the 1960s they have been challenged by a new emphasis on ascriptive values. No establishment can survive without deference, and there can be no deference without a commonly shared culture that maintains at least a modicum of consensus.[43] Throughout this century successful individuals, and their families, of Irish, Jewish, Italian, and black backgrounds, were excluded from the WASP upper class; therefore they established their own upper classes. And according to Nelson W. Aldrich, Jr., in *Old Money: The Mythology of America's Upper Class,* they bought into WASP culture even as they founded their own "schools, summer resorts, clubs—and bred their own patricians and aristocrats. They also established their own suburban enclaves and cultivated their own ethnic consciousnesses. Still, it seemed that these non-WASPs not only wanted to imitate WASP culture but yearned somehow to *be* WASP."[44] This may no longer be the case.

American society has become increasingly fragmented, and there is little or no consensus to be found regarding our political, business, and cultural life. Deference for the authority of the Protestant Establishment, or for any establishment for that matter, has been replaced in many quarters by an active, conscious hostility and opposition. Whether or not Cuomos marry Kennedys may count for very little if we adhere to no common set of social standards, obey no collective moral injunctions, and subscribe to no single culture. This situation was analyzed with great insight by Francis Fitzgerald in *America Revised,* in which she says that the message of most contemporary textbooks is that "Americans have no common history, no common culture, and no common values, and that membership in a racial or cultural group constitutes the most fundamental experience of each individual. The message would be that the center cannot and should not hold."[45] Under these conditions it is difficult to imagine the resuscitation, or reconstitution of the establishment. Then again, there are still the Kennedys and Cuomos, and countless other Irish, Italian, black, Jewish, Polish and other ethnic families who have adopted the WASP values of achievement and success, even while American society seems to be increasingly emphasizing ascriptive values in their place. As such, and I think that Baltzell would agree, they may represent our brightest prospects for the future. As of now, it is too early to tell whether they will be successful in recreating an establishment, especially one open to all talented individuals and their families, no matter what their racial, ethnic, or religious backgrounds, or whether the fragmentation of our society now underway will preclude such a development.

Notes

1. E. Digby Baltzell, *The Protestant Establishment Revisited,* edited and with an introduction by Howard G. Schneiderman, (New Brunswick, NJ: Transaction Publishers, 1991).
2. Chapter 14 below.
3. For more extensive details of Baltzell's career see my "Introduction" to the first volume of his collected papers, *The Protestant Establishment Revisited* (New Brunswick, NJ: Transaction Publishers, 1991, and my "Out of the Golden Ghetto, *Society* 29, no. 3 (March-April 1992).
4. Friedrich Nietzsche, *The Use and Abuse of History* (New York: Bobbs-Merrill, 1957), 53.
5. Francine Schwadel, "WASP With a Sting Deplores the Decline of U.S. 'Aristocracy,'" *The Wall Street Journal,* 16 December 1986.
6. E. Digby Baltzell, *Philadelphia Gentlemen: The Making of a National Upper Class* (New York: The Free Press, 1958).

7. E. Digby Baltzell, *The Protestant Establishment: Aristocracy and Caste in America* (New York: Random House, 1964).
8. E. Digby Baltzell, *Puritan Boston and Quaker Philadelphia* (New York: The Free Press, 1979).
9. Quoted in Constance Adler, "The Sound of the '60s," *Philadelphia Magazine,* November 1985, p. 169.
10. Robert C. Christopher, *Crashing the Gates: The De-WASPing of America's Power Elite* (New York: Simon and Schuster, 1989), 267-68.
11. Joseph W. Alsop, *I've Seen the Best of It: Memoirs* (New York: Norton, 1992).
12. E. Digby Baltzell and Howard G. Schneiderman, "Social Class in the Oval Office," *Society* 25, no. 6 (September-October 1988)—reprinted in *The Protestant Establishment Revisited,* and "From Rags to Robes: The Horatio Alger Myth and the Supreme Court," *Society* 28, no. 4 (May-June 1991)—reprinted in this volume.
13. Christopher Hitchens, *Blood, Class, and Nostalgia: Anglo-American Ironies* (New York: Farrar, Straus, & Giroux, 1990), 34-35.
14. Alexis de Tocqueville, *Democracy in America,* vol. 1 (New York: Knopf, 1945), 52.
15. Henry Adams, *The Education of Henry Adams* (New York: Random House, 1931), 32.
16. Richard Hofstadter, *The Age of Reform* (New York: Knopf, 1955), 136.
17. Alexis de Tocqueville, *Democracy in America,* vol. 2 (New York: Knopf, 1945), 160.
18. *The New York Times,* 21 March 1993.
19. Talcott Parsons, "Social Strains in America," in *The New American Right* ed. Daniel Bell (New York: Criterion, 1955), 125.
20. Baltzell, *Philadelphia Gentlemen,* 5.
21. Ibid., 395.
22. Alexis de Tocqueville, *The Old Regime and the French Revolution* (New York: Doubleday, 1955).
23. "Changes in the Philadelphia Jewish Community," and "The Jewish Communities of Philadelphia and Boston, 1740-1940: A Tale of Two Cities."
24. Baltzell, *The Protestant Establishment Revisited,* 48.
25. V. O. Key, Jr., *Southern Politics in State and Nation* (New York: Knopf, 1949), 181.
26. See Baltzell and Schneiderman, "Social Class in the Oval Office."
27. James Bryce, *Modern Democracies,* vol. 2 (New York: MacMillan, 1921), 557.
28. James Bryce, *The American Commonwealth* (New York: MacMillan, 1889), 406-407.
29. See my "Introduction" to James Bryce, *Hindrances to Good Citizenship* (New Brunswick, NJ: Transaction Publishers, 1993).
30. Bryce, *Modern Democracies,* 501.
31. William James, "The Social Value of the College Bred," *McClure's Magazine,* February 1908. Cf. Bryce, *Hindrances to Good Citizenship.*
32. Bryce, *Hindrances to Good Citizenship,* 119.
33. Andrew Hacker, "Liberal Democracy and Social Control," *American Political Science Review* 51, no. 4 (December 1957): 1015.
34. Ralf Dahrendorf, *Society and Democracy in Germany* (GardenCity: Doubleday, 1967), 277.
35. Tocqueville, *The Old Regime and the French Revolution,* 142.
36. Reinhold Niebuhr, *The Irony of American History* (New York: Scribners, 1952), 12-13.

37. E. D. Hirsh, *Cultural Literacy* (Boston: Houghton Mifflin, 1987).
38. E. D. Hirsh, *The Dictionary of Cultural Literacy* (Boston: Houghton Mifflin, 1988), 78.
39. Samuel Stouffer, *Communism, Conformity, and Civil Liberties* (New York: Doubleday, 1955).
40. Baltzell, *The Protestant Establishment,* 293.
41. Peter Schrag, *The Decline of the WASP* (New York: Simon and Schuster, 1970), 255.
42. Richard Brookhiser, *The Way of the WASP* (New York: Free Press, 1991).
43. Cf. Howard G. Schneiderman, "Religious Regimes and Elite Culture," in *Faith and Polity,* ed. Mart Bax et al. (Amsterdam: VU University Press, 1992).
44. Nelson W. Aldrich, *Old Money: The Mythology of America's Upper Class* (New York: Knopf, 1988), 280.
45. Francis Fitzgerald, *America Revised* (New York: Random House, 1980), 104.

1

From Rags to Robes: The Horatio Alger Myth and the Supreme Court

(With Howard G. Schneiderman)

If Horatio Alger's "rags to riches" stories are a conservative's democratic daydream, the thought of an American aristocracy may be a liberal's nightmare. There is one American institution, however, where daydream and nightmare have come together to create, in a manner of which Horatio Alger would approve, an aristocracy arising from democratic origins. Thus, Tocqueville wrote, "If I were asked where I placed the American aristocracy, I should reply without hesitation that it is not among the rich, who are united by no common tie, but that it occupies the judicial bench and bar. The more we reflect upon all that occurs in the United States, the more we shall be persuaded that the lawyers, as a body, form the most powerful, if not the only, counterpoise to the democratic element...to neutralize the vices inherent in popular government."

A century later Professor John W. Burgess of Columbia University, the virtual founder of the academic discipline of political science in America, wrote, "I do not hesitate to declare that our form of government is an aristocracy of the robe, which I venture to regard as the best form of aristocracy in the world."

At the top of the aristocracy of the robe are the justices of the United States Supreme Court, who are appointed for life by the President and who are responsible only to their own private and professional consciences. These justices, many of whom lived rags to robes stories, are uniquely qualified, as institutionalized aristocrats, to balance the leveling and all too often short-term values of democracy. This delicate balancing of the social forces of aristocracy and democracy lies at the core of our ever changing yet relatively stable political traditions.

As with so much else in American life, the gentlemanly and aristocratic traditions of our legal profession originated in England, when in 1756 William Blackstone became the first Vinerian Professor of law at Oxford, and his lectures, revised and published in the 1760's as *Commentaries on the Laws of England,* became the most widely read of all Anglo-American law texts, before or since his day. "One of the delightful ironies of American history," Daniel J. Boorstin once wrote, "is that a snobbish Tory barrister, who had polished his periods to suit the taste of young Oxford gentlemen, became the mentor of Abe Lincoln and thousands like him. By making legal ideas and legal jargon accessible to the backwoods, Blackstone did much to prepare self-made men for leadership in the New World."

At any rate, lawyers, of both haughty and humble origins, have played major roles in the history of American political leadership: thus twenty-five of the fifty-six signers of the Declaration of Independence were lawyers, as were thirty-one of the fifty-five members of the Constitutional Convention; in the first Congress, ten of the twenty-nine Senators and seventeen of the sixty-five Representatives were trained in the law. While George Washington, Andrew Jackson, and Theodore Roosevelt were amateur and voluntary military heroes before entering the presidency, and William Henry Harrison, Zachary Taylor, Ulysses S. Grant and Dwight Eisenhower were professional soldiers, twenty-four of the remaining twenty-nine presidents (John Adams through Nixon) were trained in the law (Jackson had been a lawyer and a judge as well as a military hero).

Nomination to the Supreme Court by the President of the United States, with the advice and consent of the Senate, is surely the highest honor available to the members of the American legal profession. The history of the political and personal relationships between the presidents and the justices is a fascinating one. A few days after John Marshall's death in 1835, for example, John Quincy Adams wrote in his diary of his father's appointment of Marshall to the Chief Justiceship of the Supreme Court as follows: "It was the last act of my father's administration, and one of the most important services rendered by him to his country...the office of Chief Justice is a station of the highest trust, of the deepest responsibility, and of influence far more extensive than that of the President of the United States.... Marshall cemented the Union which the crafty and quixotic democracy of Jefferson had a perpetual tendency to disolve. Jefferson hated and dreaded him." While all Federalists were pleased with Adam's appointment of Marshall, President Dwight Eisenhower, and most conservative Republicans, considered his appointments of Chief Justice Earl Warren and Associate Justice William J. Brennan, Jr., to the Court a disaster. And of course the Bork affair during the Reagan presidency and the recent resignation of Justice Brennan from the Court, followed by President Bush's nomination of Judge David Souter, of New Hampshire, to replace him, make this subject of timely interest.

The task of this essay will be limited to showing how the social class origins of the first ninety-six justices appointed to the Supreme Court (1789–1969) were related to their levels of performance on the bench. At the same time we shall compare the justices with the presidents on these two dimensions of class and performance. Off hand, one would expect the appointed and aloof aristocrats of the robe to have originated in more privileged families than the presidents who are elected by the people. After all, the Horatio Alger myth has always applied to the presidents rather than the justices who meet behind closed doors, and are hardly known by the common man, who has no say in their appointments. In a similar vein, a student of the Supreme Court, John A. Schmidhauser, once wrote: "The political variation on the Horatio Alger theme—any boy, but preferably one of humble origins, might become President—has long been one of the most satisfying of the myths of American political recruitment. This myth has been applied to national legislative and to other national executive offices. But it is hardly likely that many young men of humble origin have lost sleep contemplating their prospects for attaining a seat on the Supreme Court of the United States. Our highest judicial institution has always been veiled, in the public mind, in an aura of inaccessibility."

But, reality is always much more complicated than myths or social and political theory. Thus, in our recent study of the relationship of social class background to the performance in office of American presidents, "Social Class in the Oval Office"[1] we showed that, contrary to the "Log Cabin Myth," all but a handful of our presidents have come from upper or upper-middle class backgrounds. Perhaps more surprising, and certainly more irritating to egalitarian political theorists, we showed that presidents born with silver spoons in their mouths had far more distinguished careers in the Oval Office than did those of less advantaged backgrounds. Lincoln was the mythical exception which proved the rule. Again, contrary to conventional theory, we shall show here that the Horatio Alger story has been far more applicable to the appointed members of the aloof Supreme Court than to the popularly elected presidents. Presidents and senators have apparently used far more meritocratic and liberal criteria in their Court appointments than have the American voters in their presidential choices.

In our presidential article referred to above, we compared the social class origins of the presidents (as set forth in Edward Pessen's 1984 study, *The Log Cabin Myth*) with the two classic studies of presidential performance in office, in 1948 and again in 1962, by Arthur M. Schlesinger, Sr. and especially with the state of the art modern study undertaken in 1981 by Robert K. Murray and Tim H. Blessing of Pennsylvania State University. The Murray-Blessing panel was made up of 846 professors of American history who ranked the thirty-six presidents from Washington through Nixon into six levels of performance in office: great, near great, above average, average, below average, and failure.

There have been several rankings of the greatest justices of the Supreme Court. Only one study, however, has systematically ranked, in the style of the Schlesinger and Murray-Blessing rankings of the presidents, all the justices in the history of the Court. In June 1970, Albert P. Blaustein, of Rutgers University and Roy M. Mersky, of the University of Texas, asked a panel of sixty-five law school deans and professors of law, history, and political science to evaluate the performances of the first ninety-six justices, placing them within the categories of "great," "near great," "average," "below average," and "failure."

Unfortunately there has been no systematic effort to identify the Supreme Court justices by their social-class origins as had been done with the presidents. We have ourselves, therefore, placed the ninety-six justices, according to their social origins, at three social-class levels—upper (U), upper-middle (UM), and middle & lower (ML)—as will be seen in Figure 1.1 below.

Rating a person by social class origins is a difficult thing to do in our open-class America. The difficulty is compounded in the case of many great men who so often derive their drive to success from their mothers, who are, in turn, more often than not superior to their fathers in social-class origins, and/or in moral and intellectual stature. Thus, for example, Pessen ranked Thomas Jefferson as originating in the upper class, while many experts on the history of the Supreme Court have referred to John Marshall, who was born in an authentic log cabin on the Virginia frontier, as a self-made man. Thus, a glibly liberal professor at the Yale Law School, Fred Rodell, in his history of the Supreme Court published in 1955, wrote that Marshall's extremely conservative views were due to the fact that he "identified himself completely with the class to which he had climbed."

But Jefferson, who belonged to the class into which Marshall supposedly "climbed," was Marshall's bitter political enemy: "The Republicans," Marshall once remarked, "are divided into speculative theorists and absolute terrorists. With the latter I am disposed to class Mr. Jefferson." Actually, these famous political enemies were surprisingly similar in social origins. Through their mothers, for instance, Thomas Jefferson was the great-grandson and John Marshall the great-great grandson of William Randolph and Mary Isham, both of British gentry stock and founders of one of the leading First Families of Virginia. At the same time, both men's fathers were of ordinary origins but leaders of their respective county communities, which they represented in the House of Burgesses, in Williamsburg. Marshall's father, Thomas—as schoolmate, professional surveying associate, and comrade-in-arms, from Valley Forge through Yorktown, of George Washington—had a far more distinguished career than Jefferson's father, Peter. Professor Julien Boyd once described these two kinsmen and political enemies felicitously as follows:

> Both were Virginians. Both had been born within the frontier, though far enough on the outskirts of settlement to feel the challenging winds from the vast wilderness to the westward. Both stemmed from the distant and progenitive Randolph, deriving from him a consanguinity that neither exhibited in outward expression. Both grew up in the same kind of sturdy, self-reliant home environment, each possessing at its head a stalwart, intelligent, respected leader of the county. Both had been bred to the law under the noble teacher, George Wythe, though his tutelage of Marshall was but a brief and tenuous relationship and that of Jefferson a profound and transforming influence. Both had eagerly embraced the principles of the Revolution and had served the American cause well, the one distinguishing himself in the field and the other in legislation. Yet out of this remarkable identity of background came one of the mighty opposites of American history. The explanation of this divergence arising from similarity is as baffling as the explanation of genius....

Yet, of course, genius above all is hardly ever explained by background and the two men were almost entire opposites in temperament: Marshall a humorous and gregarious lover of men of all kinds and conditions, Jefferson a humorless and lonely lover of mankind. Perhaps it is not entirely irrelevant to note here the little known fact that the aristocratic beauty, Rebecca Burwell, the one great passion of Jefferson's youth, jilted him to marry Jacqueline Ambler. The Amblers were one of the wealthiest families in the little village of Yorktown, when young Captain John Marshall first visited the battle site and met, and later married Rebecca's beautiful daughter, Mary. Both Marshall and Jefferson, like their fathers, married well as great leaders of men had done for many centuries before them, and since. And so we have ranked John Marshall as of upper class origins.

Here we should note that, for purposes of this study, men ranked in both the upper (U) and the upper-middle (UM) classes are considered to be of *privileged* origins. On the other hand, the middle and lower (ML) ranking is an inclusive category of all those of *unprivileged* (but not necessarily underprivileged) backgrounds. About half (18) of the 32 justices of ML ratings came from solid middle class farming or small-town families, such as Justice Frank Murphy's. This pro-New Deal justice was born, in 1890, in a small farming community on the Michigan shore of Lake Huron. His biographer, J. Woodford Howard, Jr., writes of his origins in the American social class hierarchy as follows: "Murphy's father was a country lawyer. Despite financial problems which seemed endless, he was able to educate his children beyond average expectations.... Frank Murphy came from small town, middle-class and politically alert America. In class and values, he was indistinguishable from thousands of his generation."

While eighteen of the justices in this ML category had backgrounds similar to Frank Murphy's, the other fourteen justices were less privileged, ranging from the sons of poor farmers and lower status small town residents to the two most deprived future justices, Abe Fortas and Thurgood Marshall. Fortas, the son of immigrant Orthodox Jews, grew up in the ghetto of Memphis, Tennessee. Although his father, a cabinetmaker, taught himself English, his mother died illiterate. Marshall grew up in a black ghetto in Baltimore. His father was a servant at the snobbish Gibson Island Club, and his mother taught at an all-black elementary school.

FIGURE 1.1: Presidents, Justices, and Chief Justices

SOCIAL CLASS ORIGINS AND PERFORMANCE IN OFFICE							
Social Class Origins				Performance in Office			
	Pres.	Just.	C.J.*		Pres.	Just.	C.J.
U	(15) 42%	(29) 31%	(8) 57%	G/NG	(8) 22%	(27) 28%	(8) 57%
UM	(16) 44%	(35) 36%	(2) 14%	AVG	(18) 50%	(5) 57%	(5) 36%
ML	(5) 14%	(32) 33%	(4) 29%	BA/F	(10) 28%	(14) 15%	(1) 7%
	(36) 100%	(96) 100%	(14) 100%		(36) 100%	(96) 100%	(14) 100%

*The Chief Justices will be discussed below and should be ignored until then.

One further point of clarification: for comparative convenience we have included both "average" and "above average" presidents, as used by Schlesinger and Murray-Blessing, within the single category of "average" in the following table, where the social origins of both presidents and justices are divided into upper (U), upper-middle (UM), and middle and lower (ML) class levels, and their performance ratings into great and near great (G/NG), average (AVG), and below average and failure (BA/F).

The comparison of the social class origins of the presidents and justices in Figure 1.1 was immediately revealing, and at first surprising, to us and perhaps to many of our readers. Few good American democrats, especially hard-edge liberals, would expect that the Horatio Alger myth has been far more applicable to the aristocrats of the robe than to the popularly elected presidents. Yet the justices were more than twice as likely as the presidents to have originated in the middle and lower classes (ML origins: justices 33%, presidents 14%). Not only were the justices less privileged than the presidents, they were, at the same time, slightly more likely to have distinguished performance records (G/NG performance: justices 28%, presidents 22%) and definitely less likely to have poor performance records (BA/F performance: justices 15%, presidents 28%).

The performance differences by social class origins between the presidents and the justices are strikingly revealed in a quantitative comparison of the social origins of the great and near great presidents (8) and justices (27) which we have listed below in Figure 1.2, by name, term in office, and social origins (U, UM, ML).

A quantitative comparison of the class origins of these great and near great presidents and justices shows that five of the eight presidents (63%)

FIGURE 1.2: Great and Near Great Presidents and Justices

Great			Near Great		
			Presidents		
ABRAHAM LINCOLN	1861–1865	ML	THEODORE ROOSEVELT	1901–1909	U
FRANKLIN ROOSEVELT	1933–1945	U	WOODROW WILSON	1913–1921	U
GEORGE WASHINGTON	1789–1797	U	ANDREW JACKSON	1829–1837	UM
THOMAS JEFFERSON	1801–1809	U	HARRY TRUMAN	1945–1953	UM
			Justices		
*JOHN MARSHALL	1801–1835	U	WILLIAM JOHNSON	1804–1834	UM
JOSEPH STORY	1811–1845	U	BENJAMIN R. CURTIS	1851–1870	UM
*ROGER B. TANEY	1836–1864	U	SAMUEL F. MILLER	1862–1890	ML
JOHN M. HARLAN	1877–1911	U	STEPHEN J. FIELD	1863–1897	UM
OLIVER W. HOLMES	1902–1932	U	JOSEPH P. BRADLEY	1870–1892	ML
CHARLES E. HUGHES	1910–1916	ML	*MORRISON R. WAITE	1874–1888	U
*	1930–1941		EDWARD D. WHITE	1894–1910	U
LOUIS D. BRANDEIS	1916–1939	UM	*	1910–1921	
HARLAN F. STONE	1925–1941	ML	*WILLIAM H. TAFT	1921–1930	U
*	1941–1946		GEORGE SUTHERLAND	1922–1938	ML
BENJAMIN N. CARDOZO	1932–1938	UM	WILLIAM O. DOUGLAS	1939–1975	ML
HUGO L. BLACK	1937–1971	ML	ROBERT H. JACKSON	1941–1954	ML
FELIX FRANKFURTER	1938–1962	ML	WILEY B. RUTLEDGE	1943–1949	ML
*EARL WARREN	1953–1969	ML	JOHN M. HARLAN II	1955–1971	U
			WM. J. BRENNAN, JR	1956–1990	ML

*Connotes service as Chief Justice. J. Marshall, Taney, Waite, Taft, and Warren were appointed directly; White, Hughes, and Stone had previously sat as Associate Justices.

as against only nine of the twenty-seven justices (33%) were of upper class origins. Of even more importance to our Horatio Alger thesis is that while only one of the eight (12%) presidents, Lincoln, was born to an unprivileged family, thirteen (48%), or a clear plurality, of the twenty-seven justices were born to unprivileged families.

It is now time to ask ourselves why privileged origins are so much more important in determining high performance in the White House than on the Supreme Court. Moreover, how do we account for the fact that the justices of middle or lower class origins have much higher performance ratings than the presidents of similar origins? Perhaps presidential performance depends to a greater extent on the subtleties of upper-class habits of authority, whereas professional competence and superior intelligence are more essential for Supreme Court performance. Thus, thirty-one or more than one-third of the justices (35%), as opposed to only four (J. Q. Adams, Arthur, T. Roosevelt, and Taft), or about a tenth (11%) of the presidents, were members of Phi Beta Kappa in college. Further clues to this difference may be suggested by a look at the class origins of the eight great and near great Chief Justices, whose professional competence must be augmented with the subtle qualities of leadership apparently possessed also by upper class presidents. Thus five (63%) of the eight most distinguished Chief Justices were of upper-class origins, exactly the same proportion as among the eight most distinguished presidents.

Turning to the fourteen Chief Justices of the Supreme Court we see immediately, in Figure 1.1 above, that these few aristocrats of the robe were both more likely to come of upper-class backgrounds and have high performance ratings than either the thirty-six presidents or the whole group of ninety-six justices: upper-class origins of presidents 42%, justices 32%, and Chief Justices 57%; great and near great performance of presidents 22%, justices 28% and Chief Justices 57%.

The history of the Court has most often been looked at in terms of the Chief Justice's name, the Marshall, Taney, Hughes, or Warren courts for instance. We shall discuss the Chief Justices and their courts in terms of the following four historical periods which we have described in our earlier article, "Social Class and the Oval Office":

1. *The Age of Aristocracy* (1789-1850). From Washington through the death in office of Zachary Taylor.
2. *Middle Class Ascendency* (1850-1901). From the elevation of the mediocre Millard Fillmore to the Presidency through the assassination of McKinley in 1901.
3. *WASP Hegemony* (1901-1953). From Theodore Roosevelt through Harry S. Truman.
4. *Ethnic Democracy* (1953-1981). From Eisenhower through Jimmy Carter.

In both social origins and levels of performance, these four periods were distinctive and different: of the presidents who served in the *Age of Aristocracy,* ten of the twelve originated in the upper class (Harrison died the first year in office and was thus not rated) while of the eleven who were rated, three—Washington, Jefferson and Jackson—were great or near great. During the years of *Middle Class Ascendency* mediocrity was the rule, only Benjamin Harrison was upper-class born, and only Lincoln was distinguished in office (of the twelve presidents, Garfield was assassinated and thus not rated). Contrary to conventional wisdom, and James Bryce's prognostications, the half century of *WASP Hegemony* produced more distinguished presidents than any other, even the classic *Age of Aristocracy* which Bryce so admired. Thus of the eight presidents, the two Roosevelts, Taft, and Wilson were all born to upper-class privileges, and T. Roosevelt, Wilson, and Truman had near great ratings while Franklin Roosevelt was ranked by the Murray-Blessing respondents as second only to Lincoln and *above* George Washington.

It may be instructive at this point to note that both of the Schlesinger rankings of the presidents placed Lincoln at the top and Washington second. Though no such systematic rankings were done, Washington ranked first in the hearts of his countymen for the first century of our history. However, "as the United States evolved from a rural republic to an industrial democracy, and as 'equality' replaced 'liberty' as its major political concern," wrote Barry Schwartz, the leading sociological interpreter of the Washington and Lincoln cults, "the dignified restraint and aloofness of Washington's image began to undermine its popularity.... By the early years of the twentieth century, in fact, the popularity of his cult was surpassed by Lincoln's."

That the Murray-Blessing respondents placed FDR above Washington is perhaps indicative of a further move towards the values of egalitarian bureaucracy in modern America. A clue to these value changes was suggested by a breakdown of the 846 members of the Murray-Blessing panel. Thus, a small group comprising the most distinguished historians (mostly male and over 45 years of age) still placed Washington second to Lincoln. It was the younger generation of historians, especially the females, who demoted Washington; after all, a sexist, slave-owner, and aristocrat would hardly appeal to a subjective and egalitarian generation, which, incidentally, seems to place a low value on "dignified restraint."

All of this suggests that the rankings of the justices in 1970 were made in an age of equality and may be subject to change in the future. Thus Professor Fred Rodell, of the Yale Law School, rated Justice Douglas "considerably above" Justice Frankfurter in his book on the Supreme Court published in 1955; in 1970 the Blaustein-Mersky panel ranked Frankfurter as great, and Douglas as only near great.

Finally, as might be expected in our age of mediocrity, the era of Ethnic Democracy produced only John F. Kennedy of privileged origins and no presidents of great or near great stature.

The Chief Justices in each of these four periods are listed as follows in Figure 1.3, by name, dates and number of years of service, class origins, performance rankings, and appointing presidents.

As far as the Supreme Court is concerned, the *Age of Aristocracy* must be divided into two parts—before and after John Marshall. The first three Chief Justices, Jay, Rutledge, and Ellsworth, were great aristocrats and great patriots who played major roles in the founding of the Republic. Their "average" performance ratings were largely due to the lack of the Court's importance in that first, Federalist- dominated decade.

John Marshall, whose lifetime idol was George Washington, was the Father of the Supreme Court, which he dominated for thirty-four years, longer than any other Chief Justice. Liberty and freedom, Marshall was convinced, rested on the unfettered rights of private property rather than on democracy or equality; he despised the "leveling Jeffersonians." In many ways Marshall's Hamiltonian and Federalist views influenced the Supreme Court down to the Hughes Court, which finally, and wisely, compromised with the New Deal modifications of private property rights, which, in turn, began the era of leveling democracy that is still with us.

FIGURE 1.3: Chief Justices of the Supreme Court in Four Historical Periods

Age of Aristocracy (1789–1850)					
John Jay	1789–1795	6	Upper	Average	Washington
John Rutledge	1795	1	Upper	Average	Washington
Oliver Ellsworth	1796–1799	3	Upper	Average	Washington
John Marshall	1801–1835	34	Upper	Great	John Adams
Roger B. Taney	1836–1864	28	Upper	Great	Jackson
Middle Class Ascendency (1850–1901)					
Salmon Chase	1864–1873	11	U.Middle	Average	Lincoln
Morrison Waite	1874–1888	14	Upper	N. Great	Grant
Melville Fuller	1888–1910	22	U.Middle	Average	Cleveland
WASP Hegemony (1901–1953)					
Edward D. White	1910–1921	11	Upper	N. Great	Taft
William H. Taft	1921–1930	9	Upper	N. Great	Harding
Charles E. Hughes	1930–1941	11	Mid/Lower	Great	Hoover
Harlan F. Stone	1941–1946	5	Mid/Lower	Great	F. Roosevelt
Fred M. Vinson	1946–1953	7	Mid/Lower	Failure	Truman
Ethnic Democracy (1953–1980)					
Earl Warren	1953–1969	16	Mid/Lower	Great	Eisenhower

As Holmes said so well: "Time has been on Marshall's side;...the theory for which Hamilton argued, and he decided, and Webster spoke, and Grant fought, and Lincoln died, is now our corner-stone." Both Marshall and Holmes were, in their very different ways, consummate aristocrats and undisputedly the two greatest justices in the Court's history.

Marshall's successor, Roger Brooke Taney was born and raised among the Catholic, planter aristocracy of Maryland. As a second son, he turned to the law. Nominated by Andrew Jackson, he served as Chief Justice longer than anyone except Marshall. Unfortunately his name has forever been associated with the infamous Dred Scott decision (*Scott v. Sandford* 1857) which many in the North claimed brought on the Civil War. When he died at the age of 87, in 1864, he was scorned by the war-frenzied masses as well as the famous abolitionist senator, Charles Sumner. For reasons not appropriately discussed here, Taney's reputation improved during and after the 1930s and he was rightly rated great by the Blaustein-Mersky respondents.

All three Chief Justices during the next historical period of *Middle Class Ascendency,* were born in New England and made their legal and political careers in the Middle West. All were raised in privileged circumstances. Salmon Chase, though born the son of a small-town tavern-keeper in New Hampshire, came of a well-connected family, one uncle being a U. S. Senator from Vermont and another, Philander Chase, the Episcopalian Bishop of Ohio, who raised young Salmon after his father died when he was nine. Hence our rating Chase as upper-middle class in origins. Waite, son of a Chief Justice of Connecticut and a graduate of Yale, went West to Toledo, Ohio, where he became a leading member of the bar and a solid private citizen. Virtually unknown outside of Ohio when Grant nominated him, Waite turned out to be a very hard-working and respected Chief Justice, writing almost a thousand opinions during his fourteen years in office. Finally, Melville W. Fuller was born of a solid upper-middle class family in Augusta, Maine. He graduated from Bowdoin, spent one year at the Harvard Law School and began practice at the Augusta bar. After an unhappy love affair, he went west to Chicago where he married a prominent bank president's daughter, built a solid and lucrative law practice, and made wise investments, especially in real estate. Fuller was regarded as a God-fearing (Episcopalian) private citizen of little public renown in either Chicago or the state. He was virtually unknown politically when Cleveland finally picked him over several famous candidates (especially the great Associate Justice, Stephen Field, who wanted the appointment badly). A dedicated Social Darwinist, Fuller presided over a conservative court at the height of the great age of enterprise. Holmes, who first sat on the Fuller Court, considered him somewhat of a judicial lightweight, and he deserved no better than an average rating.

The period of *WASP Hegemony* produced more distinguished presidents and Chief Justices of the Supreme Court than any other period in our history; no wonder this was the great age of American world leadership. The first two Chief Justices of this period, White and Taft, were upper-class patricians of near-great accomplishment on the bench. White's father had been a sugar planter, lawyer and Governor of Louisiana; Taft's father, born on a Vermont farm, founded Cincinnati's undisputed First Family. Taft, a Unitarian, nominated White, a Catholic, for the Chief Justiceship. Taft was surely a great man from one of America's great families, yet he was only an average president and a near-great Chief Justice. Notably, Taft was responsible for the erection of the present imposing Supreme Court building in Washington.

All the Chief Justices before Charles Evans Hughes were born of privileged families; Hughes and his successor Harlan Stone were of middle class origins. Hughes had a rigidly religious upbringing. His father was a Welsh Methodist minister who immigrated to America after reading Benjamin Franklin's *Autobiography*. He became a Baptist partly because of his pious, schoolteacher wife, and held several parishes in New York state. Young Hughes went to Brown on a scholarship (because of his Baptist minister father) where he was a great social and academic success, serving as president of one of the best fraternities at Brown and other New England colleges, as well as being elected to Phi Beta Kappa. After attending Columbia Law and passing his New York bar examinations with an unmatched 99.5 score, he became a very successful Wall Street lawyer and Governor of New York before his first appointment to the court by Taft, in 1910. He resigned from the Court in 1916 to run unsuccessfully for president against Wilson, narrowly losing in the Electoral College by 4,000 votes in California. During the twenties he made some $400,000 a year as a Wall Street lawyer (a huge sum for that time) before being nominated for the Chief Justiceship by Hoover, in 1930.

Harlan Stone came from a solid farming family in New Hampshire which eventually bought a farm outside Amherst, Massachusetts, in order to raise their son in a more intellectual atmosphere. Stone graduated from Amherst—president of his class, Phi Beta Kappa, and right guard on one of the college's famous football teams. He was a successful Wall Street lawyer and Dean of Columbia Law School before being appointed to the Supreme Court by his college friend, Calvin Coolidge. Franklin Roosevelt elevated him to the Chief Justiceship during the war as a gesture towards bipartisanship (Stone was the only Republican on the Court).

Hughes was surely the greatest Chief Justice since Marshall. Stone was a great Associate Justice, dissenting along with Holmes and Brandeis and then with Cordozo and Frankfurter; he was not a great Chief Justice. It was said that whereas Hughes would guide his Court to a decision in four hours, it would take four days for the Stone Court to accomplish the same thing.

Vinson and Warren were of lower-middle-class origins. Vinson, the son of the county jailor in a small hill town in Kentucky, was a mathematical wizard and a very good athlete, both talents helping him through Centre College where he graduated first in his class and then obtained an LL.B. at its law school. As a statistically-minded lawyer he became a valuable bureaucrat under Roosevelt and Truman. He and Truman had both fought in favor of Roosevelt's notorious Court-packing plan in 1937. As president, Truman appointed Vinson as Secretary of the Treasury, in 1945, and nominated him for the Chief Justiceship the next year. Vinson was a fine public servant but a poor Chief Justice. Harry Truman, in fact, made the worst set of appointments in the history of the Supreme Court: Vinson, Burton and Minton were all failures and Tom Clark was barely average.

Earl Warren's was one of the truly great Horatio Alger stories in American history. His father immigrated from Norway to Minneapolis; after marriage to a Swedish girl, he moved to Los Angeles where he was a repair-man on the Southern Pacific Railroad when young Earl was born. When Earl once asked his father why he had no middle name (which had produced a minor passport crisis) the answer was: "Son, when you were born, we were too poor to enjoy any luxury of that kind." Earl Warren was a man of high moral character rather than intellectual or legal brilliance; at any rate, he tenaciously worked his way through the University of California, at Berkeley, earning A.B. and J.D. degrees there. He then went on to serve as a local district attorney and Attorney General of the State before becoming the first three-time Governor in California's history. Warren was a solid but liberal Republican when Eisenhower nominated him for the Chief Justiceship (some said at the time that Richard Nixon and William Knowland, leaders of the most conservative California Republicans were glad to have him relegated to the Court). Just as Taney has been forever remembered for the infamous *Dred Scott* decision, so Warren will forever be remembered for his engineering the unanimous vote in the *Brown* case in 1954, which declared that separate schools for whites and blacks were inherently unequal. John Marshall was a dedicated anti-leveller, Earl Warren a dedicated leveller and Charles Evans Hughes the diplomatic bridge-builder (in 1937) between the two philosophical positions; all were great Americans and the three greatest Chief Justices.

Finally, we shall look at the Horatio Alger myth as it applies to all ninety-six of the Supreme Court justices during our four historical periods. Thus the proportions of justices of middle and lower class origins in each period were as follows:

Age of Aristocracy	5 of 31 or 16%
Middle Class Ascendency	6 of 26 or 23%
WASP Hegemony	14 of 30 or 47%
Ethnic Democracy	7 of 9 or 78%
Total	32 of 96 or 33%

The above figures clearly show that the chances of bright and ambitious youths from the farms and small towns of America to become members of the bar, and to become appointed to the Supreme Court have steadily increased in each of our four periods, from 16% of the justices in the *Age of Aristocracy* to 78% of the justices in the period of *Ethnic Democracy*. The pivotal year was 1900: thus eleven, or 19%, of the fifty-seven justices appointed before the turn of the century, as against twenty-one, or 54%, of the thirty-nine justices appointed since then, came from middle and lower class backgrounds.

It is our judgment that the increasing opportunity for upward mobility in the legal profession in the twentieth century has been largely due to the growth of law schools, both the more ancient and prestigious such as Harvard, Yale and Columbia as well as the lesser known schools, and especially the urban night law schools which made legal careers available to the lower levels of society.

Justice Joseph Story, Marshall's philosophical right-hand man, has often been called "the American Blackstone." In 1828, while still on the Court (which then sat for only brief periods) he was appointed to the Dane Professorship of Law at Harvard where he produced "a profound revolution in legal education," and became the father of the Harvard Law School, which has been, in many ways, America's leading elite-producing institution in the style of Oxford and Cambridge in England. At the moment, ten Harvard Law School graduates are serving in the U.S. Senate, three in President Bush's cabinet, and four on the Supreme Court.

Oliver Wendell Holmes was the first justice to hold a modern university law degree when he came to the Supreme Court in 1902 (LL.B., Harvard 1869); and it was not until Charles Evans Whittaker, a poor farmer's son who earned his LL.B. at the night school of the University of Kansas City, replaced Stanley F. Reed on the Court in 1957, that all nine of its members had formal law school degrees (LL.B. or J.D.). While Reed, who had attended both the Columbia and University of Virginia Law Schools without taking a degree, had been securely bred to privilege, Whittaker's story was classic Horatio Alger. Born on a farm near Troy, Kansas, he trapped animals and sold their hides to help make family ends meet; his schooling was meager and he finally had to quit high school, after which he stepped up his trapping to save money for a legal education. In 1920, he attempted to enroll in the night program at the Kansas City Law School. At first he was turned down due to his not having a high school diploma but his persistence won out and he received an LL.B. there in 1924, having previously passed the bar examination in 1923. All through law school he worked a full day at a law firm which he joined upon graduation, became a partner in 1930, and went on to great success as a corporate lawyer and senior partner in his own firm. Appointed to the court by Eisenhower in 1957, he only served until 1962; this short length of service and the fact that he took a rather conservative position on civil liberties, probably had a lot to do with his ranking as a failure by the Blaustein-Merskey respondents.

Finally, in our age of ethnic diversity, it is important to point out that not only has the Court given increasing opportunities to those of lower and middle class backgrounds but, unlike the presidency, it has been accessible to religious minorities almost from its beginning. That Chief Justices Roger B. Taney and Edward D. White were Catholics and appointed long before the First World War, while the first Catholic president was John F. Kennedy elected a decade and a half after the Second World War, suggests that elite individuals, such as presidents and senators, are less prejudiced than a majority of the electorate. No Catholic could possibly have been elected to the White House before the Second World War, while presidents nominated and senators approved five Catholics during that same period—Taney in 1836, White in 1894, Joseph McKenna (the son of an Irish-Catholic immigrant) in 1898, Pierce Butler (another son of an Irish immigrant) in 1922, and Frank Murphy in 1940. After the war, Eisenhower, in 1956, nominated as associate justice, William J. Brennan, Jr., yet another Irish immigrant's son.

Brennan, who has just stepped down from the Court, was often thought to have been the brains behind Chief Justice Earl Warren, just as Joseph Story was Marshall's scholarly colleague a century and a half ago.

And while there have been no Jewish presidents, five Jews have served on the Court. Wilson appointed Brandeis over bitter opposition in 1916, Hoover, Cardozo in 1932, Franklin Roosevelt, Frankfurter in 1938, Kennedy, Goldberg in 1962, and Lyndon Johnson, Fortas in 1965. After Warren sent a letter to President Johnson in 1968 announcing his desire to resign from the Court, Johnson nominated Abe Fortas as Chief Justice. The Senate refused to confirm the nomination because of Fortas' involvement in a complicated financial scandal. Fortas, the first justice to do so, resigned in disgrace in 1969. (At the same time, Warren stayed on the Court until 1969, allowing newly elected President Nixon to nominate his successor, Warren E. Burger, who proved to be too liberal for Nixon, and later for Ronald Reagan).

Of course not all of the Catholic and Jewish justices qualify as Horatio Alger figures in terms of social class backgrounds. Brandeis, Cardozo, Taney, and White, were all born into privileged upper or upper middle class families. However, given the deep ethnic prejudices in American history, it is worth reiterating that the legal profession as well as the presidents and senators who appoint members of the Court have been less prejudiced than the voters. It is also worth noting that about two-thirds of all the Catholic and Jewish justices were rated as great or near great.

Franklin D. Roosevelt appointed more justices to the Supreme Court than any other president except George Washington. There is no better way to end this study of Horatio Alger and the Supreme Court than by taking a brief look at his appointments to the Court.

A millionaire by inheritance, with a pronounced Groton and Harvard accent, Roosevelt was a privileged patrician to his fingertips; but among the eight associate justices he appointed to the court, seven were of middle and lower class origins. Roosevelt had no opportunity to make a Court appointment during his first term, which was spent in a bitter fight with the early Hughes Court, which was dominated by the extremely conservative "Four Horsemen"—Willis Van Devanter of Wyoming, James C. McReynolds of Tennessee, George Sutherland of Utah, and Pierce Butler of Minnesota (three of whom were ranked as failures by the Blaustein-Mersky panel, among them McReynolds, an anti-semite who refused to speak with either Brandeis or Cardozo). The first opening on the Court occurred when Van Devanter, after finally losing his bitter battle against the New Deal, resigned in 1937. Often called a "traitor to his class," Roosevelt purposely infuriated his conservative enemies by nominating a fighting, left-wing Senator from Alabama, Hugo LaFayette Black, an entirely self-made man, who was born the son of a Confederate Army veteran, in a tiny cabin in a crossroads town in a red-dirt, cotton-chopping part of the state. With little formal schooling, he managed to earn an LL.B. from the small new law school at the University of Alabama by the age of twenty. An omnivorous reader, Black educated himself rigorously all his life.

When Cardozo died in 1938, Frankfurter was appointed to fill the "Jewish Seat." Born of middle class Viennese parents, he was brought to America at the age of twelve and spent his teens on New York's Lower East Side. After graduating with a Phi Beta Kappa key from the City College of New York, he entered the Harvard Law School, in Cambridge, which remained his spiritual home for the rest of his life. William O. Douglas, Roosevelt's next appointment to the Court, was the first-born son of an itinerant Presbyterian preacher in a small town in eastern Oregon. He had polio at the age of five and lost his father the following year. His determined and domineering mother, who called her favorite son "Treasure" during his early years, bravely raised him, and his younger brother and sister, on the wrong side of the Northern Pacific Railroad tracks in Yakimo, Oregon. For the rest of his life, Douglas bitterly resented his early poverty and his snobbish schoolmates from the establishment on the other side of the tracks. James F. Byrnes was also raised in difficult circumstances in a small South Carolina town. His father died before he was born and his doting mother took up dressmaking to earn a living. Byrnes left school at fourteen, but won a shorthand competition and got a job as a court reporter, all the time reading law and passing the state bar examinations by the time he was twenty-four. Finally, Frank Murphy and Harlan Stone, as we have already seen, as well as Robert Jackson and Wiley Rutledge, all grew up in comfortable but undistinguished middle-class families.

After James F. Byrnes resigned in 1942, the membership of the Stone Court was certainly the most brilliant in our history. Seven of the eight associate justices had been ardent New Dealers when appointed by Roosevelt, while Owen J. Roberts, a conservative Republican from Philadelphia, appointed by Hoover, was the critical swing man whose final break with the "Four Horsemen" allowed Chief Justice Hughes to preserve the Court, in 1937, by recognizing that the New Deal's egalitarian opposition to the absolute sacredness of private property was the inevitable wave of the future. As we have seen above, Stone, Black and Frankfurter were rated among the twelve greatest justices ever to sit on the court, while Douglas, Robert Jackson, and Wiley Rutledge were all of near-great stature. Five of the nine members of the court, Stone, Frankfurter, Douglas, Rutledge and Roberts, had been law school professors, and four, Stone, Frankfurter, Douglas and Roberts, were elected to Phi Beta Kappa in college.

Black, Frankfurter and Douglas stayed on the Court right through the leveling Warren era. Black, who had been the intellectual dean of the New Deal Court and a revered member of the Warren Court, was widely recognized as the greatest justice of his era when he resigned, after 34 years on the Court, in 1971, at the age of 85. The son of a Southern red-neck, Black joined the Klu Klux Klan for a brief period in his early political career and rose to become a member of the legal, political and social establishment of Birmingham, Alabama, marrying a well-born "Society Girl" on the way. He was sent to the U.S. Senate in 1927 where he vigorously opposed the national business establishment whose members bitterly resented his views, but always respected him personally. His soft-spoken Southern manners concealed a steel-trap mind and an iron will; it was said in the Senate that he "spoke with the assurance of a

Bourbon and the fiery passion of a populist." Unlike his ideological colleague, William O. Douglas, who alienated everyone close to him, including his four wives, his children, his students at the Yale law school, his law clerks and his colleagues, Hugo Black was a first rate and mature human being who had a blessed family life and never lost a friend, or the respect of an opponent, over ideological differences. While Black and Douglas belonged to the activist wing of both the New Deal and Warren courts, Frankfurter was the leading advocate of judicial restraint, in the style of his idol Holmes. Whereas Douglas refused to speak to Frankfurter for many years, personal relations were never broken between Black and Frankfurter; in 1957, during a conference, on the spur of the moment, Black passed Frankfurter a note saying, "I strongly hope nothing will happen that causes you to leave the court..."

Hugo Black's Horatio Alger career has always been an inspiration to all who have ever known or heard of him. What better example of the leveling-up character of our Supreme Court as it functions as an open but authoritative aristocracy in the midst of our ever more democratic society? Perhaps, however, not all would agree. Thus, Roy L. Brooks, a law professor at the University of Minnesota, recently wrote in *The New York Times:* "From all accounts, our society will become even more diverse as we enter the next century. Whites will be outnumbered by blacks, Hispanics, Asians, and other people of color. As our least democratic governmental institution, the Supreme Court can least afford to be managed by those from elites who have little feel for their social environment."

The lesson of this study, on the contrary, suggests that Professor Brooks' concern may be unfounded. Given the Court's history, there is every reason to think that future presidents and senators will continue to appoint to the Supreme Court men and women of ever wider class, race, and ethnic origins. Or as Tocqueville wrote of the legal profession, at the top of which stands the Supreme Court: "Lawyers belong to the people by birth and interest, and to the aristocracy by habit and taste; they may be looked upon as the connecting link between the two great classes of society."

Notes

This chapter was first published in a different form in *Society* 28, no. 4 (May-June 1991).

1. E. Digby Baltzell and Howard G. Schneiderman, "Social Class in the Oval Office," *Society* 25, no. 6 (September-October 1988). Reprinted in a slightly different form in Howard G. Schneiderman, ed., *The Protestant Establishment Revisited* (New Brunswick, NJ: Transaction Publishers, 1991. See, Howard G. Schneiderman, "Presidents, Privilege, and Performance," *Society* 26, no. 3 (March-April 1989).

2

Rich Men in Politics

There is a very good chance that W. Averell Harriman, heir to one of America's greatest railroad fortunes, will be opposed in his fight for re-election to the governorship of New York by his friend, Nelson Aldrich Rockefeller, grandson of the founder of the nation's first oil dynasty. The election has national implications, for the winner will control the country's largest delegation to one or the other of the 1960 national conventions.

Both Harriman and Rockefeller have proved themselves in a wide variety of appointive positions in the federal government under President Roosevelt, Truman and Eisenhower. Harriman, in addition, has won his spurs as a shrewd professional politician with considerable voter-appeal and campaigning stamina. Until now, Rockefeller has been content to carry out the policies of his political superiors in appointive positions. His intimates are sure, however, that this handsome, restless and responsible man-of-means wants the final prize of political professionalism—approval of the voters, elective office, and a chance to initiate policy.

The election now shaping up in New York State raises an interesting question: what kind of role have the rich and well-born played in American political life? This country is supposedly devoted to the cult of the self-made man, and a variety of traditional American ideologies could have been expected to work against the aristocrat in politics. But myth does not always correspond to reality, and our political history reveals that wealthy and well-born statesmen have consistently managed to cultivate the confidence of the voters. Both George Washington, who drove to open Congress in his coach and six, with outriders and footmen in livery, and the ostentatiously plain master of Monticello, who rode up alone and hitched his horse to the nearest post, were popular patrician heroes. And Franklin D. Roosevelt, squire of Dutchess County, carried on this tradition by becoming the egalitarian twentieth century's greatest national hero and voice of the common man.

Patrician leadership was taken for granted and openly admired during the colonial period and at the nation's founding. John Hancock, the "patriot in purple" inheritor of the largest fortune in New England, and Charles Carroll of "Carrollton," the richest man in the colonies, were signers of the liberal and revolutionary Declaration of Independence. The more conservative Constitution, as the historian Charles A. Beard emphasized, was drawn up and supported by the wealthiest men in the new nation.

Egalitarian democracy in America was a product of the frontier and factory. In the early nineteenth century, as the pioneers pushed out over the fall line of the Alleghenies and the industrial revolution began to take hold in the Eastern cities, manners and morals began to change. The folk hero of the common man first came out of the West, when Andrew Jackson challenged the money-power of the Eastern creditors, symbolized by Nicholas Biddle, old Philadelphia's most polished and arrogant aristocrat. It is usually assumed that Jackson marked the break from the older aristocratic appeal in politics to the newer cult of the self-made man. But this folk hero who led the plain people out of the banker's bondage was a typical frontier aristocrat, and not such a radical departure from the Virginia dynasty as is so often supposed. Certainly an aristocrat in bearing and conviction, even his "humble" birth has been exaggerated in the textbooks. Although the son of Scotch-Irish immigrants, his family's connections on the Carolina frontier were excellent: his uncles were large landowners as well as civic and military leaders in the Revolutionary period, and young Andrew, upon his father's death, became a landed proprietor (200 acres) at the age of three. In an environment where some of the men and nearly all of the women signed their names with an "X," the precocious boy was sent to a classical school and, at the age of eleven, was reading such news as the Declaration of July 4, 1776, to a group of thirty or forty adult citizens of his local town. In many ways the master of the "Hermitage," who had been retired as a country gentleman for ten years before being called to the Presidency, was very much in the patrician tradition of Thomas Jefferson and the older Virginia frontier. The myth may very well have changed, but the type of leadership had not.

That one must be *of* the people in order to be *for* them became an ideological staple after the age of Jackson. The log-cabin-to-President myth, as a matter of fact, was born in the cynical campaign of 1840, when the power-starved Whigs, led by Daniel Webster and the moneymen of the East, succeeded in ousting the Democrats after three terms in office. Picturing Martin Van Buren as a fastidious aristocrat with cologne-scented wiskers, forever drinking champagne out of crystal goblets, the cynical Whigs ran the old hero of Tippecanoe, General William Henry Harrison, who preferred plain hard cider and whose simple tastes fitted the Midwestern, log-cabin stereotype.

The truth may make us free, but it is often hard to come by, especially during political campaigns. In spite of log-cabin songs, log-cabin clubs, log-cabin badges and a campaign oratory akin to modern Madison Avenue methods (jingles, generals and all), the candidates themselves were actually quite different from the fictional roles into which they had been cast by the politicians. Van Buren, far from an irresponsible aristocrat, was a devoted Democrat and self-made, professional politician. And old Tippecanoe, educated by private tutors before studying medicine under the famous Benjamin Rush in Philadelphia, was the son of Benjamin Harrison, acme of Virginia's patrician-planter class, signer of the Declaration of Independence and governor of his state (the first Harrison was elected to the House of Burgesses in 1624, and the family, like the Adamses and Roosevelts, produced two Presidents of the United States).

The cynicism of the campaign of 1840 foreshadowed a general decline in the caliber of American political leadership throughout the remainder of the century. Actually the leaders of wealth and position so characteristic of eighteenth- and early nineteenth-century political life in America had been drawn primarily from the landed aristocracy. Especially after the Civil War, however, city fortunes bred a class of men who turned away from politics and public service into the counting house and factory. While old-stock Americans, of unquestionable ability, energy and lust for power were engaged in spanning a continent with rails, exploiting our natural resources and building business dynasties, political affairs, by and large, were left to the party boss and the city machine—the way to wealth and power for the ambitious immigrant. America's business gentlemen paid off the party hack and asked only to be left alone to gather gold.

By the turn of America's business century, however, a new brand of wealthy politicians was at the helm of the ship of state. As the trust gradually replaced competitive enterprise, business gentlemen discarded the less convenient aspects of *laissez-faire* ideology when they saw that monopoly profits depended on political power. In this new "billion-dollar country," the tariff became the mother of trusts, the Senate a millionaire's club, and the federal government a profit-sharing annex of Wall Street. When old Tippecanoe's grandson, Benjamin Harrison, was swept into the Presidency in 1889, wealth's domination of commonwealth was virtually complete. His famous Businessmen's Cabinet (Postmaster General John Wanamaker contributed $50,000 to the party war-chest) proved a convenient ally of a Senate composed of no less than twenty-five millionaires, representing lumber, oil, copper, sugar, silver and steel rather than geographical constituencies. And the uncrowned king was Nelson Aldrich, who ruled the Senate for thirty years in an era when boss-run legislatures, rather than the voters, chose our senior legislators in Washington.

The twentieth century, except for the business binge-and-bust during the twenties, has probably witnessed a real renaissance in American political leadership. The progressive movement ushered in the new century and produced two outstanding presidents in Theodore Roosevelt and Woodrow Wilson. Conservative and patrician in temperament and background, both men took a moralistic approach to political issues. Roosevelt, active in municipal reform and Civil Service Commissioner under Harrison before bursting on the national political scene as the hero of San Juan Hill, was of old Knickerbocker stock. Although possessed of considerable inherited means, he was hardly cut from the same cloth as the self-made millionaires of his day. Theodore Roosevelt, the patrician reformer who spoke out against the members of his class who usually "made the till their fatherland," anticipated the age of Franklin D. Roosevelt, when many men of inherited means went down to Washington to help bail out the American people from the Great Depression.

While the rich and well-born, during Fitzgerald's flaming decade, played the market and polo, it is interesting that such patricians as Averell Harriman, Dean Acheson, Francis Biddle, Sumner Welles and Joseph C. Grew, all at Groton School before World War I, should have become prominent in public service under the Democrats, the party of the urban masses. But then Franklin D. Roosevelt surrounded himself with a generation of gifted and sensitive men, many of whom were undoubtedly guilt-driven to reform by the knowledge that their immediate ancestors had "made the till their fatherland." There is no doubt that this newly-awakened sense of *noblesse oblige* in America played an important role in Roosevelt's New Deal. But there were other reasons for the re-entry of the patrician into political life.

In the first place, since the depression and World War II, government has played a larger and larger role in the lives of all Americans. Perhaps the rich men in the Roosevelt Administration, often called traitors to their class, were just the first to realize that big government was here to stay. If the costs of government were to remain high, so they reasoned, they themselves had better get into the act and do their best to see that the gigantic machinery was administered as honestly and efficiently as possible. And since the war, more and more wealthy Republicans have begun to follow the example of their Democratic friends. Instead of sitting on the sidelines, carping at that man Roosevelt, the New Deal and government in general, they have gone into politics in increasing numbers. Perhaps Nelson Rockefeller will join such men as Herter, Lodge and Saltonstall of Massachusetts, or young Freylinghuysen of New Jersey, in the slowly emerging Republican revival of the gentleman-of-means in politics.

Along with the increasing size and importance of government in American life, there has also been an increase in the power and prestige attached to governmental service. Real money-making has been handicapped by the tax structure, while elaborate expense accounts and retirement plans would hardly appeal to the more creative minds, especially those possessed of inherited wealth. Moreover, power and command have definitely shifted from Wall Street to Washington in this post-war world. The days of the Rothschilds financing the wars of Europe, or J. P. Morgan bailing President Cleveland's government out of the depression, are gone with the wind. As Dean Acheson, a brilliant example of the patrician statesman, recently wrote: "Today, more than ever before, the prize of the general is not a bigger tent, but command. The managers of industry and finance have the bigger tents; but command rests with government." Such men as G. Mennen Williams, Chester Bowles, William Benton, Adlai Steveson, Jack Kennedy, Joseph S. Clark and William Fulbright—rich, talented, and often called "egg-heads"—have surely been drawn into the political arena at least partly by the fascination of command.

Political democracy, as practiced in America today, is in many ways a great luxury. What nation in Asia could afford the multi-million-dollar campaigns we have seen here since the war? And in these costly modern campaigns, the candidate of private means has a great advantage over a less affluent opponent. While campaign contributions from outside sources are severely limited by law, there is no limit placed upon a candidate's personal expenditures. This is even more true in America than in England, for instance, where "interests" may legally finance a candidate as long as their support is open to public scrutiny.

Finally, in trying to explain why there has been an increase in the number of men of inherited wealth in politics today, one is likely to overlook an important statistical fact: it is simply that, in spite of inheritance and income taxes, there is probably more inherited wealth in the nation today than ever before. Such famous American family names as Ford, Rockefeller, Mellon and DuPont, for instance, are all in the second or third generation today. In a systematic study of American millionaires, Pitirim Sorokin found this same trend toward more and more inherited fortunes. The composition of the student bodies of such exclusive educational institutions as Princeton and Groton is another index of the status of inherited position in America. At Princeton, the sons and grandsons of alumni increased from approximately 10 percent of the entering class of 1922 to over 20 percent of the class of 1940; at Groton, while the first son of an alumnus graduated in 1915, by 1940 approximately two-thirds of the boys were from old Groton families.

American civilization, led by businessmen of daring enterprise and ingenuity, has produced the highest standards of living the world has ever known. The continuing greatness of America will presumably depend on the nation's ability to shoulder the burden of world political leadership. The recent revival of patrician participation in public life is part of a more general response to this new challenge of world leadership. The prize of power is stimulating to the old rich, and the cult of the self-made man may very well be on the wane in our world of abundant consumption which seems to prefer *Vogue* and *Esquire* to such stuff as Horatio Alger. This may or may not be a healthy thing for our country but, after all, there are few authentic log cabins for future Presidents to be born in.

Note

This chapter was first published in *The Nation,* 31 May 1958.

3

Class Authority in American History

In his famous book, *Democracy in America,* Alexis de Tocqueville wrote that "almost all nations that have exercised a powerful influence on the destinies of the world, by conceiving, following out, and executing vast designs, from the Romans to the English, have been governed by aristocracies." John Adams was also aware of the need for aristocratic institutions as a bulwark against excessive democratic tyranny. And his heavily marked-up copy of Mary Wollstonecraft's defense of the French Revolution is an excellent index of his views: Thus, where Mary wrote that "hereditary distinctions, cruelly abridging rational liberty, have prevented man from rising to his just point of elevation by his improvable faculties," Adams scrawled in longhand as follows: "Hereditary distinctions among the Greeks and Romans, and in all Europe since their times, have been essential to the liberty that has been enjoyed."

Aristocratic institutions arise in history when the more talented members of a more or less consanguine group of upper-class families not only take over the political leadership of the state, but also give tone to a literature, and authority to ideas for several generations. The leading families in Republican Rome and in England between the reigns of Elizabeth I and Victoria were two of the most successful aristocracies in Western history. Thus, of the two hundred noble consuls who served the Republic in the century before the attempted Gracchi reforms, one hundred and forty were drawn from only sixteen family lines.

In modern Europe, while the ancient French nobility degenerated into a functionless, if affluent *caste* during the centralizing reign of Louis XIV and was easily swept away by the French Revolution, the British nobility, decimated by the Wars of the Roses, was born anew in the Tudor period and played a major role in leading England through the Glorious Revolution of 1689, the Reform Bill of 1832 and to victory in the two World Wars. Thus, an Elizabethan country squire, George Velliers, founded a consanguine line which produced more than a dozen prime ministers including Lord John Russell of the Reform Bill, and England's leader in her finest hour, Winston Churchill. And a modern investigator has noted that in the one hundred and twenty-five years preceding the first labour government in 1924, of the 306 men reaching cabinet rank, 182, or 60%, were titled aristocrats (there were presumably others who were untitled younger sons and in-laws).

The thirteen English colonies along the coast of North America eventually spawned three hereditary ruling classes or aristocracies, the Knickerbocker gentry of the Hudson Valley, the descendants of the Puritan magistrates and ministers who came to Massachusetts Bay just before the Great Rebellion broke out, and the Cavaliers of Virginia whose family founders largely came to America in the 1650s after their defeat by the forces of Oliver Cromwell. The Virginians produced Washington, Jefferson, Madison, Monroe and the two Harrisons; Theodore and Franklin Roosevelt were brilliant late bloomers on their Knickerbocker family tree; and the Adams presidents, father and son, combined the Old Roman gravitas and the Puritan emphasis on the magisterial calling to found Boston's and our nation's first family.

During the Constitutional and Federalist periods, and perhaps even down to the Civil War, the Virginia planters were the preeminent aristocracy in America; but over the longer span of our history, the patrician and puritan class of Boston's best have been preeminent in molding the American leadership culture, not only in New England but in America as a whole. The term "Yankee," for instance, stood for New England in the Knickerbocker days of Irving's Rip Van Winkle, for the North as a whole by the time of the Civil War, and for all Americans who went abroad to fight in the First and Second World Wars. More seriously, all of us know of the Mathers of Puritan Boston, fewer of us are aware that the family founder, Richard, produced 70 direct descendants (28 in the male and 52 in the female line) who held pulpits (read culture, school, and college builders) in various towns in Connecticut, New York, Ohio, Michigan, and Minnesota during the nineteenth century; and Mathers were also founders, builders and leaders of Cleveland, Ohio.

We all know that T.S. Eliot and Robert Lowell were major twentieth century poets, fewer know that Eliot's grandfather was the Ben Franklin of St. Louis, founding everything including Washington University, which

to this day has been Harvard-led. And we could multiply such examples with college after college in community after community in the Old Northwest. Most important of all, of course, is the fact that the Puritans not only founded Harvard six years after landing in the New World, but, after the Mathers lost out to the liberals at Harvard, the more conservative stream went down to Connecticut and founded Yale. When liberal Yale pushed through the Half-Way Covenant, the conservatives again went west and founded Newark and Elizabethtown, in New Jersey, where only orthodox Puritans from Harvard or Yale were accepted as ministers, one of whom Aaron Burr, of a long line going back to an ancestor in the Winthrop Fleet, founded the College of New Jersey in a little sleepy town called Princeton. Once governor of Massachusetts, and governor of New Jersey at the college's founding, Jonathan Belcher, was responsible for building Nassau Hall.

Harvard, Yale, and Princeton have educated the American elite since the nation's founding in almost the same proportion as Oxford and Cambridge in England—eight presidents of the United States, including John Fitzgerald Kennedy and the Adamses, John and John Quincy.

While the Adamses are America's first family, the descendants of Governor John Winthrop have remained at the top of society far longer than any other family in American history. John Winthrop was born on the Manor of Groton, in East Anglia, in the Armada year of 1588; three centuries later, his descendent Robert C. Winthrop, was a first-family institution in Boston where he died in 1894 at the age of 85. Young John Winthrop, whose grandfather had become master of the Manor of Groton in Henry VIII's time, was a justice of the peace by the age of eighteen, was elected governor of the Massachusetts Bay Company before sailing for the New World, and served continuously as governor or assistant of the Old Colony until his death in 1649. And Winthrops continued to take the lead both in Massachusetts and in Connecticut during the Colonial period and down through the nineteenth century. Robert C. Winthrop had been Speaker of the U.S. House of Representatives, and U.S. Senator (taking Webster's place) before the Civil War; he served as president of the Massachusetts Historical Society for thirty years, and on the vestry of Trinity Church for over three decades. Appropriately enough, a Wall Street Winthrop headed one of America's sixty richest families during the Gilded Age, and today when the idea of aristocracy has been almost totally silenced by our egalitarian plutocracy, Winthrops are among the wealthier families in the fashionable areas of Long Island and Boston's North Shore.

During and right after the Revolution a talented group of extremely ambitious families from Essex County such as the Cabots, Higginsons, Peabodys and Lowells came down to Boston to fill the leadership void created by the exodus of Tory families who followed Thomas Hutchinson and the Reverend Caner of Anglican King's Chapel into exile in Canada and England. In the meantime, a host of factory towns were rising in eastern Massachusetts as every village with a waterfall set up a textile mill or a paper mill, a shoe factory or an iron foundry. Boston's best were getting richer and richer; and the portrait painter of the new nation, Gilbert Stuart, settling in Boston after 1805, painted portraits of one or more members of the following families: Adams, Ames, Appleton, Bowditch, Brooks, Coolidge, Eliot, Everett, Gardner, Gray, Higginson, Jackson, Lee, Lowell, Motley, Otis, Paine, Parkman, Peabody, Perkins, Phillips, Pickering, Prescott, Quincy, Shattuck, Warren, and Winthrop, a pretty fair index of the city's Brahmin aristocracy.

The term Boston Brahmin was coined by Robert C. Winthrop's exact contemporary, Oliver Wendell Holmes, at the very height of the literary flowering of New England. This Golden Decade opened with the publication of Emerson's *Representative Men* and Hawthorne's *Scarlet Letter,* in 1850, *The House of Seven Gables, Moby Dick,* and *Uncle Tom's Cabin,* the next year; *Pierre* in 1852 and *Walden,* in 1854. Then, in 1855, two permanently useful reference books appeared, Thomas Bulfinch, the architect's son, published *The Age of Fable* and John Bartlett, owner of the University Bookstore, the center of literary gossip in Cambridge, published the first edition of *Familiar Quotations. The Atlantic Monthly,* named by Dr. Holmes and edited by James Russell Lowell appeared in 1857, with contributions from Emerson, Motley, Holmes, Longfellow, Norton, Whittier, and Harriet Beecher Stowe marking the high tide of the Boston mind. Two years later, Holmes published an article in the Atlantic entitled *The Brahmin Caste of New England;* originally coined by Holmes to refer to a sensitive and shy "race of scholars," Brahmins soon came to be associated with upper-class Boston as a whole.

If the 1850s marked the flowering of literary New England, and of Brahmin self-confidence, the 1880s marked the passing of American literary leadership to New York and the beginning of the end of the unquestioned WASP dominance in Boston, in this country as a whole, and in the world. From our point of view the highlights of this vital pivotal decade might be listed as follows:

1880 Boston celebrates its 250th Anniversary

1881 Death of John Amory Lowell, first trustee of the Lowell Institute who also took a leading part in the founding of MIT and the choosing of six presidents of Harvard, including his good friend and protege, Charles W. Eliot; Richard Sears wins the first U.S. Lawn Tennis Championship, held the end of August at Newport, Rhode Island.

1882 Death of Emerson, and the founding of the "The Country Club" in Brookline, symbolizing both the end of the Great Generation and the beginning of the Brahmin (and WASP) flight to the suburbs. Founding of the Boston Reform Club reflecting hope for reform.

1883 Assassination of Czar Nicholas of Russia, always symbolizing to me the beginning of the New Immigration (from Southern to Eastern Europe) and the birth of the modern anti-Semitism in America. Founding of the *Sons of the Revolution,* the first WASP ancestor society.

1884 Endicott Peabody founds the Groton School and his fellow Brahmins desert their beloved Republican Party, becoming Mugwumps for Cleveland. Josiah Quincy's first political experience and of lasting import.

1885 Boston elects its first Irish-Catholic mayor, Hugh O'Brian.

1886 The year of the Haymarket Riots in Chicago also witnessed 700 strikes in Massachusetts; Josiah Quincy elected to the Massachusetts legislator as a pro-labor Democrat. ("Imagine a gentleman being a Democrat," so they said at *The Club.* But John Quincy Adams II, who died prematurely and is the least known of the four brothers in the fourth generation, was the leader of the Democratic Party in Massachusetts for many years: he ran and was defeated for the Vice-Presidency of the U.S. and for Lieutenant governor of Massachusetts; he was also offered the position of Secretary of the Navy in Cleveland's cabinet).

1888 Three-hundredth anniversary of the Armada Year; the birth of Joseph Patrick Kennedy; and the first issue of the *Social Register.*

1890 Closing of our western frontier (according to Frederick Jackson Turner),and the passing of the Sherman Anti-Trust Act, largely drafted by Senator George F. Hoar of Massachusetts and marking the first positive attempt by the Federal Government to mold the shape of American society; the Irish become a majority in Boston; (the Daughters of the American Revolution founded).

What a decade. Surely the blood-dimmed tide was loosed, and the ceremony of innocence was never quite the same again in Boston. Theodore White, a graduate of Boston Latin and Harvard, put it as follows in his latest book, *In Search of History:*

> The election of 1960 was devoid of cause only if one failed to recognize that the man himself, John F. Kennedy, embodied the cause...he was a Catholic, an ethnic from outside the main stream of American leadership...Perhaps not since the time of the Gracchi had any eighty-year period seen so great a social and racial change in a political system as did American between 1880 and 1960. between the time of the Gracchi (133 B.C.) and the Caesar's thrust across the Rubicon (49 B.C.), the Roman Republic of farmers, yeoman, citizen soldiers and patrician leaders, which Polybius described as self-governing and eternal, vanished. Its own triumphs and laws had made its capital a gathering place at once of the powerful and the dispossessed, had enfranchised Sicilians, Alpine Italians, Spaniards, Jews, Gauls. Since Roman law made Rome the only legal place of voting, the new strangers exercised an entirely disproportionate influence as they filed through the *ovile* to cast their ballots and help choose Rome's leaders. Caesar put an end to the system...[and] drove the manipulators from Rome...

White noted that America had not yet crossed the Rubicon when he wrote of Kennedy in 1978. Whenever I think of the years since the assassination of the two Kennedy brothers (just about 2000 years after the assassinations of the brothers Gracchi) I am less sure than White that it won't happen here.

At any rate, though I have written elsewhere of the sad story of WASP exclusiveness, of anti-ethnic and especially anti-Semitic prejudices, I should like to take a brief look at how and why the Boston Brahmins and their institutions have, in the long run, served to assimilate the leadership of the Irish Catholics in particular, and of the other ethnic groups too. In one way or another, their so-called enemies absorbed their Puritan-Yankee values. The acid test of Yankee success, and vital for an understanding of the political culture of Boston, is the fact that the first Irish-Catholic president of the U.S. was a product of that culture, that the Boston Kennedys are the most famous American family in the world today, and that Jack, Bobby, and Ted are the only three brothers in our history to have sat in the U.S. Senate, by far the most distinguished club in the nation.

What were these Puritan-Brahmin values that rubbed off so successfully on the Kennedys and other Boston Catholics? In the first place, the very essence of Puritanism, in both Old and New England, was the idea of the calling; the way to please God was to do one's best in one's chosen or inherited calling. John Winthrop (who referred to himself in his famous journals as "the Governor") was instructed by the writings of the sixteenth century Puritan theologian, William Perkins, who stressed the calling even more than Calvin did and placed the magistrate and the minister at the very apex of societal authority; neither Perkins nor Winthrop, nor the vast majority of Brahmin Bostonians since, have believed in equality: "At all times," wrote Winthrop, "some must be rich, some poor, some high and eminent in power and dignity; other means and in subjection." Above all, the Yankee-Brahmin, as Henry Adams wrote in his classic history of the United States in the age of Jefferson, was "ambitious beyond reason to excel."

Enemies of Calvinists and Puritans have often stressed their worship of wealth, as when William Perkins wrote: "Men are honoured in their riches." But this is only a half-truth, and Perkins went on to finish his point as follows: "I mean not riches simple but the use of riches; namely as they are made instruments to uphold and maintain virtue." Some three centuries after Perkins wrote these lines, George Peabody was piling up a great fortune as our first international investment banker. After paying J.P. Morgan's father $30,000 to handle public relations and entertainment for his firm in London, Peabody (a bachelor) lived on $3,000 a year while making more than $300,000, in the meantime becoming America's leading Victorian philanthropist both here and in England. As Godkin, the editor of the *Nation,* in New York, put it in 1871: "Boston is the one place in America where wealth and knowledge of how to use it are apt to coincide."

Finally, and perhaps the most important in the long run, the heirs of Calvinism in America were the major founders of schools and colleges, especially before the Civil War. The certificate of education replaced the certificate of ancestry above all in New England. The Boston Latin School, founded in 1635, and Harvard College, founded a year later, have been far and away the leading elite producing institutions in our history. The sons of Boston's best were educated at the Latin School from its founding through the generation of Charles W. Eliot. Thereafter just as parents moved to the suburbs, so they increasingly sent their sons off to country boarding schools, largely modeled on Round Hill School, founded in Northampton, Massachusetts, in 1829. Today, within an hour or two's drive from the top of Beacon Hill are located the American counterparts of Eton and Harrow in England: Exeter and Andover academies, founded in the eighteenth century by the Boston Phillip family, and the Episcopalian schools such as Groton, St. Paul's Middlesex and St. Marks, all founded by Boston Brahmins in the late nineteenth century.

Regardless of how his wealth was made, then, Joseph Patrick Kennedy surely fathered a family in the Puritan-Brahmin mold; after graduating from Boston Latin, he entered Harvard where he earned his letter in baseball and made a lesser final club. He then married well, to the stern and stoic daughter of John Francis Fitzgerald, congressmen, mayor and a graduate of the Latin School himself before spending a brief time at Harvard. The Kennedys raised all their children with a rigorous sense of the *right use of riches,* and their boys with ambitions beyond reason to excel in the magisterial calling; Joseph, Jr. in particular, was raised to be president. While the girls were sent to Catholic schools, the boys went to the best boarding schools where Jack, in his first year at Choate, was welcomed by Headmaster St. John in words which inspired the most famous line his inaugural address: "Always remember," St. John told his new boys, "it is not what Choate can do for you but what you can do for Choate." (And now, two decades after the address, most Americans seem primarily interested in what their government can do for them). Then Jack spent a year at Princeton before going on to Harvard where he joined a club that is now famous. He was a middling student until his senior year when he wrote a thesis which was later published as a book. And when he went on to the White House, he used Harvard men and Harvard more than any other president very much in the style of Franklin Roosevelt.

I should like to end, however, on a sad but hopeful note. It is often in history that new men, from Cicero to Webster appreciate and apply the manners of the class to which they have aspired (and attained) with far more zest and conviction than those who are, as they say, to the manor born. Thus after dinner, in the fall of 1972, when McGovern was running for the presidency and Harvard was running wild, I was taken to

Kennedy's final club for a drink or two by one of those professional alumni. It was interesting to observe that, while several blond-haired WASPs apparently took their club for granted and were oblivious if not rude to the two old men sipping scotch, a thoughtful and polite undergraduate, of Italian background and a resident of a Boston suburb was charmingly informative as we engaged in a half hour's conversation. This should not have been surprising, of course, since social mobility and class authority are handmaidens to the American dream.

Note

This chapter is published here for the first time. It was originally presented as the Lowell Lecture, on 30 September, 1980, at the Kennedy Library in Boston, Massachusetts.

4

The Forging of an Aristocracy

Harvard College was founded and governed for almost two centuries by the state-church establishment in Massachusetts. *The Forging of an Aristocracy: Harvard and the Boston Upper Class, 1800–1870,*[1] by Ronald Story, is a thorough and extremely interesting analysis of how, between 1800 and 1870, Harvard gradually became a privately endowed institution supported and governed by upper-class Boston. In 1780, when the Massachusetts constitution was written, for instance, the Board of Overseers was composed of the president of the college and the governor, lieutenant governor, councilors, and senators of the state, as well as the Congregational ministers of Cambridge, Watertown, Charlestown, Boston, Roxbury, and Dorchester. A hundred years later, these magistrates and ministers had been replaced by Harvard alumni drawn primarily from the ranks of Boston's upper-class business and professional community.

Harvard continued to prosper under state control in the nineteenth century so long as the Federalists, the party of the rich and well-born in Boston and elsewhere in the state, dominated all branches of the state government. The real break came in 1824 when the federalist party was finally defeated forever in Massachusetts; the triumphant Jeffersonian-Republicans cut off all state funds.

The transformation of Harvard from a communal to a class institution was no easy task: it was led by a small group of increasingly affluent, upper-class Bostonians who, in 1842, founded the Harvard Alumni Association and in 1855, the "Club of the Graduates of Harvard College," which later became the Boston Harvard Club; even then it was not until 1865 that the Massachusetts legislature finally transferred control of the college to the Harvard alumni who were henceforth to choose the Overseers "voting at Cambridge on Commencement Day." The margin of victory was a single vote in the senate and a "slender majority" in the house.

Ronald Story shows how the privatization of Harvard turned it into an elite institution in which the socializing function became as important as teaching and research. And the goal of the socializing process was the cultivation of gentility in the style of Oxford and Cambridge in England. Under the leadership of Edward Channing, professor of rhetoric after 1819, the so-called Harvard accent was modeled on "the purity and simplicity of the English style."

Story carefully shows how the privatization of Harvard was part of a more inclusive development of an associational rather than a solely familistic upper-class in Boston; at the same time, as Boston's brahmins were building Harvard into the most highly endowed private institution in America, they were also building up a solid group of other cultural and medical institutions such as the Lowell Institute, the Athenaeum, the Massachusetts Historical Society, the Massachusetts General Hospital (McLean Asylum), the Perkins Institute for the Blind, and so forth. All of these institutions were founded before the Civil War and formed the core of what Tocqueville saw as our American associational democracy, a democracy unlike anything found on the continent of Europe where all education and most cultural institutions have traditionally been founded and supported by the state.

As there was very little to criticize in this excellent book, it was all the more boring to have the author close on a now-fashionable anti-elitist note: "For the forging of the Brahmin aristocracy, then," he writes in the last paragraph of his book, "the consequences of the great institutional developments of the antebellum era were altogether happy. For the forging of a viable society with a coherent culture, they were far less so." He, of course, produces no evidence for this final concession to current tribal sentiment.

Notes

This chapter was first published in *The American Historical Review* 86, no. 2 (April 1981).

1. Ronald Story, *The Forging of an Aristocracy: Harvard and the Boston Upper Class, 1800–1870* (Middletown, Ct: Wesleyan University Press, 1980).

5

The Log Cabin Myth

The "Horatio Alger" and "Log-cabin-to-presidency" myths are deeply imbedded in our American traditions. All white American mothers have been led to believe that their sons have a chance to become president. Even Edward Pessen, the author of this delightful book, *The Log Cabin Myth: The Social Backgrounds of the Presidents,*[1] dedicated it to his three grandsons, "presidential timber, all."

Pessen does a thorough and convincing job of analyzing the backgrounds of our presidents from Washington to Reagan; but he does not say that background is more than one factor among many; he is no environmental determinist. *The Log Cabin Myth* is an important book about, as the author puts it, "a suprisingly neglected theme." Many of us believe James Bryce's observation that most presidents were self-made men of humble origin. However, this systematic analysis of the social backgrounds of our thirty-nine presidents reveals that a large majority of them had upper or upper-middle class origins.

Pessen uses the sixfold class hierarchy developed by W. Lloyd Warner, adding two border levels of his own. Thus, of the sixteen presidents born to the highest status, Washington, Jefferson, Madison, J. Q. Adams, W. H. Harrison, Tyler, Taylor, B. Harrison, Theodore Roosevelt, Taft, and Franklin Roosevelt are ranked as upper-upper; Polk and Kennedy, upper-upper to lower-upper; and John Adams, Monroe, and Wilson as lower-upper. The next sixteen presidents are ranked by Pessen as follows: Pierce, Hayes, Cleveland, Harding, Coolidge and Truman lower-upper to upper-middle; Jackson, Van Buren, Buchanan, Grant, Arthur, McKinley, Hoover, L. B. Johnson, Ford, and Carter were upper-middle. Three presidents, Lincoln, Eisenhower, and Reagan, were on the borderline between the upper-middle and lower-middle. Finally, Pessen ranks

Fillmore, Garfield, and Nixon as lower-middle and only Andrew Johnson as upper-lower.

Pessen does a thorough, and thoroughly convincing, job of researching and analyzing the social backgrounds of these men. He takes into account the status not only of their fathers but also of their mothers, and where need be, their grandparents. Lincoln, for instance, was by no means born to such lowly origins as the log-cabin mythmakers would have it; his grandfather owned a 200-acre farm in Virginia which he inherited from his father; and the president's father, often described as lazy, shiftless, and a failure, was actually a skilled carpenter and farmer who owned "two farms of six hundred acres, several town lots, livestock and horses, property that was quite close to the total owned by the wealthiest man in the area" at the time of his famous son's birth.

Lincoln married extremely well, into the "bona fide Kentucky aristocracy." In this connection, it is interesting that all our presidents except Nixon, Ford, and Carter made judicious marriages: Jefferson's wife "inherited 135 slaves and more than 11,000 acres of land two years after their marriage." Lyndon Johnson married the daughter of "the richest man in the county."

While Pessen very successfully challenges Bryce's humble-origins theory of the presidency, he has no quarrel with Bryce's famous dictum that "few great men have been elected president." Here I tend to disagree. Our four wartime presidents, Washington, Lincoln, Wilson, and Franklin Roosevelt, have been absolutely first-rate.

I am even more in disagreement with the last page of this book where the author argues that "in a true social democracy, one would expect to find the highest office occupied by men and women who represent a cross section of the society, socially and occupationally. The intelligence and other qualities ideally required of a political leader would seem to be as available among skilled mechanics, farmers, teachers, and architects as among politicians and lawyers; no less common among men and women of modest income than among the unusually well-to-do." But his appeal to common-man [sic] rhetoric contradicts what little he has to say about our presidents' ability as related to their social origins. Thus, he notes that only six presidents—John Adams, Jefferson, Madison, John Quincy Adams, Taft, and Wilson—were possessed of "sheer intellectual brilliance." He does not say that earlier he ranked all these men as upper-class in origin. Also of high social origins were the only four men—John Adams, Jefferson, Madison, and Wilson—whom he describes as political philosophers of note.

In spite of some disagreements in interpretation, I found this book extremely well argued and interesting. We are all in the author's debt for filling a void in the historical record.

Notes

This chapter was first published in *Contemporary Sociology* 14, no. 2 (March 1985).

1. Edward Pessen, *The Log Cabin Myth: The Social Background of the Presidents* (New Haven: Yale University Press, 1984).

6

Gentlemen in Crisis: The Union League of Philadelphia

It has been said that if three Americans were dropped out of an aeroplane flying at 5,000 feet, by the time they had reached the ground they would have formed an association and elected themselves president, vice president, and secretary and treasurer. "Americans of all ages, all conditions, and all dispositions," wrote Tocqueville, "constantly form associations. They have not only commercial and manufacturing companies, in which they all take part, but associations of a thousand other kinds, religious, moral, serious, futile, general or restricted, enormous or diminutive.... Wherever at the head of some new undertaking you have a government in France, or a man of rank in England, in the United States you will be sure to find an association."

Benjamin Franklin was the greatest association-founder in American history, and his adopted city of Philadelphia is marked today by an infinite number and variety of voluntary associations, from the Masons, Mummers, Odd Fellows and Kiwanis to cricket clubs, country clubs, men's clubs and so forth. Along south Broad Street, under the shadow of Billy Penn's statue atop City Hall and close by the famous Academy of Music, stands the Union League Club, a handsome Victorian pile and one of the city's architectural landmarks today. For more than a century now, The League, as it is known by its members and knowing citizens of the city in all walks of life, has stood for good fellowship and selective dogoodism in the tradition of Franklin, as well as patriotism, social exclusiveness, and the guardianship of the virtues of the Republican Party.

In *Gentlemen in Crisis: The First Century of the Union League of Philadelphia, 1862–1962,*[1] Maxwell Whiteman, archival and historical consultant to the League, has given us an excellent and exhaustive study of the League's first hundred years from its founding in 1862. In 386 fact-packed pages, including 584 footnotes, he has not only covered a wide variety of the club's activities but also placed them within the context of the history of the city, the State of Pennsylvania, and the nation.

In the election of 1860, though Pennsylvania went for Lincoln, Philadelphia did not. Situated close to the Mason-Dixon Line and a textile center, the city was dominated by an establishment both intermarried with Virginians and Charlestonians and admirous of the chivalrous virtues of the South. John Clifford Pemberton, for instance, was not only a member of one of the oldest Quaker-turned-Episcopal clans in the city but was also the Confederate General who surrendered to Grant at Vicksburg on July Fourth, the same day his Philadelphia playmate George Gordon Meade defeated Lee at Gettysburg. Thus when the talented author and handsomest clubman in the city, George Boker, and some of his idealistic friends, founded an association to support Lincoln, the Union cause and the rights of Negroes, the Proper Philadelphia Establishment was shaken to its roots. Within the city's more exclusive social circles, wrote Boker, "the President was vulgar, the administration was vulgar, the war was vulgar, and the people who waged it were of the common sort, who would shortly receive a merited castigation from the gentlemen of the South...."

Like so much else in American history, the League was born in idealism. Its first motto was "God and Our Country" and Lincoln found it to be "an organization free from political prejudices and prompted in its formation by motives of the highest patriotism." Beginning with the nonpartisan ideal of preserving the Union, the League gradually became a partisan supporter of the national Republican Party. The heyday of the League as well as the Republican Party was of course the age of McKinley. In 1900, when the Republican National Convention was held in Philadelphia, League members, along with a large majority of the men who still unquestionably dominated our economy and society, reached a peak of optimism about America and the world. In the course of the century, the nation's population had risen from 4 to 80 million, and the WASP gentlemen of the League were still proud of the thousands of hard-working immigrants who had come to our shores in ever increasing waves.

Although many members were tempted to withdraw from political commitments and enjoy their club for its social fellowship alone, the League continued to play an important role in the Republican Party at both the national and state level. A very important point brought out in this book, but unfortunately left unanalyzed or discussed in much detail, is the fact that almost from the beginning the League made a firm decision to stay out of local Philadelphia politics. Though League members became governors and senators of the state, and cabinet members in various Republican administrations in Washington, gentlemen of the League remained aloof from the corrupt politics of the Republican machine that dominated the city government from the last decades of the nineteenth century until after the second World War. Though machine leaders like the Vare brothers were pointedly excluded from membership in the League, no attempt was made by the gentlemen of the League to run for local office or to officially back reform candidates. No wonder Henry Charles Lea, distinguished historian and leading Victorian civic reformer, finally resigned from the League. When Lincoln Steffens came to Philadelphia and found it both corrupt and content, League members were certainly aware of the accuracy of his conclusions. Yet they apparently were unwilling to do anything about it.

In the 1920s, during the last-gasp fling of old-stock America and its bastion, the Republican Party, the League became more aggressively Republican. It lost its former faith in the immigrant and stood out for the restriction of immigration. Even though the members were forced to admit that Franklin Roosevelt was "a gentleman of culture and a graduate of Groton and Harvard," the New Deal days were a trial to the League. The Republican Era, if not the Republican Party, had had its day, and gradually League members were looked upon as "reactionaries" who had not changed from the days of McKinley. It even became "difficult to obtain prominent Republican political figures to speak at the League."

At any rate, in spite of the depression when many League members were forced to resign for financial reasons, and the post World War II suburban era when urban club life in general declined, the League is still an active force in the social and business life of the city. During the Eisenhower years, even their political spirits were raised a notch or two.

I should like, finally, to mention Mr. Whiteman's excellent discussion of the staff members of the League, most of them originally veterans of the Civil War. In our increasingly uncivil age it is appropriate that he should discuss this source of civility in any good club in America. It is surprising how many of them, doormen, bartenders, waiters and managers, served the League for five and more decades. It is a tribute to the League that this vital source of civility has been respected and recorded by Mr. Whiteman.

This is far and away the best club history I have ever come upon and reading it is a rewarding way to relive the history of America and Philadelphia since the Civil War.

Notes

This chapter was first published in *The Pennsylvania Magazine of History and Biography* 100, no. 2 (April 1976).

1. Maxwell Whitman, *Gentlemen in Crisis: The First Century of The Union League of Philadelphia, 1982–1962* (Philadelphia: The Union League of Philadelphia, 1975).

7

Cadwaladers and Others

Two hundred years ago this past summer, 55 delegates from twelve colonies (egalitarian and antinomian Rhode Island sent no one) met in Philadelphia to revise the Articles of Confederation and ended up writing the Constitution. The style of the age was more aristocratic than democratic. Since these 55 gentlemen trusted one another, they met in complete secrecy from May to September. George Washington, who silently presided over the meetings, was the very personification of aristocratic and class authority in this classic age of deferential democracy.

In the defiant democracy that marks our tragic age of unmatched mistrust, secrecy has become akin almost to treason. Now when we are attempting to untangle a web of lies that seems to have held sway at the very top levels of our government, perhaps we might benefit from some understanding of the values of more aristocratic ages when a gentleman's word was his bond. A first-rate, analytical book on aristocracy might provide some perspective on our present time of troubles.

Unfortunately, Stephen Birmingham's 23rd book, *America's Secret Aristocracy,*[1] is neither first rate nor analytical; it is, rather, an unsystematic collection of anecdotes about so-called old families in America, such as the Hudson River patrons of New York, the Brahmins of Boston, the F.F.V.'s (First Families of Virginia), the pre-1849 Spanish grandees of California, and so forth. Since the book includes 26 chapters in some 334 pages, nothing is covered in depth. In chapter 14, for instance, Mr. Birmingham dissects the aristocracies of Boston, Philadelphia and Charleston, S.C., in just 16 pages. He devotes more space to the old saw about how Proper Boston Ladies inherit, rather than buy, their hats than he does to the accomplishments of the Adams men, or Lowell families. A large part of his discussion of Charleston's aristocracy is taken up with a tedious anecdote about how in the 1950s an imposter with a British accent was totally taken in by Old-Family Society. And his swift look at Proper Philadelphia is somewhat out of focus.

Mr. Birmingham seems to worship the Livingston and Jay families, often for the wrong reasons. Thus, he carefully tells us that when John Jay married Sarah Livingston in April 1774, he was of newer wealth and status than she. He tells us almost nothing about the careers of John Jay and of Sarah's kinsman Robert R. Livingston, friends at King's College (predecessor of Columbia) and youthful law partners, who went on to become two of the leading statesmen and jurists of our Founding Fathers' generation. Much later in the book, Mr. Birmingham discusses John Jay Chapman, mainly because he was a Jay; while he goes into some detail about Chapman's eccentric and tragic aristocratic style of life in the mid-19th century, he writes hardly a word about the fact that Chapman was a leading cultural, political and moral critic of his age, according to such scholars as Edmund Wilson and Lionel Trilling.

Similarly, he mentions Mr. and Mrs. S. Dillon Ripley several times, largely, of course, because Mrs. Ripley was born Mary Livingston; the fact that her husband is a fine ornithologist and largely responsible for building the Smithsonian into the absolutely first-rate institution it is today is more or less ignored. Perhaps Mrs. Ripley anticipated the tone of this book-to-be when she once wrote; "It seems to me that these old families would be better off if they spent less time glorifying their families' past, and more time thinking about what they could do to help America's future."

Not only are Mr. Birmingham's selections of facts often superficial; his information is sometimes quite inaccurate. In discussing the Society of Mayflower Descendants, for instance, he notes that "the second boat to arrive at the Plymouth Colony" was the Arabella. On the contrary, the Arabella never carried any *Pilgrims* to the New World; rather it was the flagship of the Winthrop fleet of *Puritans* and it landed at Salem. In Proper Philadelphia, everybody knows that "when a Biddle gets drunk, he thinks he's a Cadwalader"; but Mr. Birmingham has it that drunken Biddles think they are Ingersolls; two chapters later, he notes that "the Ingersolls, Willings, and Chews have been outflanked by Biddles, Cadwaladers, Pews, and Campbell's Soup Dorrances." Old Philadelphians will react to this not quite appropriate sentence much as they did as children when an annoying peer scratched the blackboard with his or her fingernails. Finally Mr. Birmingham's historical sense is nicely revealed when he writes that *Fortune* magazine "had forgotten FDR's relative President Theodore Roosevelt, who was also Groton-educated." Groton was founded in 1884, while Roosevelt graduated from Harvard in 1880.

To close on a more positive note, it is my impression that this book will sell very well. Mr. Birmingham and his editors have a clever sense of the marketplace: the word "Secret" in the title suggests conspiracy, which has great appeal in our mistrustful age; and any book on the superficiality of aristocracies flatters the snobbish, egalitarian mind.

Notes

This chapter was first published in *The New York Times Book Review,* 27 September 1987.

1. Stephen Birmingham, *America's Secret Aristocracy* (Boston: Little, Brown & Company, 1987).

8

Scenes from American Life

If the sociology of the theater is ever written, it is my judgment that *Scenes From American Life,*[1] by A.R. Gurney Jr., will be recognized as both a theatrical landmark and a cultural artifact dramatizing the disintegration of the American WASP upper-class in our dehumanizing age.

The sociology of class goes back to the classic works of Karl Marx (1818–83) whose turgid writings were devoid of persons and filled with moralistic battles between good and evil classes and abstract conceptual systems such as capitalism and socialism, bourgeois and proletariat. At the same time, his contemporary, Charles Dickens (1812–70), wrote of Victorian England in terms of Pickwick, Pip and Miss Havesham, David Copperfield, Oliver Twist and a host of others. Dickens has left us a *moral* world of enchanting, if often diabolical characters while Marx's *moralistic* world of abstractions was, in my judgment, a major force in ushering in what Max Weber saw as the "disenchantment" of the modern world.

F. Scott Fitzgerald opened his short story, *The Rich Boy,* as follows: "Begin with an individual, and before you know it you find that you have created a type; begin with a type, and you find that you have created—nothing... There are no types, no plurals. There is only a rich boy, and this is his and not his brother's story." And Fitzgerald has left us a vivid gallery of individuals from Anson Hunter (his rich boy) and Amory Blaine to Jay Gatsby, Daisy and Tom Buchanan, Dick Diver and Rosemary, and Monroe Stahr.

Bad art, according to Fitzgerald, ends up as sociology. But traditionally the artist and the sociologist have been interested in quite different things. The sociologist has no interest in Mrs. Thomas Buchanan as woman with a "low thrilling voice," but only as she is an abstract example of a female age cohort, a race, an ethnic group or a class, who plays the proper gender roles of a rich suburban housewife. While Fitzgerald suggests the corruption of the WASP upper-class after the First War through the characters of Daisy and Tom Buchanan, and their good friend, the cheating lady golfing champion, Gurney is more direct and sociological, replacing characters with a few anonymous actors and actresses playing a variety of upper-class roles. *Scenes From American Life* has no heroes or heroines, cheaters, degenerates like Tom or corrupted dreamers like Jay Gatsby.

Fitzgerald's contemporary, Phillip Barry, wrote his most successful plays about the upper-class during its Indian Summer in the twenties and thirties. Gurney, born in 1930, writes of this same class during its Cold Winter of discontent and disintegration in the seventies and eighties. Barry, an outsider like Fitzgerald, was enchanted by the members of the leisure class enjoying their leisure, among them Tracy Lord and C.K. Dexter Haven, Philadelphia Main Liners who had once sailed away in marital bliss aboard their True Love ("My, she was yare.") Gurney a birthright insider in upper-class Buffalo, was almost totally disenchanted with his own class, especially when he wrote *Scenes From American Life.*

The play opens in 1930 (between the Crash and soon-to-be-hated FDR) at a reception after a typical upper-class-Episcopalian christening service: the Bishop takes his martini from the Maid with a tray and the godmother is slightly tipsy. The play is mainly about the developing generation-gap and other trials and tribulations of upper-class parents and children during the sixties. Gurney's methodology is nicely indicated in his written instructions to whomever directs the play: "The size of the cast may vary. The play is probably impossible to do with less than four men and four women,..." he wrote. "It is very important that the roles be *evenly* and *variously* distributed, that sons play fathers, that mothers play daughters, and so forth...Otherwise the play will seem to be the story of *one* or two families, whereas is *should be* the story of *many*..." (italics mine) The play, in other words, is to be about a class and not the development of individual characters within a class milieu. The class, not its members, is Gurney's main concern.

Perhaps another way of illustrating Gurney's innovative method is by listing the roles (there are no *parts*) the actors must play in the order of their first appearances in Act I: Father, Bishop, Mother, Godfather, Godmother, Guest, A Woman, A Maid, Nelly, Man, Woman, Referee, Uncle

John, Aunt Helen, Timmy, Minister, Grandfather, Girl, Man, Nancy, Mark, Group Leader, Another Man, Woman Who Giggled, Bert, Marge, Steve, Missy, Howard, Ted, and Miss Jones. It is hard to imagine a modern Cary Grant or Katherine Hepburn agreeing to act in a play like this.

In the hopeful and humane inter-war years, Barry and Fitzgerald were still writing in the tradition of Charles Dickens. In our steadily dehumanizing age, Gurney, I think wrote *Scenes From American Life,* and his later play, *The Dining Room,* more in the tradition of Marxian sociology. These two innovating plays are definitely not bad art in Fitzgerald's sense but rather deliberate attempts to sociologize the stage as it were. In an age when methodology is the message, in other words, I am suggesting that Gurney may well prove to be a far more innovative playwright than many people today realize.

Notes

The remarks from which this chapter is adapted were originally presented by E. Digby Baltzell serving as a member of a panel including Helene Keyssar, professor of communications, University of California at San Diego; Calvin Trillin, a prominent author and reviewer for *The Nation* and *The New Yorker,* and A. R. Gurney, Jr., the author of *Scenes from American Life.* This panel discussion of *Scenes from American Life* was titled "Perspectives on a Society in Transition: America in Drift?" It was held 7 February 1988, at the Long Wharf Theatre in New Haven, Connecticut.

1. A. R. Gurney, Jr., *Scenes from an American Life,* presented at the Long Wharf Theater, New Haven, Connecticut, 22 January–6 March, 1988.

9

From Patrician to Professional Elite

Alexis de Tocqueville saw the American legal profession as providing an aristocratic anchor in our egalitarian and drifting democracy, all too prone to anarchic individualism. In the years leading up to the Civil War, wrote Roscoe Pound, the legal profession was "not so much a bar but so many hundreds or so many thousands of lawyers each a law unto himself." In response to this state of anarchy, between the end of the Civil War and the coming of the First World War, a series of modern bar associations were founded all over the nation in order to set standards of admission into the bar and to regulate the professional conduct of those admitted. *The Association of the Bar of the City of New York* (ABCNY), founded in 1870, and the subject of Michael Powell's *From Patrician to Professional Elite,*[1] was the first bar association in America and played a leading role in the bar association movement which followed: the American Bar Association (ABA) was founded in 1878, and by 1916 there were more than six hundred bar associations at all levels of government, city, county, state and national.

Most of the metropolitan bar associations were founded and more or less dominated by WASP elites until World War I, after which most of them became inclusive and democratic. The ABCNY, a conspicuous exception, was dominated by New York City's WASP upper-class until the end of World War II. All the presidents, for instance, were old stock WASPs and listed in the *Social Register* before 1920 when James Byrne, an Irish-Catholic, was elected to the office. Byrne was a Harvard graduate and had been listed in the *Social Register* since 1913; he was also, in 1920, the first Irish Catholic to be made a member of the Harvard Corporation. While upper-class partricians dominated the presidency in the inter-war years, the ABCNY slowly became an elite rather than upper-class association in the 1950s and 1960s still dominated by large corporations and Wall Street lawyers but of broader ethnic and class origins. The first Jew, Louis Loeb, was elected to the presidency in 1956; by this time, fifteen percent of the ABCNY membership was Jewish in a bar which was 60 per cent Jewish. Like Byrne, a quarter century earlier, Loeb had all the right credentials: of an old line, German Jewish financial family and a graduate of Exeter and Yale, he was a Republican and a partner in Lord, Day and Lord, a very proper Wall Street firm.

In 1964 another Jew, Samuel Rosenman, son of an immigrant and born in the South, became president; a friend of Franklin Roosevelt who placed him on the state supreme court while Governor, Rosenman was an active *Democrat* and New Dealer, and later a close ally of mayors Wagner and Lindsay. Two New York ethnic Jews followed in the presidency in 1970 and 1976; both were democrats and distinguished members of the bar—Bernard Botein, a distinguished Appellate Court Judge, and Adrien DeWind, very active in the Jewish community and a partner in a large law firm. By this time, the Jewish membership in the ABCNY had almost doubled since 1955 to 25 per cent. This gradual change from a class to an elite, yet continually exclusive, association allowed for a continuity of values and elitist sense of responsibility (not explicitly stated as a virtue but implied throughout Powell's excellent and judicious analysis).

Closely related to the changing composition of the ABCNY was the changing influence of the association on the ethical practices of the whole bar; without going into the fascinating details covered by Powell's historical analysis, it should be said that up until the late 1960s the ABCNY Committee on Grievances retained its authority over the ethical behavior of the whole bar. Throughout the 1970s however, its authority was continuously questioned until, in 1980, the policing function was taken over by the Appellate Division Disciplinary Committee, a fine example of Tocquevillian sociology: when upper-classes and societal elites lose legitimacy the government fills the authority void.

Fortunately, this book was rooted in the comparative method, the very essence, I should think, of the best historical sociology. Thus Professor Powell began this study partly at the suggestion of John P. Heintz and Edward Laumann who were in the process of completing *Chicago Lawyers,* their classic study of the Chicago Bar Association (CBA). While the ABCNY has remained exclusive and elitist, the CBA was probably the most inclusive and democratic of the large metropolitan bar associations.

Powell makes judicious comparisons between the two bars throughout this book. He carefully refrains from any value judgements as to which model has been more effective over the years. He never comments, for instance on the following statement on the hierarchy of the CBA: By the mid-1970s, according to Powell, "Jewish and Catholic lawyers were as likely to be members of the CBA as were Protestant lawyers.... Furthermore, throughout the 1970s, ethnic Jewish and Irish Catholic lawyers, engaged in the *personal-plight practice of law as solo practitioners or in small firms, dominated the presidency of the CBA* " (italics mine).

I should have liked at least a brief comment on this oz-like world where lawyers with the lowerst professional prestige hold the highest offices, especially in such an otherwise excellent book.

Notes

This chapter was first published in the *American Journal of Sociology* 96, no. 2 (September 1990).

1. Michael J. Powell, *From Patrician to Professional Elite* (New York: Russell Sage Foundation, 1988).

10

The Rich and the Super-Rich

The Rich and the Super-Rich: A Study in the Power of Money Today,[1] by Ferdinand Lundberg, is both fascinating and exasperating. It has everything, and something for everybody: plot; fact; fiction; overstatement; understatement; statistics; epithets; pronouncements of conspiracy, crime and wealth; and a whole new jargon, including "finpol," "pubpol," and "churchpol." The main plot tells how great families of large inherited fortunes rule modern America, a supposedly free and democratic society which, in Lundberg's considered and judicious opinion, has become the "Banana Republic *par excellence,*" where "mindless conformity" is the rule in a "Garrison State" in which "Jefferson could not be elected dog catcher. . . ."

In the course of trying to analyze my feelings about this curious book, I have come to the conclusion that its great appeal is to be found in its *methodology* which is not unlike my own methodology when playing the role of character-analyst or palm-reader at charity bazaars or church fairs. On those occasions, my methodological rule is to cover everything from as many sides as possible; thus the customer will be sure to be satisfied with my scientific accuracy, because he will remember what appears to be true and flattering to him and forget the rest.

After wading throughout the 801 pages of this heavy book the careful and attentive reader will surely be convinced of several things: (1) that there is a sizeable group of American families possessing great inherited wealth; (2) that new wealth and new fortunes are harder to come by today than before 1929 or the First World War; (3) that, contrary to the famous Berle and Means thesis, the separation of ownership and control of the American corporate octopus is not as wide as those more gullible than Lundberg have supposed; and (4) that consequently our great democracy is *really* an oligarchical plutocracy by default (this in spite of the fact that Lundberg, who loves conspiratorial theories of evil of all shades, devotes several pages to Senator Joseph Clark's analysis of the "Senatorial Establishment," which the senator and other multimillionaires have been unable to overcome).

The reader will put this big book down with the feeling that he has taken in so many facts that he cannot digest them. If he hoped for understanding, he is disappointed. What does it all mean?

The lack of meaning is due, I suspect, to the author's purpose and point of view; when the chips are down and the facade of statistical tables and endless documentation is seen through, one comes to realize that Lundberg is far more interested in debunking than in understanding modern American society, especially the rich. This book, then, is valuable primarily because it is another excellent and fascinating example of the alienated tone of modern American intellectual life. The book, in other words, will sell well and have a wide appeal among a variety of men and women who tend to hate America, the rich in general, and themselves in particular.

Antiestablishmentarians, who will agree with Lundberg that "religion is part of the political process of keeping the common man in chains," will be delighted by the following diagnosis of the modern temper: "If one, for example, can believe without any difficulty in the Virgin Birth of Jesus and that Jesus walked on the waters, changed water into wine, and performed other unnatural acts, then one will experience little difficulty in accepting Everett M. Dirksen and Lyndon B. Johnson, to name no others, as great statesmen, and little difficultly in believing that some fifty-nine-cent cosmetic will make one irresistible to the opposite sex." Of course Mr. Lundberg does not seem to have noticed that it is just in our age when fewer and fewer people *do* believe that "Jesus walked on water" that more and more people have place their faith in fifty-nine-cent cosmetics; nor has he asked himself whether "enlightened" ages such as our own are more likely to produce or elect greater statesmen than in earlier and darker ages when religious faith was more widespread. But he is more interested in being entertaining by debunking conspiracies than in making a reasoned analysis.

Antiestablishmentarians will smile when they read that "the United States does not have anything like a ruling class, according to an extensive assortment of fully house-broken professors...." For of course most professors, and especially sociologists, are merely apologists for the hidden members of the American ruling class or oligarchy.

To take another carefully reasoned causal connection from among the many strewn throughout this book: "The country now possesses," Lundberg writes quite correctly, "a large section of disoriented young, neither at school or at work and getting into a variety of headline-making mischief from congregating in unseemly hordes to sedulous extra-curricular copulation and drug addiction." This statement of possible fact is then followed by this explanation: "No elected representative ever passed on the decisions that produced these results. The decisions were made quietly by quiet men in quiet corporate boardrooms." How? Because, of course, the rich are naturally responsible both for "house-broken professors" and for decisions made by their hired executives in boardrooms to encourage "copulation and drug addiction."

But what else would one expect in a book in which a diverting chapter on "Crime and Wealth" ends on the following note: "We must confess, then, to failure in the attempt to find members or agents of any Mafia, Cosa Nostra, or underworld syndicate of any kind high in the business world, although the established entrepreneurs, securely installed, give a lusty account of themselves in the matter of lawbreaking. Comparatively, they make the Mafias and Crime Syndicates look like push-cart operations."

Lest this review be thought to be part of a larger conspiracy against the antiestablishment science of Ferdinand Lundberg, I hasten to suggest that the infectious style of a very popular author sometimes rubs off on an admiring and envious reviewer. For example, after all these 801 pages, I am not at all sure that some clever members of the oligarchy of established wealth in America are not, by this time, quite high up in the Mafia hierarchy. Anything is possible for those infected with the conspiracy theory of history.

Notes

This chapter was first published in the *American Sociological Review* 34, no. 3 (June 1969).

1. Ferdinand Lundberg, *The Rich and the Super-Rich: A Study in the Power of Money Today* (New York: Lyle Stuart, 1968).

11

The Peabody Influence

"In an address before the Phi Beta Kappa Society of Harvard University two years ago," wrote President Eliot, in 1890, "I have endeavored to show, among other things, that democratic government, as distinguished from aristocratic or autocratic government, has no quarrel, as has been alleged with the biological law of hereditary transmission.... On that occasion I had no time to do more than to mention some of the means of perpetuating good family stocks in a democracy. It seems to me, however, that the principal means of preserving family lines in democratic society ought to be discussed; because the family, rather than the individual, is the important social unit; because perpetuation of sound families is of the highest social interest...."

One of the soundest families yet produced by this democracy are the Peabodys who first came to the stern and rockbound coast of Puritan New England in 1635.[1] Probably originating as a fiercely individualistic clan in highland Wales, the family came to America from the home counties around London and settled primarily on the North Shore of Boston. They were a healthy and hardy, God-fearing tribe who seemed to possess, from the beginning, an instinct for leadership and public service, great intellectual curiosity, and more than their share of business acumen.

By the end of the colonial period, some five generations of Peabodys had already begun to make a name for themselves in history, as judges, lawyers, clergymen, intellectuals and soldiers—with Wolfe on the Plains of Abraham, at Bunker Hill, Ticonderoga and Louisbourg. But it was Joseph Peabody of Salem who, in the fourth generation, must be credited with founding the family fortune. He began his way to wealth when he shipped out of Salem on the privateer *Bunker Hill* in 1777. After more than a dozen privateering ventures under the Gardners of Salem, young Joseph went in for himself, put money away, married, and finally settled down to raise a family on Essex Street. He soon had enough money to build a wharf and counting house on Derby Street. In 1817, having never spent more than $3,000 a year on himself and his family, he was honored by his neighbors as the most important man in Salem and the wealthiest merchant in the United States. He died in 1844 in the same house on Essex Street where he had taken his young wife many years ago.

If Joseph of Salem was the first founder of a family fortune, George Peabody of Danvers (now Peabody), Massachusetts, was to become the wealthiest and most famous member of the family. Not a very good student, and born to one of the poorer branches of the family, young George was apprenticed to a Captain Proctor who ran a general store in Danvers. After completing his contract of indenture, and gaining additional experience as a storekeeper in Newburyport, George went south, bought a horse and peddled merchandise through the towns and villages of Pennsylvania, Maryland, and Virginia during the War of 1812. After the war, in 1814, he went into a partnership with Elisha Riggs (total capitalization of $7,000,including Peabody's total savings of $1,700). By 1829, when their partnership dissolved, Peabody was thirty-four years old and rich by the standards of that day. The firm continued under Peabody's sole ownership, with branch offices in Philadelphia and New york but centered in Baltimore, an excellent port for trading with Europe.

In 1835, the state of Maryland was in deep financial trouble. Peabody seemed the logical choice to send abroad to seek a loan in London, the financial capital of the world. He was successful in the amount of some $8,000,000. He was now the toast of Baltimore but was honored even more when he returned the State's draft of $60,000, his commission for obtaining the loan. Though he could hardly afford this *largesse* at the time, it paid off manifold, especially in London where the British bankers were much impressed with the gentility and honor of this unusual Yankee. His international reputation now made, in 1837 he set up his famous banking house in London where he soon knew everyone from the Governor of the Bank of England to Wellington and the Queen. Unmarried, and like Joseph of Salem rarely spending more than $3,000 a year on his private life out of an income of more than $300,000, his fortune multiplied and his philanthropic interests, especially after the Civil War, began to absorb all his time. In the meantime, in order to carry on his firm's business in London he had hired, in 1854, a youthful Yankee merchant from Hartford, Junius Spencer Morgan, whose family line was not unlike Peabody's own. As Peabody was a public relations expert long before the term was ever coined, young Morgan was at once provided with an entertainment allowance of $25,000 a year, all of which he was expected to spend.

George Peabody was probably the nation's first systematic philanthropist; he spread his gifts throughout the United States, primarily among educational and cultural institutions. When he died in 1869, he was mourned on both sides of the Atlantic. There were countless Peabodys who made names for themselves during the nineteenth century, especially the three sisters from Salem—Elizabeth, an authoress and the nation's first lady-publisher, whose famous Boston bookshop became the gathering place of the Transcendentalists; Sophie, Hawthorne's devoted wife; and Mary who, with her husband, Horace Mann, revolutionized education in America.

When old George Peabody's body was brought back from London to be buried at Peabody, Massachusetts, Junius Spencer Morgan dropped by after the service to ask young Samuel Endicott Peabody to join him as a partner in the London firm. Thus the Peabody influence was carried down into the twentieth century by Samuel Endicott's son, Endicott, who was sent to Cheltenham and Cambridge where he absorbed British traditions of class leadership which he eventually brought to Groton School, which he founded in 1884 (with Junius Spencer Morgan's son as one of the original trustees). Over the years, the surrogate Peabody family at Groton was somehow to inspire such twentieth-century American leaders as Franklin D. Roosevelt, W. Averell Harriman, Dean Acheson and Francis Biddle.

This is a delightful and inspiring book.

Notes

This chapter was first published in *The Pennsylvania Magazine of History and Biography* 93, no. 3 (July 1969).

1. Edwin P. Hoyt, *The Peabody Influence: How a Great New England Family Helped to Build America* (New York: Dodd, Mead & Company, 1968).

12

The Celebrity and the Gentleman

The pathology of modern American life and leadership is most sadly seen in the rapid erosion of privacy, certainly an essential aspect of all high civilization. Privacy is unknown in primitive cultures. Lewis Mumford has often stressed the fact that privacy is the creature of civilization and its decline indicative of reversion to barbarism. The term "courting," he once wrote, originated in the sixteenth century when wit and charm as well as physical passion became part of love-making in court society where private rooms were available for the first time. He also has pointed out that modern architecture's love of free-flowing space at the expense of doors and walls, the suburban developer's love of picture-windows facing the neighbors if not the passing crowd, as well as the decline of the parlor in favor of the automobile and movie-house as courting atmospheres, are all part of an age dominated by public-relations barbarians in Brooks Brothers suits.

Perhaps only a people who had lost all sense of privacy would have consented to discuss their intimate sexual life with a zoologist who subsequently became America's most famous social scientist, when he rescued sex from the privacy of the bedroom and placed it on statistical tables for all to see and compare with their own experiences. And it was surely no accident that the late Dr. Kinsey was most severely criticized for his biased sample, which of course contained a disproportionate number of cases from the enlightened and educated classes rather than the ignorant masses, who presumably had more of a sense of privacy and were therefore harder to interview.

Cleveland Amory's *Who Killed Society?* is an amusing, chatty, name-dropping, exhaustive and sometimes suggestive saga of the war between privacy and publicity in America.[1] Although he made his well-deserved reputation with a sympathetic and charming study of Proper Bostonians who were still guarding their privacy long after their sense of sin had slipped away, this latest book is the story of rootless men and women of talent and ability whose social world centers around New York and Washington and is ruled by the guardians of "Publi-ciety," where publicity and the "name" name has taken over. In this new world, millionaires are a dime a dozen, "contacts" have replaced "background," publicists and gossip columnists have replaced genealogists and society editors, and journalists who a generation ago received their guest lists—if they got them at all—via spies or at the back door now receive invitations to dinner and in many cases have cars sent for them by their hostesses. Whereas the favored few used to have affairs behind closed doors, some even enjoying the delights accompanying a sense of sin, in our age when public relations have made private relations old hat, nobody now gives a damn who you sleep with—or where—as long as you dine with the right people, in the right restaurants, and with the right columnist at an adjoining table.

Cleveland Amory is an author who knows all there is to know about his subject. But he who tells all is a bore, and one hates to think how many nostalgic, proper octogenarian gentlewomen (with souls as hard as nails) he must have talked and gossiped with in the seven years he spent gathering the anecdotes for this book. There is, however, an underlying theme to the book, which is important, well-documented and interesting, but unfortunately underplayed, because, I think, public relations and sales appeal demanded it. In other words, the book is written on two levels. On the surface and emphasized for promotion purposes, it is a book primarily about publicity-seeking personalities—mostly effeminate men and asexual women—who once made up the "400," or Society with a capital "S," and now make up Cafe Society or what the author calls "Publi-ciety." Actually, as he points out, nobody killed Society; it has only changed its form and name. Publicity and shallow values were the stock-in-trade of Ward McAllister, *the* Mrs. Astor (which one I could not possibly recall) and the other dominant dames of the Society era; the same shallow values, perhaps more vulgarly and more blatantly displayed, are still the stock-in-trade of *the* Mrs. Mesta, *the* Miss Maxwell, Cholly Knickerbocker No.1 and No.2 and the 35 society editors who now swarm over Washington cocktail parties. The "gossip truth," after all, has held sway among the fashionable in America from Tocqueville's day to this.

In addition to this detailed study of the changing modes of fashionable society, which appropriately ends its tale of suicide, divorce and boredom with a discussion of seven unsolved and hushed-up Society murders, the underlying theme is a discussion of the aristocratic idea in egalitarian America. In contrast to the fashionable world of effeminate men and masculine women (Miss Maxwell of course never had time for sex: "I wouldn't subject myself to it. I never was interested for one minute, ever. I married the world—the world is my husband. Sex is the most tiring thing in the world."), Amory rightly points out that an aristocracy is always dominated by men. The aristocrat's castles are his home and his club (invaded by women since World War II), and he more often than not feels ill-at-ease in a cafe or ballroom as well as at the majority of chatty cocktail parties. His values are built upon family, potency, pride, privilege and above all, privacy.

As a welcome escape from the world of the *professional* socialite (the aristocrat in America is unfortunately often referred to as a socialite) and the celebrity, a minor part of this book does an excellent job on the gentleman in America. Amory shows how American society can stand up to, and even surpass aristocratic Europe when it comes to producing a core of aristocratic families. Even in the decade of the 1950s, for example, *Mayflower*-descended Robert Fiske Bradford was Governor of Massachusetts, Sinclair Weeks Secretary of Commerce, Robert Cutler Assistant to the President, Christian Herter Secretary of State, one Lodge Ambassador to the United Nations and his brother Governor of Connecticut and Ambassador to Spain. John Cabot Ambassador to Brazil and another Cabot perhaps the country's No.1 Marshall Plan authority, one Saltonstall in the Senate and another the head of Exeter Academy, Charles Francis Adams the head of Raytheon, and a Lowell a Pulitzer Prize winner in poetry (eleven Cabots listed in the 1960 edition of *Who's Who*).

This book, then, is an excellent and definitive study of both the celebrity and the aristocrat; it is too bad that its title, its tone of anecdote and the sales pitch of its publishers all lay such stress on the former at the expense of the latter. But perhaps this is because our egalitarian ideology allows room for the self-made celebrity while dismissing the aristocrat as beyond the democratic pale. Yet, in the long run, even the most successful celebrities, who so often end up in a consuming self-hate, long for some kind of aristocratic privacy. Thus Billy Rose, celebrity *par excellence,* has finally grown tired of running in public. When *Life* magazine in 1958 wished to run a fourteen-page spread on his house, he refused saying, "I have outgrown that sort of thing. I am trying to be a gentleman."

Notes

This chapter was first published in the *National Review,* 11 February 1961.

1. Cleveland Amory, *Who Killed Society?* (New York: Harper, 1960).

13

White Protestant Americans

White Protestant Americans: From National Origins to Religious Group,[1] by Charles H. Anderson, is part of the series Ethnic Groups in American Life, edited by Milton M. Gordon, which will include other monographs on Jewish Americans, Japanese Americans, black Americans, Mexican Americans, and so forth. The author has written a sensible and solid book on a slippery subject—slippery because there is some question as to whether "white Protestants" are best understood as one of the many "ethnic groups" in American life. Thus, the traditional sociology of ethnic relations in this country has largely concentrated on minority groups, especially those whose members came here after the Civil War from southern and eastern Europe or Asia and subsequently suffered various forms of discrimination in the course of their attempts to rise out of pariah and lower-class status into the mainstream of middle-class life. White Protestants, on the other hand, have always been and still are both a majority of our population and situated in the higher levels of middle-class life. They have been considered Americans rather than hyphenated Americans, discriminators rather than objects of discrimination. This has been the case ever since sociology became a recognized science in the early years of the twentieth century.

The author has, nevertheless, handled this problem wisely and well by taking a historical, or what I should like to call an up-hill-and-down-dale, approach. In other words, Part 1 of the book is devoted to a discussion of how the various non-English, national-origin groups from northern Europe, faced with an established, British hegemony, gradually melted into a new white Protestant majority in the course of the eighteenth and nineteenth centuries. The author brings a wealth of judiciously selected detail to show how this process worked for the members of the various national-origin groups—Scots and Ulstermen, Swedes, Norwegians,

Finns, Dutch, and Germans. The language barrier was, of course, the main factor determining the rate of assimilation; time and place of first migration were also important. Thus, the Scots and Ulstermen were highly educated and spoke English, came early, and were rapidly assimilated into the very highest levels of the social structure, as such men as Thomas Jefferson, Patrick Henry, James Wilson, Washington Irving, and John Paul Jones illustrated so well. The Continental, with his different language and culture, of course, took longer to melt into the pot. But even they melted differently; for example, the Dutch in New York had an experience different from that of the Germans in Pennsylvania (some of whom, such as the Amish and other sectarians, still remain apart). In this connection, and considering our long interest in the Protestant ethic, I should have liked the author to have placed more emphasis on religion (regardless of national origin) as a vital factor in assimilation. One has the impression, for instance, that it was the Calvinists, whom Weber incidentally used as the prototypical example of the Protestant ethic, who assimilated fastest, while the Lutherans and the Sectarians were more likely to lag behind in their religious and ethnic islands. There is no space to go into details here, but it is indicative that all the major denominations, except the Lutherans, have had at least one president of the United States; and the Calvinists (Presbyterian, Reformed, or Congregational), whether Dutch, English, German, Scots, or Irish in national origin, have produced more presidents than any save the Episcopalians, many of whom were, like the Roosevelts, of Calvinist background.

After Part 1 has shown how the non-English stock struggled uphill to form part of the Protestant-British dominant majority which ruled America from the Civil War to World War II, Part 2 shows how the Protestant hegemony went downdale after World War II. Unfortunately, this book is weak in analyzing just how, when, and why this waxing and waning of Protestantism took place. At any rate, "Protestantism in America today," wrote Will Herberg in 1960, "presents the anomaly of a strong majority group with a growing minority consciousness." No doubt the use of the term "WASP" is now used, within this new context of competing ethnic groups without a hegemonic majority, as a kind of compensatory and negative epithet not entirely unlike such older epithets as "wop" and "kike" which are no longer permissible in polite society. Perhaps there is a crisis in American leadership today partly because we are now all marginal men, doubting our right to rule in an age when who's to say who's right and no values are any longer sacred. This book is weak in that it makes no attempt to analyze this very vital problem. Thus, Part 2, like Part 1, is largely descriptive—and, strangely enough, largely descriptive of Catholic-Protestant differences; "anti-Semitism," "Jew," and "Jewish" are not to be found in the index.

But men are always better judged by what they do than what they do not do. This author has done a fine job of documenting the rise and fall of white Protestanism in America.

Notes

This chapter was first published in the *American Journal of Sociology* 76, no. 6 (May 1971).

1. Charles H. Anderson, *White Protestant Americans: From National Origins to Religious Group* (Englewood Cliffs, NJ: Prentice-Hall, 1970).

14

Blue-Blood Blues

In our rootless and resentful age of increasingly classless bureaucracy, George Bush purportedly has a "class problem," which I should like to look at here from a historical perspective.

Throughout most of this so-called Century of the Common Man, the subject of class in America has had much the same closed-closet status as masturbation and fornication: ladies and gentlemen simply did not talk about such things in mixed company or in public. Since the '60s, however, when every damned thing was dragged out of the closet, and ladylike and gentlemanly manners were dismissed as elitist, everybody has been free to talk about anything, anywhere at anytime, few suspecting that a world without closets might already be well on its way to barbarism. In this new climate of opinion, I should not have been taken by surprise when one of my students at Penn during the '70s came up to me after class and asked: "What's *your* class background professor?" "None of your business, my boy," I replied with a smile. Nor should I have been enraged as I watched Diane Sawyer rudely ask George Bush, in front of millions of TV viewers, to explain why people thought of him as a wimp. Had I been Bush, I would have kicked her, but Bush did his best to answer her patiently and politely. I suspect that Sawyer hardly remembers that people like her once thought of Franklin Roosevelt as the equivalent of a wimpy preppy (or featherduster), although the term "wimp" was not coined until our present unisexual age, and the term "preppy" was never used, especially when referring to a graduate of Groton School, where Roosevelt was educated in the British tradition of the Christian gentleman by his headmaster and later lifelong friend, Endicott Peabody, who *never* referred to Groton as a prep school.

Even Walter Lippmann, the George Will of his age, was somewhat deceived by FDR's accent and easy patrician charm. In his now famous column in the *Herald Tribune,* Lippmann wrote of candidate Roosevelt, in 1932, as "a highly impressionable person... without very strong convictions.... He is an amiable man with many philanthropic impulses, but he is not the dangerous enemy of anything." All too eager to please and too cautious to take political risks, Roosevelt, Lippmann concluded, was merely "a pleasant man who, without any important qualifications for the office, would very much like to be president."[1] What Lippmann and many others failed to take into account, according to Lippmann's biographer, Ronald Steel, was Roosevelt's "tenacious will." Perhaps we should remember that George Bush also possesses a tenacious will beneath his obvious good manners.

In spite of our cherished "Log Cabin" myth, President Bush is now part of a long tradition of aristocratic and patrician presidents. Washington, the two Adamses, Jefferson, Madison, Monroe, and the two Harrisons, in the 18th and 19th centuries, and the two Roosevelts, Taft, Wilson, and Kennedy, in the 20th, were all born to families of the very highest social status in their respective communities; Washington was one of the wealthiest men of his day.

But of course everybody knows that wealth and privilege are a great help to anyone seeking high office in America; less obvious, however, is the fact that high performance in office is also correlated with privileged origins. Thus, of our six greatest presidents—Lincoln, Franklin Roosevelt, Washington, Jefferson, Theodore Roosevelt, and Wilson—all save Lincoln were born to privilege. On the other hand, of the five presidents—Lincoln, Eisenhower, Fillmore, Andrew Johnson, and Nixon—born with the least advantages, only Lincoln and Eisenhower performed above average in office, while Fillmore, Andrew Johnson, and Nixon were well below average, if not outright failures.[2]

George Bush is also part of a venerable WASP establishment tradition of Skull and Bones men in the nation's service: President William Howard Taft, his son, Senator Robert Taft, Henry Stimson, Averill Harriman, Justice Potter Stewart, William and McGeorge Bundy, and the late Malcolm Baldrige. Stimson—who served in high appointive offices under Theodore Roosevelt, Taft, Wilson, Coolidge, Hoover, Franklin Roosevelt, and Truman—was Andover Academy's most distinguished alumnus when he gave the graduation address to George Bush's class of 1942.

Traditions are produced by a cumulative of successful experiments down through the ages. Or as Oliver Wendell Holmes Jr. once wrote: "A page of history is worth a volume of logic." The patriarchal family, for instance, has proved to be empirically successful through hundreds of generations, while the egalitarian family is largely the reasoned product of our age alone. And, from all historical evidence, Bush's privileged class origins should have been, from the beginning, an asset rather than a liability; indeed, perhaps the preppy, wimpy, elitist issue has been a problem for media intellectuals alone. By and large I have always assumed that liberal intellectuals have resented *other* people's privileges far more than the average man on the street, or on the factory floor. Thus, Frank Greer, a Democratic consultant, was quoted by *Newsweek* as saying during the presidential campaign: "If I were managing Bush, I wouldn't be filming commercials in Kennebunkport, I'd be in the working-class neighborhoods of Houston...."

Fortunately, intellectuals are sometimes divided on issues, and *Newsweek* also noted that Faith Popcorn, a social trend analyst of some wit, thought that "the elitist thing is just the ticket" for George Bush. "Money could be his flag—how everyone can aspire to getting some," Popcorn continued. "And, after all, there is a return to fashion of good families, good schools, quality. The Kennedys didn't hide it. Why should he? If Ralph Lauren can sell the Polo line to the country, why can't Bush sell polo to the masses...? But he needs a style of his own. Maybe he needs a Scottie." It is my impression that the political forecasters would have profited far more from Popcorn's wit than from Greer's elitist and patronizing conventional wisdom.

Finally, if one may be allowed to bare one's private fantasies, I should suggest that if all the young girls growing up in America today were to marry the first boy they ever kissed, in the style of our First Lady, our beleaguered land would be well on its way to solving its tragic problems of poverty, AIDS, and abortion.

Notes

This chapter was first published in *The New Republic,* 3 April 1989.

1. *The Herald Tribune,* 8 January 1932. Reprinted in Walter Lippmann, *Public Persons* (New York: Liveright, 1976), 113–16.
2. Cf. E. Digby Baltzell and Howard G. Schneiderman, "Social Class in the Oval Office," in *The Protestant Establishment Revisited,* ed. Howard G. Schneiderman (New Brunswick: Transaction Publishers, 1991), 241–59.

15

Dilemmas of Democracy: Tocqueville and Modernization

More essays and reviews on Tocqueville's work have appeared during the past decade than at any other time since his death in 1859. "Of all the projections of social development written at the juncture of the industrial and democratic revolutions in Western Europe, or, at least at the moment of greatest psychological impact, Alexis de Tocqueville's remains one of the most enduring and remarkable," writes Professor Seymour Drescher in the Introduction to *Dilemmas of Democracy: Tocqueville and Modernization.*[1] "It takes its place beside the optimistic vision of a scientific-industrial society, forecast by the Saint-Simonians and Positivists, and the specter of total crisis and transformation prophesied by Marx."

Unlike Marx, Tocqueville was immediately recognized and widely acclaimed by his contemporaries. Soon after his death, however, his work went into eclipse while that of Marx became more and more influential. The differential patterns of acceptance of these two thinkers provide us with an interesting problem in intellectual history. A reading of this excellent book, which attempts to place Tocqueville's writing on modernization within the intellectual and social climate in which he lived and worked, adds to our insight as to why Marx became so important during the first half of the twentieth century, and why Tocqueville has only been revived in our time. First of all, Tocqueville was far less of a partisan or ideologist than Marx or, for that matter, Saint-Simon. Systematizers create partisans and followers, and Professor Drescher rightly notes that Tocqueville "was at once analytically lucid and systematically ambiguous." And, indeed, this is just why he is quoted today as an authority by men on politically and intellectually opposite sides of various ideological fences. Tocqueville, in other words, has admirers rather than followers in an age which is sick of systems and seems to prefer piecemeal reformers to single-minded preachers of perfection at the end of history.

In contrast to Marx and so many twentieth-century, liberal reformers, Tocqueville feared the centralization of political power far more than the concentration of wealth; he might even have seen the concentration of private property as a secondary power or countervailing force in our age of tremendous concentration of power in public property or the state. It is, indeed, understandable how so many men in our day would be likely to sympathize with Professor Drescher's statement of Tocqueville's position in the following sentence: "Since the increasing independence of man from man," he writes, "was the propensity, even the disease of modernization, the increasing dependence of man upon the state was *the* social question of Tocqueville."

Any good critic must not only sympathize with the author's point of view but also must point out his weaknesses. This, Professor Drescher does with great insight. He does an excellent job, for instance, in showing how Tocqueville, partly due to his aristocratic bias in seeing middle-class businessmen as basically hedonistic, failed to see the connection between modernization and Protestant asceticism. He makes his point with insight and humor in the following paragraph: "Whatever the relationship between the Protestant ethic and the spirit of capitalism, by Tocqueville's hedonistic business psychology, the brothel or the harem should long before have produced modern commercialization, with Don Juan as this ideal type, rather than Benjamin Franklin or Richard Arkwright." This is by far the most interesting book I have read on Tocqueville in some time.

Notes

This chapter was first published in *The Annals of the American Academy of Political and Social Science,* March 1969.

1. Seymour Drescher, *Dilemmas of Democracy: Tocqueville and Modernization* (Pittsburgh: University of Pittsburgh Press, 1968).

16

Tocqueville and the Problem of Democracy

At the close of World War II, the works of Alexis de Tocqueville were largely out of print and often unobtainable. He was hardly ever quoted in the textbooks of sociology, although Charles Horton Cooley, one of the founders of the discipline, referred to him frequently in his classic book, *Social Organization*—which was also out of print for many years.

As everyone now knows, things have changed. Tocqueville has now been brought back into the scholarly literature of sociology and political science and is quoted constantly with approval in the popular press, as well as in the smaller journals of opinion on both the Left and the Right, from *Dissent* and *The New Republic* to the *National Review*. There has also grown up a considerable body of interpretive literature on this great master.

Professor Marvin Zetterbaum's excellent little book, *Tocqueville and the Problem of Democracy*,[1] is a welcome addition to this growing literature. While sympathetic to Tocqueville, he is not uncritical. In the very beginning of this book, the author rightly sees that Tocqueville was one of the first social theorists to go beneath the political forms of democracy and back to the underlying social system. Professor Zetterbaum correctly emphasizes the fact that Tocqueville saw that Equality—equality of conditions—was the most powerful social force behind what we rather loosely call democracy.

Though Tocqueville tried to present a neutral position as between his two ideal-typical, polar constructs of aristocracy—hierarchy, freedom, and family—and democracy—equality of conditions, social mobility, and individualism—there is no doubt as to where his sympathies lie. He was, although he knew at first hand its abuses, quite definitely on the side of aristocracy and, although he saw its undoubted moral advantages, quite definitely fearful of democracy.

Professor Zetterbaum does an excellent job of analyzing the problem of determinism and inevitability in Tocqueville's work. Of great importance here, he shows how Tocqueville probably masked his moral preferences behind the intellectual screen of transcendental determinism.

This then is an excellent book. I, for one, am not altogether sure that the growing literature on Tocqueville is a good thing, and for two reasons. First, I would hate to think that such a monstrous thing as "Tocquevilleism" might be the result. Though Marx without Marxism would be hardly possible, "Tocquevilleism" would be a contradiction in terms. Moreover, though legions of sensitive intellectuals have been proud of being Marxists, I doubt if anyone who admires the spirit of Tocqueville would even approve of being called a "Tocquevilleist." Secondly, while there is much in Marx which lends itself to interpretation, there is no work on Tocqueville, including the book here reviewed, which has been able to clarify "what Tocqueville really meant." He said what he meant, and, above else, was crystal clear. For some men commentaries have clarified the original, but never in the case of Tocqueville.

Notes

This chapter was first published in *The Annals of the American Academy of Political and Social Science,* January 1968.

1. Marvin Zetterbaum, *Tocqueville and the Problem of Democracy* (Stanford, CA: Stanford University Press, 1967).

17

The Rise and Fall of the Elites

The Rise and Fall of the Elites: An Application of Theoretical Sociology[1] is the first edition in English of a long essay by Vilfredo Pareto which marked his turn from econometrics to the study of sociology. Written at the turn of the century (1901), this classic essay outlined the basic ideas for which he later became famous, especially in the United States after 1936, when an entire issue of *The Saturday Review of Literature* was devoted to an analysis of the four volumes of his classic work, *The Mind and Society*. Pareto is now out of vogue; in their comprehensive reader, *Class, Status and Power*, Reinhard Bendix and Seymour Martin Lipset apparently do not consider it appropriate to include even a brief example of his work. It is hard to believe that he was the rage at Harvard in the thirties, under the leadership of Lawrence Henderson and Elton Mayo.

Frankly the publication of this essay, at this time, seems, to this reviewer at least, a waste of the publisher's time and money. The introductory essay by Hans Zetterberg is far more edifying than the rest of the book, which includes nothing that could not already be found in the other translated writing of Pareto. But, then, we live in an affluent age.

All this is not to say that contemporary students of society have nothing to learn from reading Pareto, including his well-known, and often tiresome, biases against all forms of tender-mindedness or humanitarianism. We are all captives, more or less, of the conventional wisdom of our times, to say nothing of the trained incapacity of contemporary professional standards and theories. All of us might ponder upon, in other words, the following lines which Pareto quoted with approval from Taine's analysis of the French Revolution:

> At the end of the 18th century, a horror of blood prevailed in the upper, and even in the middle class; refinement of manners and idyllic dreams had weakened the mili-

tant will power.... Everywhere the magistrates were forgetting that the maintenance of society and civilization is infinitely more valuable than the lives of a handful of offenders and fools. They forget that the primary objective of government, as it is of the police force, is the preservation of order through force.

Notes

This chapter was first published in *Social Forces* 48, no. 1 (September 1969).

1. Vilfredo Pareto, *The Rise and Fall of the Elites: An Application of Theoretical Sociology* (Totowa, NJ: Bedminster Press, 1968).

18

Five Contemporary Ben Franklins

If three Americans were dropped from an airplane at 10,000 feet, by the time they had reached the ground they probably would have formed an association and elected themselves president, vice president, and secretary-treasurer. Alexis de Tocqueville, visiting America in the 1830s during the Jacksonian era, saw the vital role of voluntary associations in organizing common action and maintaining freedom in America's increasingly individualistic and egalitarian society. "Where ever," he wrote, "at the head of some new undertaking you see a government in France, or a man of rank in England, in the United States you will be sure to find an association." Tocqueville also saw associations as important secondary powers serving as intermediary buffers between a multitude of equal, and equally weak, private citizens and an increasingly centralized state: "Governments," he wrote, "should not be the only active powers; associations ought, in democratic nations, to stand in lieu of those powerful private individuals whom the equality of conditions has swept away." It is the genius of Americans to have replaced aristocratic with associational *noblesse oblige,* expressed today through the exercise of leadership in nonprofit organizations.

Benjamin Franklin was surely America's first and most famous association founder. In founding the nation's first free library, first university, first hospital and, along with his Quaker friends, the first abolitionist society in America, he would have been proud to have been called our first All-American dogooder: His favorite book in his youth was Cotton Mather's *Essays to Do Good.* Franklin first broke into print in Boston using the pen name Silence Dogood.

Even though the power of the national government has grown enormously since Tocqueville's day, our society still carries on a vigorous associational life in the best Franklin tradition: According to the June

11, 1980 issue of *Agenda,* for instance, there are more than 75,000 nonprofit associations in the state of Pennsylvania today.

Who are Philadelphia's present Benjamin Franklins? What kind of men are carrying on his dogood traditions? In order to shed some light on these questions, I have interviewed five men: William Warden Bodine Jr., president of the World Affairs Council of Philadelphia; John Whiley Eckman, president and chairman of the Rorer Group, Inc.; Frank C.P. McGlinn, vice president, Western Savings Bank; Isadore M. Scott, chairman of the board, Tosco Corporation; and Robert Montgomery Scott, partner in the Philadelphia law firm of Montgomery McCracken Walker & Rhoads. These five men between them are presently serving on the boards of about one hundred nonprofit associations.

Along with president Bill Bodine, Frank McGlinn, John Eckman and I.M. (Scotty) Scott sit on the board of the World Affairs Council. John Eckman is a life trustee, R.M. (Bobby) Scott a term trustee, and Scotty an associate trustee of the University of Pennsylvania. Scotty, Eckman and Bodine are leading members of the board of the University City Science Center. Eckman has started a term as president, and Scotty and McGlinn as members of the board, of the Historical Society of Pennsylvania. Eckman is chairman and Scotty a member of the board of the Wistar Institute. Eckman, McGlinn, Bodine and Scotty have served on the boards of the United Fund and United Way over many years (in the fall of 1938 when Scotty first arrived in Philadelphia from West Virginia he was asked to solicit for the Community Chest in North Philadelphia, which he did), Bobby Scott is president of the Philadelphia Museum of Art, and Scotty is a vice president; finally, Scotty and McGlinn serve on the board of the Philadelphia Award.

An historian of England during the Puritan Revolution, when members of the merchant and gentry classes were replacing the nobility as leaders of society and in charitable giving, once wrote: "Power, as history has so often demonstrated, flows inevitably to those unafraid to assume the burdens of responsibility." In any society, city, class or club it is always a small minority of persons who are willing or able to assume responsibility. Any student of colonial Philadelphia soon learns how Franklin assumed responsibility for the leadership of one dogood institution after another in the years between his founding of his famous "Junto" in 1727 and his death in 1790; and also how very few men worked closely with him over the years. And so it is in the city today where, for instance, McGlinn, Scotty and Bodine are currently serving on 28, 25 and 19 boards respectively.

Consider an example. The Historical Society of Pennsylvania has an endowment of only half a million as compared to Boston's historical society which boasts of $10 million. The Pennsylvania society recently appointed James E. Mooney to aid in its rejuvenation. Eckman (chairman of the society's board of managers), Scotty, and McGlinn have been brought in, as one of them put it, to replace the traditional Philadelphia Club type managers.

Or consider the University City Science Center: Its president, Randall M. Whaley, has visions of expansion with a capital fund and building program which will create a World Science Center and make the whole city a kind of Geneva. Bill Bodine has dropped some of his board memberships to take on the chairmanship of this funding drive along with his close friend and cohort, Scotty, as vice chairman.

These five modern Franklins are a varied and interesting group of men. Bill Bodine and Bobby Scott are of old Philadelphia roots and Harvard alumni. Bodine's grandfather was one of the founders of the United Gas Improvement Company (UGI), and Scott's great grandfather was assistant secretary of war under Lincoln and surely one of the most creative and charming presidents in the history of the Pennsylvania Railroad. Frank McGlinn is a Philadelphian of old Quaker roots on his mother's side and Irish-Catholic on his father's. After graduating from William Penn Charter School, he went to the University of North Carolina; of the 3,500 students, there were forty Republicans and forty Catholics, and he was the only one on campus who was both. In 1936 he founded and was first president of the Carolina Republican Club as well as a Big Man On Campus. Al Smith, his boyhood hero, bolted the Democrats and voted for Landon in 1936 and Wilkie in 1940; Frank worked hard for both men (assistant sergeant at arms at the Republican National Convention, in 1936). McGlinn is the only one of this group of five to serve his political party actively over the years since 1936. He also appears to be the only one to have been extremely active in his religious community: among many other honors he is a Papal Knight and closely involved at both LaSalle and Villanova universities.

Scotty was born of immigrant Jewish parents in a small mining town in West Virginia. Beginning in a one-room schoolhouse, he graduated from the local high school and went on to take an A.B. (Phi Beta Kappa) at West Virginia University and a J.D. from the law school of Washington and Lee. He came to Philadelphia in 1938 where he married Joan Rosenwald, fought in the war, raised three children, made some money, and served—in the cheerful, charismatic, and utterly charming style of Benjamin Franklin—in so many dogood organizations over the years that a mere listing of them would consume the rest of this article.

John Eckman is a native of New York. After graduating from Trinity School, he went away to Yale and thence to the Wharton School where he graduated in 1943, in a U.S. Naval uniform as the first Battalion Commander of the Naval R.O.T.C. unit. Nine days later he was ordered aboard a light cruiser (where he lost the use of one eye in a plane accident). He eventually went to submarine school and by V-J Day was an officer on a submarine in the Argentine from whence he commanded a captured German U-Boat and brought her back to the States. After the war, Eckman spent several years with the then fashionable-Philadelphia drug firm, Smith Kline & French, before going on to eventual leadership of the Rorer Group of pharmaceutical companies (during the past fifteen years under his leadership Rorer has acquired no less than 20 additional companies in various parts of the world). Eckman valued his navy experience highly and learned a great deal from navy ways of doing things.

Scotty, McGlinn, Bodine and Eckman, now in their sixties, all served in World War 11; Bobby Scott, only 51, did not. The tremendous dedication to serving their community since the war was both reflected in and a product of the war experiences of Scotty, McGlinn and Bodine; all three won the Purple Heart for wounds received in action.

Scotty served in North Africa, Italy and Austria and, among other honors, was awarded the Legion of Merit, Silver Star, Bronze Star, Crown of Italy, Degree of Cavaliers Officials, and the Czechoslovakian Medal of Merit, First Class.

Bill Bodine says, tongue in cheek, that he dropped out of Harvard in his sophomore year in order to "save the world for democracy." Among his many decorations were the Legion of Merit, Croix de Guerre, and the Bronze Star. A young battalion commander Bill was "shot up in the Battle of the Bulge" and eventually wound up for recuperation in one of those stately homes of England, which included a butler and fine wine cellar; week-ends were spent with his father's old St. Paul's School friend, Ambassador Gilbert Winant. To make a fascinating story short, Bill met

General Eisenhower one night at the embassy, was taken on as Ike's aide and travelled with him to many capitals of the world (he met his wife, Louise Dilworth from Pittsburgh, in Paris during this tour of duty). In our interview, Bill revealed that his war experiences were more important than anything else in his formative years: at Harvard "I think I was pretty well on the way to being, if not a full-time bum, at least a part-time bum. And I debated a long time about staying in the military."

McGlinn spent his war years in the Navy, minesweeping in the Gulf of Mexico, the Atlantic, the Mediterranean, and around Japan: "My ship blew up in the Mediterranean. A mine blew us up. It didn't go down though. It should have but it didn't. We had been sweeping with another ship and they went down in three minutes. We had complete watertight integrity. I was trapped for awhile, but the crew used torches and got through the hatches and got me out." Frank's war experiences were not only traumatic but seemed to deepen his religious convictions. "When the war was over I was gung-ho and got involved with things like the Red Cross. I was grateful for what they had done when I blew up on the minesweeper." As he had been in Hitler's Germany before the war broke out and of course fought against the Nazi idea, it "seemed natural to work for the National Council of Christians and Jews," even though "in those days the Catholic Church did not look kindly on such ecumenical work . . ."

In the same spirit, McGlinn served as president of the World Affairs Council before Bodine. As he put it, "most of the boards you go on involve something you are interested in or feel an obligation to do." And McGlinn surely has a tremendous sense of obligation: not only does he serve on more boards than any of this group (than any in the city, I am sure), but he seems to have a photographic memory and brings a wealth of information about all aspects of the city's life and people to any board meeting. He has also been in the habit, according to his friend Bodine, of keeping a list of rising young men and women who would be likely candidates for future board responsibilities. As a sociologist, finally, I was fascinated with his detailed knowledge and statistics on minority and especially Catholic movements up the ladders to the top in the banking business—LaSalle, Villanova, and St. Joe's graduates catching up to the Penn or Princeton people over the postwar years. Though Bobby Scott was too young for the Hitler war, his three years as special assistant to our ambassador to the Court of St. James, Walter H. Annenberg, was a very important experience in serving his nation. Born to considerable wealth and, like his father and grandfather before him, a product of Groton, he had the obligations of public service drilled into him at school. "There is certainly an element of having been brought up with as much as I have which creates a certain feeling that I must participate and contribute to make the world slightly better. I believe that very strongly."

Inherited wealth and privileges were also strong motivating forces for Bill Bodine. Like his father, he went to St. Paul's School where obligations were stressed almost to the same degree as at Groton (both Bodine and Bobby Scott, incidentally, were leaders at these two schools, one president and the other vice president of their respective senior classes). Bill was rather articulate about his family education in public service. "First," he said, "I grew up in a family that sort of brainwashed me that was what one did...rightly or wrongly, we got indoctrinated over the years with the feeling that one owed something to his or her community...I feel I would have done my father in if I had not carried on his traditions." Then he continued: "I don't think I ever said it out loud to anybody, but I felt a certain satisfaction that when my father was no longer around, I succeeded him on the boards of the Bryn Mawr Hospital, the Episcopal Academy and the Harvard Alumni."

If Bobby Scott and Bill Bodine are motivated by the obligations of inherited privilege, Scotty is motivated by the simple pride in the privilege of being an American: "you see, I was brought up in a little town in West Virginia, where I was taught that anything that happened in America was my responsibility. From my earliest days, I was taught that this is my country. We waved the American Flag and played the "Star Spangled Banner" and if you didn't have tears coming down your face there was something wrong with you."

All five men mentioned that they had met and gotten to know a large number of fine people on the various boards upon which they served. All of them frankly enjoyed knowing "movers and shakers" in their city and country: "I could rattle off a hundred people whom I would not have met, or maybe just barely have met, who today I can call close friends," said Bodine. He then continued with a war analogy: "Serving in the United Way last year was somewhat like going to war...for a period of weeks it almost was war...We had a Cardinal battling us on one side, and the media on the other...and like the fellows who served in the military together, we somehow have a bond...they run into one another thirty years later and start to tell the same exaggerated stories they were telling in the trenches together..."

For all of these five men, boardsmanship is a kind of calling, in the old Calvinist or Puritan sense. All emphasized the fact that one never seeks board membership; one gets asked or persuaded. Or as Scotty put it, "I never sought a board in my life; there are people who seek them...it's pathetic."

All five of these boardsmen seem to be workaholics to a greater or lesser degree. Golfing or country club life in general has little appeal, even though some belong. All, however, are members of the Union League in Center City. In spite of his taking a great deal of time and care with his leadership at the Academy of Music and at the Museum of Art, Bobby Scott logs in over 3,000 hours a year at his law firm. "It's a seven-day week. It's not a hardship; I don't mind working seven days in here (his law offices)...I don't play golf." Scotty follows in pretty much the same mold: "I work seven days a week...I work long hours and I enjoy every doggone bit of it." Scotty works at home on most weekends: "I got out of my pajamas yesterday (Sunday) at five o'clock. Last weekend I was in my pajamas all day Saturday and Sunday, home working. I love it. I'm not doing anything I don't want to do." At 68, Scotty is trying to slow down a bit, especially at night: "I used to go to all those dinners in Philadelphia at night, honoring this or that...I remember one time I had five lunches and five dinners at the Bellevue in one week . . ."

A large number of social scientists have conspiracy theories about interlocking directorships and the power structure, largely because of a lack of an historical imagination or first-hand knowledge of the real world or real people. From Franklin's day to this, of course, the richness, variety and freedom of our society has depended on the very few men and women in each generation and community who are willing to shoulder the burdens of responsibility and leadership. One doesn't have to be a sophisticated manipulator of statistics or chi square techniques to know that one always gives important tasks to the busiest man in the community.

John Eckman, as sea-salts often do, has a more colorful way of putting it: "do you want to know what Eckman's Law is?" John asked at our interview at the Penn Faculty Club. "Eckman's Law is that the percentage of time a boat spends underway is in inverse ratio to its size...By that I mean, you give a kid a little outboard and he's in it all day long. Guys who have hundred-foot yachts use them two weekends a year. A logical extension of that is that somebody who has everything, or a lot of time, usually does nothing with it."

These are five of the Benjamin Franklins of Philadelphia in the 1980s. They exemplify the many people who carry on the dogood tradition Ben established; who keep alive the associational *noblesse oblige* so correctly identified by Tocqueville as a special trait of the American character. These individuals are asked to assume responsibility because they have demonstrated their ability and willingness to carry responsibility. They have been preceded by countless others in the same role; they will be followed by still others; and our society is uniquely benefited by their work.

Note

This chapter was first published in *Agenda* 2, no. 7 (September 1981).

19

The Architecture of Frank Furness

Fame is fickle. The Rev. William Howard Furness (1802–1896) and his son, the Shakespearean scholar Horace Howard Furness (1833–1912), are recorded in our own Plutarch, the *Dictionary of American Biography.* Frank Furness (1839–1912) is not. Today, when his father and brother are rarely recalled, Frank Furness has become a kind of cult hero, not only among Philadelphia architects and lovers of architecture but elsewhere as well. Not long ago the University of Pennsylvania wanted to tear down Furness's library (1888–1891). Today the "Furness Library" and Kahn's Richards Medical Research Towers (1959), are considered by many the only creative buildings on the campus. Frank Furness, a pugnacious misanthrope in the City of Brotherly Love, redbearded, bull-dog-faced, scowling, dressed in the loudest tweeds, swearing like a trooper—Furness is the only noted American architect who won the Congressional Medal of Honor—has been resurrected as the Victorian ancestor of the present "Philadelphia School."

As part of the Furness revival, and published on the occasion of an exhibition of his work, *The Architecture of Frank Furness*[1] by James F. O'Gorman, is a vital and visually beautiful exposition of a life and a life's work.

An artist's work must be examined in terms of its historical roots, in terms of the climate of opinion of his own time and of his critics' time, in terms of his social background of family, class, and place, and of his personal qualities. The presentation and analysis of the works themselves is, of course, the most important of all. This book succeeds brilliantly on all counts.

An essay by James F. O'Gorman forms the first part and critical core of the book. In the kind of parsimonious prose which marks an author's sure feel for his subject, O'Gorman deftly outlines American architecture in terms of its dialectical dependence on French and English traditions, emphasizing the importance of Furness's two years' apprenticeship in the atelier of Richard Morris Hunt. He nicely places Furness in his own generation by contrasting him with his almost exact contemporary, H. H. Richardson. While Richardson was "the force that shifted the direction of American architecture away from the picturesque," the work of Furness "remained firmly within the bounds of the picturesque"—which may be one of the reasons for his oblivion and recent rediscovery. In personality, the gregarious Richardson, forever entertaining at his Brookline home, was the opposite of the Philadelphia "curmudgeon" who sought refuge from his critics by riding horseback at his country place. In the Boston tradition, Richardson sought and found fame. Furness, like his fellow Philadelphian Eakins, shunned it.

O'Gorman does an especially fine job on Furness's family and class background. The Furnesses with their New England antecedents were one of the most intellectually distinguished families in Philadelphia's upper class. And Frank Furness's generation was perhaps the most creative in the city's history. Richardson's work won him national recognition. Furness was infinitely a Philadelphian; almost all his work was done there, and almost all his clients came from the ranks of Philadelphia's upper class. The symbolic and pecuniary center of this elite was the Pennsylvania Railroad. It was said that its children ended their prayers with "God bless mommy and daddy and the Pennsy." It is indicative of Furness's place in Victorian Philadelphia that he built the Broad Street Terminal and several other stations for the Pennsy. And when the railroad developed suburbs along its main line to the west, it commissioned Furness to design the Bryn Mawr Hotel, a stunning edifice where Mary Cassatt, sister of the Pennsy's president, was a well-known guest. Furness also did much work for the Reading and the Baltimore & Ohio Railroads (he built the Reading station at Chestnut Hill, Philadelphia, at about the same time that Richardson did a station in Chestnut Hill outside Boston). He built a host of private houses in town and in the Main Line suburbs. For proper Philadelphians at play, he built the Merion Cricket Club, the Undine Barge Club, and the armory for the First Troop, Philadelphia City Cavalry.

Philadelphia history—as opposed to antiquarianism—has been a somewhat neglected subject. If someone wishes to do a study of Philadelphia's Victorian age, he could not do better than to begin with the "Checklist of the Architecture and Projects of Frank Furness" which forms the third section of this book. The second part, "Catalogue of Selected Buildings," is an excellent visual presentation. The special photography is simply outstanding.

Notes

This chapter was first published in the *Journal of Architectural Historians* 33, no. 4 (December 1974).

1. James F. O'Gorman, *The Architecture of Frank Furness* with a catalogue by George E. Thomas and James F. O'Gorman,(Philadelphia: Philadelphia Museum of Art, 1973).

20

Philadelphia, the Crossroads of America

The city that greeted delegates from far and wide to the Constitutional Convention was a city in its golden age, and it was also one in which the visitors could be comfortable. Philadelphia served as capital of the American colonies and the new nation for most of the time between September 1774, when the First Continental Congress met at Carpenters Hall, and September 1800, when President John Adams and his wife, Abigail, moved to the new capital in Washington.

During this quarter-century of nation-founding, the leading members of our greatest generation walked the streets of the city where three of the most famous documents in our history were written and published: the Declaration of Independence in 1776, the Constitution in 1787, and President Washington's Farewell Address in 1796.

Washington came to Philadelphia from Virginia as a delegate to the First Continental Congress in 1774 and made many trips between the Potomac and the Schuylkill in the ensuing years. In the spring of 1775 he attended the Second Continental Congress, where he was unanimously elected commander of the Continental Army. While General Sir William Howe occupied the city during the bitter winter of 1777–78, Washington was encamped and busily drilling his raw troops at Valley Forge.

His most important trip to the city came after the war was won, in the spring of 1787, when he reluctantly left Mount Vernon for Philadelphia on May 9th to attend the fateful convention, convened to alter the Articles of Confederation and create a more centralized union. He arrived in Philadelphia four days later and was escorted through the city by the First Troop of Light Horse. He made a formal call on Benjamin Franklin and spent the night at the great mansion of his old friend Robert Morris, where he remained throughout the convention.

Born in Liverpool, England, Robert Morris came to Philadelphia as a young man from the Eastern Shore of Maryland and took a job in 1747 with the great merchant-banking house of Charles Willing & Sons; he formed a partnership in 1754 with Charles' son, Thomas, and the new firm, Willing & Morris, became the "House of Morgan" of the day, playing a primary role in financing the Revolution. Thomas Willing, whose style and bearing reminded contemporaries of Washington, was the leading Philadelphia gentleman of his time. He was made president to the private Bank of North America at its founding in 1781 and then served as first president of the quasi public First Bank of the United States from 1791 to 1797. Under the leadership of Thomas Willing and Robert Morris, Philadelphia was the cradle of American finance at the nation's founding.

In January 1789, the presidential electors cast their ballots unanimously for Washington; in April, he was inaugurated in New York City, the first temporary capital of the United States. The next year, the House of Representatives, by a close vote, chose Philadelphia temporary capital until 1800, when the permanent capital on the Potomac would be ready. Washington returned to Philadelphia at the end of 1790.

We shall now take a look at why Quaker Philadelphia became the ideal political capital of the emerging nation in what is known, because of his importance of the development of the city, as the Age of Franklin.

By the end of the 18th century, Philadelphia was the most sophisticated city in North America. During the middle years of the century, a rich variety of social and cultural institutions were founded and built, largely by Franklin and other ambitious and talented *auslanders* who came to seek their fortunes in Philadelphia from Europe and the New World.

Born in Puritan and provincial Boston, Franklin found his natural home in more tolerant, cosmopolitan and friendly Philadelphia, arriving here at the age of seventeen in 1723. A year later, he helped organize the Carpenters' Company, which later built a hall in time to host the First Continental Congress; about the same time, he and his like-minded new friends founded the Junto, a "society meeting weekly for their mutual improvement in useful knowledge"; later the group founded the Library Company, the first circulating library in America.

Franklin also helped to found the American Philosophical Society (1743), the first learned society in the colonies, which was eventually housed in a building facing Fifth Street in State House Yard. About the same time (1790) the Library Company built a distinguished Georgian structure on Fifth Street in time to serve as a temporary Library of Congress.

When Franklin walked into Philadelphia, with one Dutch dollar in his pocket, on a Sunday morning in 1723, Boston was the largest and oldest city in the colonies; Philadelphia was the newest about half Boston's size. While Boston hardly grew at all between 1740 and 1776, Philadelphia's population increased by more than 200 percent; it had passed both Boston and New York by 1760 and by the outbreak of the Revolution, the city had a population of 40,000. Among other large colonial cities at the Revolution, New York had a population of 25,000; Boston, 16,000; and Charleston, S.C., 12,000.

Philadelphia was centrally located, important when people traveled on foot and by carriage and horseback. In addition to its size, wealth and central location, Philadelphia also was the most cosmopolitan city in the colonies.

Virginia, Pennsylvania and Massachusetts (in that order) were the largest colonies at the nation's founding. While the white populations of Virginia and Massachusetts were largely British in origin, Pennsylvania had the most ethnically heterogeneous population in colonial America. By 1740, each of its three major immigrant groups—English, German, and Scots-Irish—constituted about a third of the total.

Pennsylvania was also the most religiously tolerant. Anglican Virginia and Congregationalist Massachusetts had established churches, but all religious establishments were alien to the Quakers, and Philadelphia became the most hospitable city in the colonies. Pennsylvania was tolerant not only of all Protestant sects and churches, but of Catholics and Jews. The first Catholic church in Philadelphia, St. Joseph's was built by Jesuits on an inconspicuous spot in Willings Alley in 1732; it grew steadily and a second church, St. Mary's was completed in 1763; a third, Holy Trinity, opened in 1789 (it was the first German Catholic church in the colonies). By the middle of the 18th century, Pennsylvania had 11 Catholic congregations, next in number to Maryland (15). There were at the same time, very few Catholics in either Virginia or Massachusetts, and certainly no Jewish communities.

On the other hand, Philadelphia had a Jewish congregation as early as 1745, and its first synagogue was erected in 1782. Early Jewish merchants were readily assimilated into the city's elite social life. David

Franks, for instance, was a charter subscriber to the exclusive Dancing Assembly at its founding in 1748. Though he remained a Jew all his life, his beautiful daughter, Rebecca, was baptized at Christ Church and became one of the great belles of the Revolutionary War period. Haym Solomon, a Polish Jew who came to Philadelphia in the early days, worked closely with Robert Morris and the Continental Congress as a broker in helping to finance the Revolution.

Although the established Congregational church in Massachusetts had a long history of intolerance, the Anglican establishment in Virginia was mild and tolerant, and the big men from Virginia at the Constitutional Convention were heartily in sympathy with Philadelphia's long tradition of separation of church and state. Madison and Jefferson led the move for disestablishment in Virginia which came to pass after 1776. Washington was a strong believer in religious tolerance and a secular state: thus in 1775, as commander-in-chief in Boston, he did away with the annual anti-Catholic celebration of "Pope's Day"; he did not wish to offend his Catholic soldiers.

In Philadelphia, Washington attended St. Mary's Church at least twice, once when he was a delegate to the Continental Congress, and once during the constitutional convention. Along with Stephen Girard, he was one of the main benefactors of St. Augustine's, at Fourth and New Streets, completed in 1801, which became the largest Catholic church in the diocese. Finally, though Washington regularly attended Christ Church, both in 1787 and after 1790, he was never seen at the communion rail, as his wife Martha often was.

The men of 1787, met in a secular and rationalist spirit, neither calling on God to back their opinions, nor, like the less temperate French, calling on the goddess of Reason. And Franklin's city was an ideal host to men of such sentiments.

Many Southern aristocrats, who so often took the lead in 1787, also felt at home in Philadelphia, for reasons of kinship. Dr. William Shippen, a kinsman of Thomas Willing's and a pioneer in anatomy, married Alice Lee, daughter of the prominent Lee family of Virginia, in London, where he was studying medicine. The grand Shippen house, at Fourth and Locust Streets, was thus the natural gathering place for the Virginia aristocracy, among them the brother of Chief Justice John Marshall, who married Robert Morris' daughter. When Charles Willing's daughter married William Byrd 3d of Virginia, Willing built them one of the four great houses in the Willing compound (between Third and Fourth and Willings Alley and Locust Street). After Byrd committed suicide in 1777, Benjamin Chew, chief justice of the colony and a Tory, bought the house; two of his daughters married distinguished men from Maryland: Charles Carroll, son of the signer of the Declaration of the same name, and Col. John Edgar Howard, an old friend of Washington's who became a U.S. Senator in 1796 and returned to live in Philadelphia. Thus began a long upper-class Philadelphia habit of marrying Southerners.

The ever-bickering Pennsylvania Assembly finally decided to build a State House for the Province of Pennsylvania, in 1730; it purchased a plot of ground on Chestnut and Fifth and Sixth Streets. Two important leaders of the building committee were Andrew Hamilton and Dr. John Kearsley, brilliant *auslanders* who had come to the city at about the same time as Franklin, from Maryland and England, respectively. Hamilton, whose date and place of birth are unknown, made the term "Philadelphia Lawyer" famous when he successfully defended Peter Zenger in an early freedom-of-the-press case in New York. Kearsley became the father of Philadelphia medicine, training in his home a brilliant group of young men who went on to found the Pennsylvania Hospital, the first medical schools of Philadelphia and New York, and the College of Physicians of Philadelphia. Son of an English vicar, he was a staunch Anglican, and he designed, financed and built the present Christ Church (1727), and designed St. Peter's as well.

The State House (now Independence Hall) was flanked to the east by Old City Hall (used by the U.S. Supreme Court 1790–1800), and to the west by Congress Hall, constructed in 1787–89 as the Philadelphia County Court House. Washington (second time) and Adams were inaugurated here. This governmental complex (with the neighboring intellectual resources next door) has been called "the earliest planned group of buildings in America;" it served as an ideal setting for the nation's founding in the 18th century, and it makes an ideal national shrine today.

Note

This chapter was first published in *The Philadelphia Inquirer,* 28 April 1987.

21

The Divided Metropolis

In recent years Philadelphia has become a veritable laboratory for sociological and historical research, largely due to two invaluable sources of data being compiled at the Urban Archives of Paley Library at Temple University and by Theodore Hershberg's Philadelphia Social History Project at the University of Pennsylvania. *The Divided Metropolis: Social and Spatial Dimensions of Philadelphia, 1800–1975,*[1] edited by William W. Cutter III and Howard Gillette, Jr., is a collection of ten articles on Philadelphia, several of the authors using these two excellent sources. The book begins with a discussion of the consolidation of the city in 1854 and ends with a summary article on the centralizing and decentralizing forces in the city's development; in between are eight articles which discuss how neighborhoods are related to transportation, architecture, social class, and so forth.

I found all the articles save one to be sophisticated and informative. Two were of special interest: George E. Thomas's analysis of architectural patronage and social status makes, it seems to me, a major contribution both to sociological theory and to the history of architecture. His use of maps and photographs is excellent.

The second article that particularly impressed me was Meredith Savery's theoretical and historical analysis of neighborhood stability and change. Savery uses two very different neighborhoods to test hypotheses—Strawberry Mansion and East Mount Airy—the former a modest streetcar suburb, predominantly Jewish between 1929 and World War II and overwhelmingly black today; the latter a middle-class railroad suburb wedged in between Germantown and Chestnut Hill. Savery notes that reformers—especially those responsible for the National Neighborhood Emergency Act (1977)—have worked to promote "community, continuity, and heterogeneity." She then goes on to show, in the case of these two very different neighborhoods, how in actual historical fact neighborhoods are marked by continuous change rather than continuity and are most communal during periods of homogeneity. Strawberry Mansion was a homogeneously Jewish neighborhood in the 1930s just as it is homogeneously black today.

The sixth article on work and residence, by Stephanie W. Greenberg, betrays all the worst characteristics of pseudoscience. Of the article's twenty-eight pages, for instance, half are text, nine are given over to tables, and five to footnotes, all this to suggest that availability of jobs tends to affect living patterns. One wonders what excuse there is for the following equation found at the bottom of Table 6-1: "Index of Relative Clustering:

$$C_i = \frac{1}{G_j} \sum_{j=1}^{404} \left(g_{ij} \bullet \frac{g_{ij}}{G_i}\right); \quad C_t = \frac{1}{G_t} \sum_{j=1}^{404} \left(g_{ij} \bullet \frac{g_{ij}}{G_t}\right); \quad I_{rc} = C_i/C_t;$$

where G_t = total manufacturing jobs; G_i = total jobs in industry i; g_j = all jobs in tract j; g_{ij} = jobs in industry i located in tract j."

That the bureaucratic mind attracts bureaucratic money is attested to in a footnote where Greenberg gratefully acknowledges support for a larger study, of which this article is a product from the National Institute of Mental Health (MH16621), the National Science Foundation (SOC 76-20069), and, God forbid, the National Endowment for the Humanities (RC25568-76-1156).

Notes

This chapter was first published in *The Journal of American History* 67, no. 4 (1981).

1. William W. Cutter III and Howard Gillette, Jr., editors, *The Divided Metropolis: Social and Spatial Dimensions of Philadelphia 1800–1975* (Westport: Greenwood, 1980).

22

Class in Suburbia

Class in Suburbia,[1] by William M. Dobriner, is a fascinating book. Its author happily combines a thorough knowledge of the scientific—and journalistic—literature with a lively imagination, conceptual clarity, and a sense of humor: he finds mobile commuters horrifying the old residents of a three-hundred-year-old village with their demands for such educational frills as "plastic gymnasiums and marble swimming pools."

The main task of the book is to destroy and modify the myth that suburbs are: (1) warrens of young executives on the way up, (2) uniformly middle class, (3) homogeneous, (4) hotbeds of participation, (5) child-centered and female-dominated, (6) transient, (7) wellsprings of the outgoing, "other-directed" life, (8) arenas of adjustment, (9) Beulah Lands of return to religion, and (10) political Jordans from which Democrats emerge as Republicans.

The author attributes this myth to the classic book, *The Organization Man,* by William H. Whyte. Contrary to Whyte's immediately postwar findings—which may have been right for the time and the suburbs selected—Professor Dobriner, a sociologist at Hofstra College on Long Island, proceeds to show that our suburbs have become, as of the 1960s, increasingly heterogeneous, significantly different from one another, and less and less independent of, or different from, the rest of the metropolitan complex. In the 1960s, for instance, he found the following residents of a single street in Levittown, Long Island: a Catholic second generation Italian housepainter, a Protestant "old American" college professor, a Jewish second-generation automobile mechanic, a Catholic second-generation Italian plumber, a Protestant "old American" salesman, a Catholic third-generation German blue-collar worker, a Protestant "old American" skilled worker, a Jewish second-generation clerk, a Catholic "old American" research physicist, a Catholic third-generation Irish semiskilled factory worker, and a retired elderly couple who had just moved in.

Perhaps the most important part of the book is devoted to contrasting Levittown, Long Island, as of 1950–1951, when it was a more or less homogeneous, relatively educated, and transient community—as studied by a Yale graduate student—and in 1960–1961 when the author—armed with census data and his own interviews—found it to be increasingly heterogeneous and divided along class lines much like any older community. In other words, he attempts to show that the concept of a "class" is much more useful and accurate variable than "suburban" in predicting and understanding behavior. In Levittown today, for instance, there is a tragic division between those residents of lower-class origins and values who want to spend a minimum on education and are not upwardly mobile themselves nor driven by mobility aspirations for their children and their middle-class and mobility-oriented neighbors who want only the best education for their children. Most tragic of all is the fact that due to the prohibitive cost of education in a new community like Levittown in the first place, and due to the increasingly lower-class control of the school board, the teachers in Levittown eventually set up an association whose task it was to advertise their dissatisfaction systematically—in the *New York Times*—and to act as their agent in obtaining jobs elsewhere in the states.

Suburbia, then, is only an apparent, and temporary, escape from the class, ethnic, racial, and religious conflicts which mark our modern cities.

Notes

This chapter was first published in *The Annals of the American Academy of Political and Social Science,* March 1964.

1. William M. Dobriner, *Class in Suburbia* (Englewood Cliffs, NJ: Prentice Hall, 1963).

23

Goodbye to All That: Upper-Class Origins of American Sport

"The Battle of Waterloo," according to the Duke of Wellington, "was won on the playing fields of Eton." Whether or not the Great Duke ever made this immortal statement, the fact remains that the chivalrous code of the British gentleman ruled supreme in the century between the battles of Waterloo and the Somme, where, on July 1, 1916, the British army suffered 60,000 casualties; 20,000 officers and men, including more than their share of Old Etonians, made the ultimate sacrifice on that terrible summer day (a sum equal to 40 per cent of all the Americans killed in the eight years of Vietnam War.) On July 22nd, the later-famous poet and classicist, Robert Graves, was reported dead in a letter sent to his mother by his commanding officer. Actually Graves miraculously survived his severe wounds and wrote *Goodbye To All That,* a classic autobiography outlining both the end of his own innocence and the decline of the chivalrous code of his class, in post-war England.

In France, a few days after the Armistice of November, 1918, an American aviator and squadron commander, Captain Hobey Baker, was killed while testing one of his squadron's Spad bi-planes. He was a legendary hero in his days at St. Paul's School and Princeton and is today the only athlete to be included in the Ice Hockey Hall of fame, in Canada, and the Football Hall of fame, in America. We shall have more to say of Baker below. In the meantime, Arthur Mizener, a biographer of F. Scott Fitzgerald, once wrote of Baker's sporting code as follows: "When Hobey Baker limped into his opponents' dressing room to shake hands and thank them for a wonderful game after he had been ruthlessly hammered all evening long, it was not because he was a fool or even because he was a man gritting his teeth and carrying out the sportsman's code. It was rather because that code was so deeply ingrained in him that he was incapable of treating an opponent according to his mere deserts: always he treated him according to his own honor.... The Flanders Fields kind of gallantry is out of fashion at the moment, but it was neither an easy or despicable achievement...with his almost incredible skill and grace, his perfect manners, his dedicated seriousness, Hobey Baker was the nearly faultless realization of the idea of Stevenson, Dean Acheson, and John Kennedy, who were significantly influenced by the Princeton, the Yale, and the Harvard for which Hobey Baker was the perfect hero."

Although Hobey Baker's gentlemanly ideal still motivates a goodly minority of men in America to this day, it reigned supreme in the innocent years before the First War, when Harvard, Yale and Princeton men were leaders in business, in law and medicine, in the arts and literature, and especially in sport. We shall begin with football, the American equivalent to cricket as the primary school of manly manners in the pre-war years. We shall follow with brief discussions of ice-hockey and rowing, the two other favorite upper-class team sports: similarly with tennis and golf, as well as, squash racquets and court tennis, still upper-class sport to this day.

At this point, it should be emphasized that baseball, our national pastime, has never been a class sport. Virtually from the beginning, first-rate baseball has always been organized professionally. The pioneering Cincinnati Red Stockings, for instance, went professional in 1869 and, as a major sports encyclopedia has it, "the success of professional baseball through 1871 sounded the death-knell of the sport as an amateur game of importance." While college football has often drawn crowds of 100,000, most college baseball games attract less than a thousand.

And the egalitarian and democratic mores of baseball have always been quite different from once-class-rooted mores of amateur football or tennis. Thus the booing of umpires' decisions, the booing of opponents, (and often the home team, as in Philadelphia), applauding opponents' errors and arguing with umpires, rattling the pitcher, and various forms of skullduggery and downright cheating have long been colorful and characteristic staples of summers afternoons at the ballpark; anything goes on a ball field if "the ump don't see it." All this is not to say that baseball is not loved among the classes as well as the masses, readers of the *New Yorker* as well as readers of the *National Inquirer.* Thus, a prominent Philadelphia lawyer, art collector and civic leader, R. Sturgis Ingersoll, was a graduate of St. Paul's and one of Hobey Baker's roommates at Princeton. He was an avid baseball fan all his life and for many years legal council for the Philadelphia Phillies; his firm still handles the Phillies in the person of a young partner, William Webb, a Dartmouth Alumnus.

"If Wellington was right that the Battle of Waterloo was won on the playing fields of Eton, then it's a good bet that the battles of the Marne, Chateau Thierry, Guadalcanal and Anzio were won on the playing fields that trace their histories back to some goings on in New Brunswick on an afternoon long ago." The writer of these lines, in 1949, was referring to the first football game played on a cold November day in 1869, between Rutgers and Princeton, on College Field, in New Brunswick, before a hundred or so curious onlookers, including an absent-minded, Rutgers professor who soon left shouting: "You men will come to no Christian end." And the professor missed the birth of "the American autumn madness."

That first football game was actually soccer. In the meantime Harvard had played two games with McGill in 1873, one game by soccer rules and the other by rugby rules. Harvard too to Rugby. When the first Harvard-Yale game was played in New Haven, in 1875, the rules were a confusing compromise between soccer and rugby. Finally in 1876, Harvard and Yale played rugby as Oxford and Cambridge, Eton, Harrow, Rugby, and all other English public schools played it. Princeton observers liked the English game and initiated a meeting in the late fall when the Intercollegiate Football Association was formed by representatives of Harvard, Yale, Princeton and Columbia. The rules of the English Rugby Union were adopted with modifications.

Just as James Dwight, Harvard 1874, was the father of American Lawn Tennis, so Walter Chauncey Camp, Yale 1880, was the father of American Football. Camp, as a freshman, played in the first Harvard-Yale game to follow the rugby rules, in 1876, and in 1878, participated in the first meeting of the football associations rules committee, where he served every year until his death while attending a committee meeting in 1925.

Walter Camp and Yale dominated American football from 1876 until 1908, when Percy Haughton, a graduate of Groton School and Harvard '99, became the first professional coach at his Alma Mater (also first in the Big Three). Haughton, an imperious and aloof aristocrat, wrested control of the rules committee from Camp in the winter of 1909–10 and led Harvard through its football Golden Age. One of his greatest players was Eddie Mahan, fellow Marshall with his friend, R. Norris Williams of the class of 1916; Mahan was captain of the team in 1915 which defeated Yale 41-0, and the star of Haughton's greatest team which went undefeated and beat Yale 36-0, in 1914.

While the Big Three dominated football before the First World War, the changing composition of the All-American teams from 1889 to 1916 shows how players from other institutions were steadily absorbed into this elite group: Pennsylvania, a football power almost from the very first, contributed 33 All Americans, and other "Ivy League" colleges—Cornell, Columbia, Dartmouth, and Brown—had all produced All-Americans by 1906; six of the big ten—Chicago, Michigan, Minnesota, Wisconsin, Illinois and Ohio State—had done so by 1916.

Football All Americans, 1889–1916

Ivy League		Other Colleges	
Yale	81	Army	9
Harvard	72	Michigan	8
Princeton	51	Chicago	6
Penn	33	Minnesota	4
Dartmouth	8	Illinois	2
Cornell	6	Wisconsin	1
Brown	5	Ohio State	1
Columbia	3	Penn State	1
		Other Colleges	17

Just as Yale clergymen went out and founded churches, academies and colleges all through the West throughout the nineteenth century, so football stars of Old Eli spread the gospel of Muscular Christianity as football coaches in colleges all over the nation, in the years between 1890 and the First War.[1] And the greatest of them all was Amos Alonzo Stagg who chose to work his way through Yale rather than accept a full scholarship at Dartmouth because he was a staunch Presbyterian and wanted to study in the Divinity School. He was chosen on the first All-American team in 1889 and pitched the Yale nine to five championship seasons; rather than accept a more lucrative contract to play professional baseball, he decided to devote his life to the moral education of young men, on the gridiron rather than in Sunday School. In 1892, Dr. William Rainey Harper, first president of the University of Chicago, under whom Stagg had studied Hebrew at Yale, appointed him an associate professor and football coach at $2,500 a year. He went on to coach The College of the Pacific and elsewhere until his final retirement from coaching in 1960 at the age of 98, for reason of his wife's health: "My wife, the best assistant coach ever had... my buddy, the mainstay and center of my life for 59 years, needs me. I will stay by her in every way."

Stagg died at the age of 103. Four days before his hundredth birthday, Allison Danzig, one of the greatest sportswriters of his age (now enshrined in the Tennis Hall of Fame), wrote a touching and inspiring article on Stagg in the *New York Times,* from which I quote the following paragraphs:

> But it is not because of his prowess as an athlete that Alonzo Stagg is being feted this week as has been no other American in sports... not because he was the most fertile and prolific mind football has known in devising and originating plays, formations and techniques that helped to shape the patters of the American game that evolved from English rugby into the spectacular running, passing, passing test of skill, brains and brawn that attracts millions annually.
>
> It is for his unparalleled service in teaching the young to shoot square, for seventy years; the spartan ruggedness and simplicity of his life in devotion to an ideal, and the granite-like integrity that never compromised for victory and set new standards of sportsmanship in college athletes. It is for these, and a durability surpassing that of Michelangelo and Titian, that Stagg, a throwback to the Spartan mold, who endured semi-starvation to get an education and prized working with you far above the many opportunities for commercial gain he rejected, has been honored over and over....

Nineteen-thirteen was the first year that Yale, Harvard, Princeton and Pennsylvania did not place a majority of men on the All-American first eleven; and, except for 1914 when Houghton's championship team at Harvard included five All-Americans, they never placed a majority again.[2] Thus the year marked the end of upper-class dominance of America's most popular collegiate game. By this time, Princeton had become an ideal symbol of upper-class college life in America. That Princeton's ideal of the gentleman-athlete-scholar was important up to the Second World War is attested to in the following list of Rhodes Scholar winners. It should be added that all through these years, Princeton and the Uni-

Rhodes Scholars 1904–1940
(Institutions with more than 10 winners)

Ivy League		Other Colleges	
Princeton	61	Univ. of Virginia	26
Harvard	46	Williams	13
Yale	43	U.C. Berkeley	13
Brown	22	Bowdoin	12
Dartmouth	20	Haverford	11
Penn	10	Swarthmore	10
Cornell	10	Stanford	10
(Columbia	02)	North Carolina	10

versity of Virginia were well-known for having honor system that worked; they still do, so they say.

In the Princeton class of 1914, three-fourths were educated at private schools, including fifteen graduates of St. Paul's School. Among them was Hobey Baker, the last national sports hero to come from the inner ranks of the Eastern Seaboard, Old-Stock Establishment. One of the best all-around athletes in Princeton history, he was the captain of the ice-hockey team in his junior year and football captain in 1913. "The whole atmosphere was electric when he was playing," wrote John R. Tunis, "Everybody would just stand up when he got the puck or caught the punt. Never wore a headguard in football and I remember that great shock of blond hair—Hobey standing waiting all alone. He was the only player on the field you looked at, the only player you saw…Everything he did was dramatic—because he was a vivid character—had *panache,* as the French say. He did everything with a kind of showmanship that wasn't showmanship because it was natural to him…Never was anybody like Hobey Baker." A well known photograph of Hobey Baker now hangs in the cellar bar of the Nassau Inn, in Princeton. It is flanked by the photographs of two other Tiger immortals, Dick Kazmaier and Bill Bradley (who may one day become Princeton's third President of the United States).

Hobart Amory Hare Baker was born on Philadelphia's Main Line, fourteen days before Williams in January 1892. His father, a Presbyterian-turned-Episcopal clergyman was an old Princeton halfback. His mother, Mary Pemberton, was descended from Israel Pemberton, "King of the Quakers" in early eighteenth century Philadelphia. Hobey was named after his mother's uncle, Dr. Hobart Amory Hare, dean of the

Jefferson Medical School in Philadelphia, and a kinsmen of two Episcopalian bishops, John Henry Hobart, of New York, and William Hobart Hare, a Philadelphia bishop who devoted his life ministering to the Sioux Indians of South Dakota. As Hobey's parents were divorced (and ostracized by Proper Philadelphia Episcopalians) he and his brother, Thornton, were virtually raised at St. Paul's School, in Concord, New Hampshire, where his father's cousin, the Rev. James Potter Conover, was a master. "Aunt Mary" Conover, daughter of the school's first rector, brought the boys up, both in Concord and at Newport during the summers. Conover had brought ice hockey and squash racquets from Canada to the school which thus became a pioneer in both sports. He took a special interest in Hobey who is still a legend at this cradle of American schoolboy ice-hockey (the team once beat Princeton varsity which had won the Big Three championship the same year). Hobey was a first-rate, club tennis player and often played at the Newport Casino. He, of course, played baseball in the spring at St.Paul's.

F. Scott Fitzgerald, one of the most gifted authors of the second American renaissance in literature, entered Princeton in September, 1913. His first and commercially most successful novel, *This Side of Paradise,* was a romantic tale of the years when "war rolled up the beach and washed the sands where Princeton played." To Fitzgerald's generation, Big Three football was a deadly serious game played by gentlemen in a Tennysonian, Round-Table spirit. As it was before the age of specialization, courage and tenacity were primary virtues when all participants played both offence and defence, many remaining in the field throughout the game. As Fitzgerald walked around the campus as a freshman, later described in *This Side of Paradise,* he noted the pictures of the football captain, Hobey Baker, along with ubiquitous Gibson Girls, in the store windows along Nassau Street (still unpaved); and he watched a group of upperclassmen marching across the campus, singing "Going Back to Nassau Hall" and headed by Hobey Baker, "slim defiant, as if aware that this year the hopes of the college rested on him..." In an age brought up on the exploits of Frank Merriwell, young men still had high hopes for their heroes.

Their social system of the Eastern Seaboard upper-class was reflected at Princeton in the club hierarchy which Fitzgerald ranked, in *This Side of Paradise,* as follows: "Ivy, detached and breathlessly aristocratic;[3] Cottage, an impressive melange of brilliant adventurers and well-dressed philanderers; Tiger Inn, broad shouldered and athletic, vitalized by an honest elaboration of prep-school standards; Cap and Gown, anti-alcoholic, faintly religious and politically powerful; flamboyant Colonial, literary Quadrangle; and the dozen others, varying in age and position." Hobey Baker and his St. Paul's friends were members of Ivy, while Fitzgerald was proud of his election to Cottage.

Hobey Baker was the product of the narrow but rounded, class culture which molded his peers at St. Paul's of Groton, Harvard, Yale or Princeton. It was not always the best preparation for the cold, cold world of business; while working at a job at J.P. Morgan, obtained through an influential Ivy Club Alumnus, he was so restless and bored that he took flying lessons at the Signal Corps, at Mineola, Long Island, before leaving for the city in the morning; with his army flying mates, he did acrobatics over the new Palmer Stadium at the Yale game in November, 1916 (word spread through the crowd that it was Hobey); he was one of the first American officers to go to France with the Lafayette Escadrille; "The war in the air," wrote John Davies, in *The Legend of Hobey Baker*, "was a gentleman's war, and the roster of American pilots, at least at first, read like an Ivy League reunion." Hobey often met with his friends at the Paris apartment of Cole Porter, an extremely wealthy Yale contemporary he had known in college; he rose to become commander of the 141st Squadron (its symbol was a Princeton Tiger); and he was killed in a plane crash, as we have seen, soon after the Armistice. Perhaps it was a fitting end to a Princeton and upper-class legend. George Santayana's *Last Puritan* died in much the same senseless way. What he wrote of his Puritan hero might just as well have applied to Hobey: "There was even a touch of grandeur, almost of triumph, in a life finished roundly, that seemed in action and not a succession of involuntary predicaments...." Perhaps Scott Fitzgerald was thinking of another Princeton legend when he wrote "the death of Johnny Poe with the Black Watch in Flanders started the symbols crashing for me..."

The Poes of Baltimore created an incredible family legend at Princeton, unique in the history of American football. John Prentice Poe, nephew of the poet, Edgar Allen Poe, graduated from Princeton in 1854, and served as Attorney-General of Maryland for many years, and produced six sons—who played football for Princeton:

S. Johnson Poe '84	Halfback
Edgar Allen Poe '91	Quarterback
John P. Poe '95	Fullback

Neilson Poe '97	Halfback
Arthur Poe '00	Left End
Gresham S. Poe '02	Right End

Edgar Allen Poe, blessed with the famous name, became attorney-general of Maryland like his father. He was quarterback on the first All-American team in 1889 and captain of the Princeton football and lacrosse teams in both his junior and senior years; he and two of his younger brothers were members of the Ivy Club, as befitted an Ivy man. He married a wealthy Philadelphia widow and served on Princeton's board of trustees. Arthur Poe was the best football player in the family and the only one to reach the Hall of Fame. He had a flare for the dramatic, beating Yale almost single-handedly in 1898 and 1899, picking up a fumble and running 100 yards for the only touchdown in the game in 1898, and kicking a field goal for a last minute win the following year.

John Prentice "Johnny" Poe, Jr., a legend as an undergraduate "stood behind the door when fear went by;" served as a human tackling dummy, admonishing his teammates to hit him harder each time he got up; and coined the famous phrase, "A team that won't be beaten can't be beaten." After college he enlisted in the Spanish-American War but saw no action. Bored with the "scramble for the almighty dollar", in 1907, when war broke out between Honduras and Nicaragua, "El Capitain Poey" fought first on the Honduran side and ended up with the Nicaraguans. Soon after August 1914, he went to England and joined up with the Black Watch and was killed in action early in 1915 in the fighting around the coal field of Loos.

Neilson Poe returned as assistant football coach at Princeton in 1942, just sixty years after the first Poe brother played for Old Nassau, in 1892. In 1917, at the age of forty-one, "Net" Poe reported for officers training at Plattsburg, New York, in July 1918, in the second battle of the Marne, he took command of his unit when the captain was killed, and a day later was wounded with shrapnel through both arms and the right side of his body; still hospitalized when the war ended, he was awarded the Distinguished Service Cross, the second highest award for heroism in combat. He returned to Princeton to coach football, in 1919, living in room 24, in the Nassau Inn, where he died at the age of 86 (all the brothers except Johnny lived past seventy) a few days before the Yale Game in November 1963; he not only missed the game but never saw the Yale Game issue of the Princeton Athletic News which had a reproduction of an oil portrait of him on the cover, and featured one story on the Roper years and another on the Poe legend.

The spirit of Hobey Baker and the Poe brothers has had a hard time at Princeton since that sad November when Net Poe died and President John F. Kennedy, who entered Princeton with the class of 1939 before transferring to Harvard, was tragically assassinated in Dallas. While Kennedy's classmates scored below the national average in their SATs and were more or less content with Gentleman C's, Princeton is now a co-ed, and atomized, meritocracy of SAT virtuosos, pounding out pre-professional A's in ever larger numbers.

In watching the tennis team these days, one becomes quickly bored by the technically excellent, but joyless, styles of the players: opponents never chat while changing courts and generous gestures such as "nice shot" or "nice try" are hardly ever heard. One heard from student friends that the coach of the men's team, a Harvard Ph.D, and a power in NCAA tennis circles, is far more interested in uncovering some future John McEnroe in the number one spot than in teaching all the boys down the line to improve their games in order to better enjoy tennis in later life.

As an index, incidentally, of the declining amateur spirit at Princeton, it is of interest that, while 90 boys participated in the college tennis championships, in the fall of 1913, there is no such tournament today. Finally, one suspects that female Princetonians are being schooled for professional success rather than ladylike stature. The coach of the woman's tennis team recently had to default one of her best players because of blatant cheating. At about the same time, the reputation of the gentleman's honor code suffered a bit when the media reported that a senior, and honors student, had been caught plagiarizing. What was most modern about the story was that her case was taken to court, in Trenton, and that Princeton was threatened with a law suit for "deprivation of livelihood should it fail to award her a degree." Thank God Princeton won out.

In other words, the "fair, gracious, charming and honorable spirit" which Fitzgerald found characteristic of the Princeton of Hobey Baker and the Poe Brothers has been slowly dying in the quarter century since Kennedy's assassination. While working in the Fitzgerald collection at the Princeton library, for example, Jeffrey Hart, captain of the Dartmouth football team in 1951, Dick Kazmaier's year at Princeton, wrote an essay entitled "When Did Hobey Baker Die?" which concluded that Hobey's Princeton died in the 1960s, ending on the following note:

> It is quite possible that Princeton today has a faculty superior to that of Fitzgerald's Princeton, and I am aware that much useful scholarship is being produced.... The students may be cleverer, on the whole, but there is not Edmond Wilson here, I think, no Fitzgerald, no John Peale. There has occurred somewhere along the line an enormous lesion of identity and style, a wound that is mortal rather than intellectual....
>
> Perhaps the whole disaster is a sort of generally applicable metaphor for the apparent hatred of style and distinction that had invaded our lives.

Surely, the hatred of style and distinction has invaded American tennis in general and at Flushing Meadow in particular to perhaps an even greater extent than at Princeton.

At about the time that Hobey Baker's uncle brought ice-hockey from Canada to St. Paul's, Malcolm Chase, three times intercollegiate singles champion in tennis, and some other tennis players, saw the game and brought it down to Yale. In the meantime, a group of St. Paul's alumni bought an old ice-house at Sixty-six Street and Columbus Avenue and converted it into the first artificial ice-skating rink in Manhattan. The first hockey league in the United States was formed in New York in 1896; the first league game was played between the St. Nicholas and Brooklyn Skating Clubs. In the St. Nicholas line-up were three top-ranking American tennis players, H.W. Slocum, R.D. Wren, and W.A. Larned, who between them had won the U.S. Singles Championships 14 times. The National Hockey League (professionals) was organized in Montreal in 1917.

Because of his captaincy of Football, Hobey Baker declined re-election as Princeton ice-hockey captain for 1913–14 in favor of his old St. Paul's friend, Wendel Kuhn. Princeton won the intercollegiate championship that year, losing only one game (out of three) to Harvard. That game was one of the longest and most exciting of all time. It was played in January, 1914, in the Boston Arena to a capacity crown of six thousand (sold out for weeks). Though Princeton was favored, two of its leading players did not make the trip, one because of injuries and the other, a graduate of pious St. Paul's, because of too many Chapel cuts. The score remained at 1-1. After the regulation 40 minutes and two five minute overtime periods. The captains agreed on a "sudden death final overtime. After twenty three minutes, a Harvard wing dashed down the ice and took a shot which was deflected into the air and fell, twenty-three feet form the Princeton goal, at the feet of an awkward but dedicated substitute. Instead of dribbling it in, he lofted a shot that miraculously got past the Princeton goalie and won the game. The substitute was Laverett Saltonstall, later Governor and U.S. Senator from Massachusetts, who captained a Harvard crew that spring which was the first American eight ever to win at Henley.

According to David Halberstram's fascinating book, *The Amateurs: The Story of Four Young Men and Their Quest for an Olympic Gold Medal,* rowing is the most purely amateur collegiate sport in America. Great oars have rarely been the first-rate athletes but rather big men with masochistic zest for punishment and driven by the Puritan ethic of accomplishment and excellence. And they have often been born to privilege. Tiff Wood, Beacon Hill Bostonian and a graduate of St. Paul's and Harvard,[4] rowed on the 1972 Harvard Freshman crew that won the Thames Cup at Henley, and on two of the greatest crews in Harvard's history, in his junior and senior years. It was "hard to understand," wrote Halberstram, "the son of Beacon Hill spending so much time and subjecting himself to so much pain to attain an honor that no one else even understood. Perhaps in our society the true madness in search of excellence is left to the amateur." And Tiff Wood, two Yale men, and an outsider from California, were solely driven by the quest for excellence and the honor of winning, at the very same time that Conner and McEnroe were playing before boisterous crowds at Flushing Meadow for ever mounting monetary rewards. Most mediocre men admire money, few appreciate excellence.

Rowing is as old as civilization. The earliest sweeping oarsmen were slaves under their Egyptian and Roman rulers. No doubt the Romans introduced oarsmanship to the British; by Henry VIII's time, the Thames was the most congested inland waterway in the world, and by the time of his death, there were 3,200 licensed oarsmen on the river. In the early nineteenth century, English university men got the idea of making rowing into a sport, and the first Oxford and Cambridge boat race took place in 1829, just two years after the first cricket match between the universities was held at Lord's. Collegiate rowing in America dates from the first Harvard-Yale boat races, in 1852, which have been held annually (with few exceptions) down to the present. In our age of affluence, the annual race, now held on the Connecticut River, at New London, is a major social event each spring, as many millions of dollars worth of yachts line the course. Other Eastern colleges formed the Intercollegiate Rowing Association in 1899, Pennsylvania winning the first race which was held for many years on the Hudson River, at Poughkeepsie. Cornell, with its ideal location on Lake Cayuga, won most of the races between 1900 and 1930; in the thirties, California and Washington crews won most often. Rowing, an expensive sport, grew rapidly among school and college boys and girls in the affluent years following World War II.

In that September, 1913, when Fitzgerald arrived at Princeton as a freshman, the Intercollegiate Tennis Championships were being held at the Merion Cricket Club, along Philadelphia's Main Line. Harvard won everything: Norris Williams defeated his teammate Watson Washburn in the singles; in the doubles final, Washburn and J.J. Armstrong defeated Williams and E.H. Whitney, captain of the Harvard team in the most exciting match of the tournament—Williams and Whitney, after winning the first two sets and leading 5-1 in the third, lost their touch, the final three sets, and the match.[5]

George Church, a Princeton friend of Hobey Baker, defeated Norris Williams to win the Intercollegiates in 1914; Williams won it in 1915, to be followed in 1916 by Colkat Caner of Harvard. After the war, Charles Garland, Williams' doubles partner and close friend for many years, won the title for Yale, in 1919; another Yale man, L.M. Banks, won in 1920, all were won by men from the older Eastern Seaboard, 29 or 80 percent, from Harvard (16), Yale (8), and Princeton (5), and three from Pennsylvania, two from Columbia, and one each from Cornell (Larned) and Brown (actually Malcolm Chase won it for Brown and twice for Yale).

Finally, in 1886, Godfrey M. Brinley won it for Trinity College, Hartford. Brinley graduated from St. Paul's School in 1884, and, after Trinity and ordination in the Protestant Episcopal Church, went back to the school where he served as a master between 1888 and his death in 1930. Always called "The Deacon," he took the lead in athletics, especially tennis and cricket, and charmed the boys with his booming sermons in the chapel. Over the years, the better tennis players in the school, including Hobey Baker, often played on Brinely's private court, hidden away in the woods near the school pond. As with college football tennis was democratized after the First War. After Philip Neer, of Stanford, won the title in 1921, the center of collegiate tennis gradually moved to California. Never again was the old stock establishment able to dominate the game their fathers had brought from England just over a hundred years ago.[6]

While the tennis intercollegiates were being played at Merion in 1913, the Intercollegiate Golf Championships were being played at the Huntingdon Valley Country Club, in a fashionable northern suburb of Philadelphia. Nathaniel Wheeler won the individual championships for Yale; a Harvard man won it in 1914, Yale in 1915, and Harvard again, in 1916. Before the First War, golf was even more class-limited than tennis. Thus of the 21 intercollegiate golf championships held between 1897 and 1916, *all of them,* were won by boys from Yale (9), Harvard (8), and Princeton (4). The Big Three monopoly in golf was broken when the first championship held after the war in 1919 was won by A.L. Walker, Jr. of Columbia. Ivy League schools still dominated the championships throughout the twenties, Tom Aycock, Jr. of Yale winning in 1929. George T. Dunlap Jr., of Princeton, winner in 1930 and 1931, was the last Ivy League Champion.

Squash racquets has long been the most popular upper-class, winter racquets game. Invented in the 1850s by the boys at Harrow School, in England, it was brought to America by Hobey Baker's uncle, the Reverend James Conover, who had seen the British game while playing cricket in Canada. The first organized game in the United States was played in 1882, at St. Paul's where the boys played on English courts (square) according to American rules until after World War II. The first intercollegiate championship, held in 1932 at Trinity College, was won by Beekman Pool, of St. Paul's and Harvard, the second championship was won by William G. Foulke, of St. Pauls's and Princeton. Of the fifty championships between 1932 and 1982, 40, or 80 per cent, were won by Harvard (20), Princeton (10), Yale (6), and Pennsylvania (4). The two great centers of the game have been Harvard University and the cricket clubs of Philadelphia. Stanley W. Pearson, a contemporary of Tilden at the Germantown Cricket Club, was the only man to win the National Singles Championship six times (1915, '16, '17, '21, '22, '23). The Pearsons of Philadelphia are squash's first-family dynasty. Stanley Pearson Jr., an all around athlete at Princeton, won the Intercollegiates in 1939, the National Singles in 1948, and the National Doubles in 1948 and 1949.

Eleanora Sears, the beautiful Boston Brahmin, won the first National Singles Squash Championship for women, in 1928. Since then the majority of women's champions have come from Boston or the Philadelphia area (Princeton and Wilmington). Betty Howe Constable, wife of the famous football star and a resident of Princeton, won the National Singles title five times, not in a row. Today, Alicia McConnell, the professional at Heights Casino in Brooklyn, is the greatest woman squash player in the world. She won the Intercollegiate Singles three times for Penn, and the National Singles seven times between 1982 and 1988.

The origins of lawn tennis, and all other racquet sports, go back to royal or court tennis, the game of kings which went through its Golden Age in Europe during the 16th and 17th centuries. In 1571, Charles IX of France noted that it was "one of the most honourable, worthy and health exercises which princes, peers, gentlemen and other distinguished persons can undertake." Henry VIII was champion of England in his day (it probably did not pay to beat him). In 1519, the Venetian Ambassador wrote of young Henry as follows: "His Majesty is 29 years old and ... much handsomer than any other sovereign in Christendom.... He is extremely fond of tennis, at which game it is the prettiest thing in the world to see him play, his fair skin glowing through a shirt of the finest texture." Henry built a Royal Tennis Court at his favorite palace, Hampton Court, in 1529; it is still in use today.

Royal or Court Tennis is the most exclusive game of them all, there being some thirty courts and about 2000 players in the entire world (about one-fourth in America). An audience of a hundred spectators is considered a huge crowd. Although there are courts at Oxford and Cambridge, court tennis in America is too expensive even for the Big Three, though Richard Sears, the first U.S. Court Tennis Champion, was a Harvard man, and most champions since have been graduate of Harvard, Yale or Princeton, or, as with the greatest champion of them all, Jay Gould, very rich men's sons who felt no need for college degrees. While Jay Gould won eighteen championships in a row, the next most frequent champion, Alastair B. Martin, a Princeton graduate, won it once before World War II and seven times in a row afterwards (he is enshrined in the Tennis Hall of Fame, in Newport). The first Court Tennis court in the United States was privately built in Boston, in 1876; courts were subsequently built at the racquet club of Boston, New York, Philadelphia and Chicago, as well as at Tuxedo Park, New York, and at the Newport Casino.

During the Gilded Age, Jay Gould was the most hated speculator on Wall Street. His son, George, became a country gentleman, built a great palace, *Georgian Court,* in Lakewood, New Jersey, and devoted himself to his children, his polo, and horse and dog breeding. *Georgian Court* included one of the few private court tennis courts in the world. When the court was finished, young Jay Gould, named after his grandfather, was twelve years old. In the spring of 1900, Frank Forester a professional at the Prince's Club, in London, was brought to Lakewood to teach the Gould boys the game. Jay was soon an addict, playing with Forester every morning seven days a week; in the afternoon, he also began playing with some of the world's best players; by 1904, Georgian Court was a kind of court tennis mecca for British, French and American champions. In 1906, before he was eighteen, Jay won the Gold Racquet tournament at Tuxedo and the National Amateur Court Tennis Championship at the Racquet and Tennis Club, in New York. He then went abroad and became the first American to win the British championship. As we have seen, Jay Gould went on to win 18 singles championships in a row (1906–25, none held 1918–19); he also won the doubles every year except two (he had three partners, all members of the Philadelphia Racquet Club). Finally Jay Gould was the only amateur to hold the world open championship which he won in March 1914 at the Philadelphia Racquet Club.[7]

When Nathaniel Thayer and Hollis Hunnewell built their private court in Boston, in 1876, they hired a professional and a young locker boy, Tom Pettitt, from England. Pettitt soon became the best professional player in America also winning the world championship at Hampton Court, in 1885. When the Newport Casino was opened in 1880, Pettitt was hired as the professional in both court and lawn tennis; he remained at the Casino for 65 years until his death in 1946; he was enshrined in the Tennis Hall of Fame, 1982.

Ranking next to Pettitt as a great professional was Pierre Etchebaster, a product of the Basque country in northern Spain, who taught at the New York Racquet and Tennis Club for many decades; he won the world championship in 1928 and retained the title until his retirement in 1954, at the age of sixty. Pierre was enshrined in the Tennis Hall of Fame in 1978.

Before ending, something should be said about the relationship between the laws, or written rules, in the games of life and the unwritten class codes which have supported them in our best Anglo-American traditions. Our legal system for example, is deeply rooted in the English common law, which in turn, was an historical product of an accumulation of unwritten customs going back to tribal Britain. In a similar sense, the Anglo-American sporting traditions are deeply rooted in unwritten class codes of honor and decency, originating in England and brought to America, especially in the half-century leading up to the First War. The written rules of cricket, football or tennis have been supported by the unwritten class codes which reigned at Oxford and Cambridge as well as Harvard, Yale and Princeton in the pre-war years. In other words, in a very important sense, the so-called *majesty* of the law has always depended on the support of a *nobility* of unwritten class customs.

And when these unwritten class codes disappear, as they surely have done in American Tennis Circles since 1968, written rules of behavior, such as the penalty-point system, soon degenerated into a kind of pettiness which both the anxious authorities and the players come to despise. But perhaps honor and decency simply cannot be mechanistically defined in a written code. Take, for example, the mechanistic new concept of "sexual harassment" which is plaguing our college campuses these days. The issue came to a head at Princeton in May, 1987; after two marches up and down Prospect Street (Princeton's "frat row"), one of which produced criminal action against a student who dropped his pants, President Bowen felt obliged to urge the students, in the daily campus newspaper, to show some "mutual respect and just plain decency" toward one another. But this old fashioned appeal to traditional "decency" apparently did not satisfy undergraduate leaders (especially those at the Women's Center) and the Princeton authorities are now engaged in drawing up a *written* "social honor code." And it will presumably be just as successful as the penalty point system used at Flushing Meadow. Just as Fitzgerald or Hobey Baker could not possibly have conceived of their peers dropping their pants on Prospect Street or raping a debutante date from Bryn Mawr, they also would not have conceived of a need for a stop watch to clock the time one may bounce the ball before serving nor the need for verbal abuse penalties to curb the use of the F-word on the court within hearing distance of lady spectators. Someday, we Americans may come to see that honor and decency must be cultivated, not legislated.

In the course of human history, little is entirely lost and nothing is entirely new. Thus in the Fall of 1910, a young Philadelphia gentleman, Hobey Baker, came down from St. Paul's to a fashionable WASP college, in the sleepy little town of Princeton, New Jersey; at the same time, a modern Norseman, born in a tiny hamlet in the mountains of Norway, Knute Rockne, came over from an Irish-Swedish neighborhood in Chicago to Notre Dame, a small Catholic college of 400 boys set in a sleepy Indiana town not unlike Princeton. Both boys were highly exceptional, Hobey was hard-working and an average student, Knute was bright and graduated *Cum Laude,* both were all-around athletes and campus idols, and both were captains of their respective football teams in the Fall of 1913. While Hobey was a hero, Princeton's team was undistinguished. The Notre Dame team was entirely unknown when it took its first trip East, in 1913, to play Army, on the plains of West Point, and beat them 35-13, largely due to the innovative passing combination of two bosom-buddies and roommates, Charlie Dorias, quarterback, and Knute Rockne, end (cadet Ike Eisenhower who was forced to give up football the previous year because of a knee injury, was in the stands that day). In the fall of 1918, Rock was made head coach of Notre Dame and, in December, Hobey's spad biplane crashed in France. Rock, who shared Hobey's values, brought the spirit of honorable amateur sportsmanship to countless sons of immigrants from all over Europe, through his brilliant coaching career. And he always looked with disdain on the professional athlete: for example, one of the finest men he ever coached and captain of the famous 1924 team, Adam Walsh, once wrote about his deceased idol: "When George Halas, and the Chicago Bears offered the Four Horsemen and myself $35 a week and living expenses, plus 50 percent of the net gate to split among us, we did not take it because Rock didn't want us to. Because I knew how he felt, I did not play any pro football." In the early 1930s, Knute Rockne, like his spiritual kinsman, Hobey Baker, died in a aeroplane crash.

In our greedy age of aimless affluence, the spirit of Hobey and Rock has been taking a terrific beating in American sport. I like to think, however, that it still lives on in the spirit of Joe Paterno, who would rather remain a moral mentor at Penn State ("It's a good to lose once in awhile," he said on TV the other night), than move to the money-made world of NFL Football.

James Wilkerson, tennis coach in MacGregor Park, in a black ghetto of Houston, Texas, surely dwells in the same moral universes as Lonny

Stagg, Knute Rockne and Joe Paterno. His two proteges, Zina Garrison and Lori McNeil, are now playing world-class tennis, the first black women to do so since Althea Gibson. "Wilkinson is a purist, seemingly unconcerned with the trappings of success and celebrity," writes Peter Bodo in *Tennis* magazine, "At home he drives a battered green Datsun so old that the paint has blistered off the roof under the merciless Houston sun. As a youth in the country near San Antonio, Wilkerson picked cotton, read the Bible and developed staunch, traditional values. He is not a deal maker, a hand shaker or a scene maker."

Rockne was once asked to name his best teams. "I don't know yet," he replied. "I'll have to wait and see how the boys turn out in life." In the same vein, Wilkerson told Bodo: "You always have to ask yourself what you want at the end of the road. I guess I'm interested in two things: getting the best performance out of the girls and helping them grow. I'm not as concerned with Zina's marketability than in how she's going to feel when the smoke clears, when she retires at 32 or 33. She ought to end up a healthy aware person. That's got nothing to do with how much money you've made—even Chris or Martina will tell you that."

Notes

This previously unpublished chapter was written in 1993.

1. Between 1890 and World War I, fifty-three Yale men became head football coaches at the colleges listed below:

Army	Fordham	N.Y.U.	U.S.C.
Auburn	Illinois	North Carolina	Springfield
California	Indiana	Northwestern	Stanford
Carnegie	Iowa	Notre Dame	Syracuse
Chicago	Lehigh	Ohio State	Tulane
C.C.N.Y	Louisiana	Oregon	Vermont
Colorado	Michigan	Pacific	Virginia
Columbia	Minnesota	Pennsylvania	Washington
Cornell	Missouri	Purdue	Western Reserve
Dartmouth	Navy	Rutgers	West Virginia
Duke	New Hampshire	Sewanee	Williams

2. Endicott Peabody, grandson of the founder of Groton School, who was selected as a guard on te 1941 team, was the last Brahmin All-American.
3. The Ivy Club's first section were members of the Class of 1880. Woodrow Wilson, along with eight other members of the Class of 1879, was an Associate Graduate Member of the club.
4. Up until World War II, St. Paul's was the leading rowing school in America; and it still remains at the top levels.

5. William T. Tilden, Jr., representing Penn, was defeated in the first round by a Harvard man.
6. Harvard, Princeton, and Yale produced 80 percent of the intercollegiate singles champions between 1883 and 1920; the other Ivy League schools contributed all the others. Between 1920 and 1967, however, U.S.C., U.C.L.A., Stanford, and other California schools produced 47 percent of the singles champions; southern schools contributed another 34 percent during this period. From 1968 to 1987, 60 percent of the intercollegiate singles champions camefrom California schools, and another 30 percent came from southern colleges and universities.
7, Though the Goulds were New Yorkers, Jay always represented the Philadelphia Racquet Club. Goulds were not welcomed by New York's best clubs because Jay, the family founder, had ruined, so they said, quite a few men of the best families on his way to the top.

24

The Sixties

A counter-culture is a minority culture marked by a set of values, norms and behavior patterns which directly contradict those of the dominant society. According to the *Oxford English Dictionary*, the word was added to the English language in the late 1960s and early 1970s, referring to the values and behavior of the American younger generation of the "sixties" who were revolting against the dominant cultural institutions of their largely affluent parents. Although the word entered the language in response to this particular generational conflict in America, the idea is as old as the Judeo-Christian history of the West; Christianity itself was a counter-culture in Jewish Jerusalem and later in pagan Rome. Both J. Milton Yinger, a leading American sociologist of counter-cultures, and Christopher Hill, a leading British historian of the English Revolution, refer to the Bible in their books on counter-cultures:

> These men who have turned
> The world upside down
> Have come here also.
> (Acts 17:6)

The driving force of Christianity has been built on the dialectical tension between the Old and New Testaments, between law and Gospel, between the Ten Commandments and the Sermon on the Mount. Perfectionists in every generation have usually appealed to the Gospel of love as against the culturally-rooted laws symbolized by the Ten Commandments. Thus among the multitude of seekers spawned by the English Revolution of the 1640s and 1650s, the followers of such sects as "The Family of Love" were not unlike the flower people and hippies of the "Love Generation" in the American "sixties."

Sectarian and counter-cultural movements have usually had two aspects, radical activists who seek politically to revolutionize society, and bohemians who withdraw from society to live in isolation. Thus John Lillburne, the most popular man in Cromwellian England, led his Levellers in political revolt, but eventually withdrew from political activism and became a Quaker; so Staughton Lynd, a guru of the student New Left who went to Hanoi with Tom Hayden, also became a Quaker. Theodore Roszak, in an excellent, early book on the counter-culture, includes both "the mind-blown bohemianism of the beats and hippies" and the "hard-headed political activism of the student New Left" within counter-culture.

At the close of the Second World War, Americans were confident and proud of their institutions which were rooted in Calvinist cultural values. These included faith in reason, science and technology, a Puritan ethic of hard work and self-improvement, representative democracy limited by law and Constitution, and finally, a mildly patriarchical family where divorce was still relatively taboo, parental authority assumed, and family church attendance higher than in any other Western nation. Order and authority in this confident society were shaped by a hierarchical, yet increasingly open, and opportunitarian, class system led by elites drawn from, or being assimilated into, a secure and hegemonic WASP establishment.

This optimistic booster society launched the longest economic boom in American history, which produced an unprecedented baby-boom lasting well into the sixties. These baby-boomers went to college and on to graduate and professional schools in increasing numbers. Meanwhile, a prophetic minority as described by Jack Newfield, of them became disenchanted with the materialistic values of white America and attempted to turn them upside down in the 1960s, the most anti-authoritarian, anti-elitist and disestablishmentarian decade in American history. In the course of the decade, the hegemony of a WASP establishment over an open class system was replaced by a governmental bureaucracy, bent on levelling downward rather than upward, creating a classless society of ranks based on credentials rather than ability.

Coming of age in the shadows of the Holocaust and Hiroshima, and faced with the dehumanizing aspects of ever more rationalized and impersonal institutions such as the multiversities at Berkeley and Michigan, many members of this generation found all forms of racism and ethnic prejudice as well as war unacceptable; reason, scientism and technology-worship were major parts of the problem rather than any solution; hard work and social mobility became the "rat race" to be avoided at all cost (better an independent and honest carpenter or plumber than a conforming and conniving bureaucrat); self-improvement through self-denial gave way to the *Playboy* ethic of self-indulgence, love-making courtship rituals to "having sex"; husbands and wives were replaced by more or less permanent "significant others" (lasting relationships were honestly feared); Synagogue and Church attendance, as well as nineteenth-hole rituals at the suburban country club, were left to up-tight parents while their children fled in search of meaningful lives in the student civil rights movement in the South, New Left politics on the very best campuses of the nation, and escape through drugs and various Eastern religious cults in the urban Bohemian scenes like the East Village, in New York, or Haight-Ashbury, in San Francisco, as well as the bohemian fringes of their favorite campuses from Berkeley to Harvard Yard. The Quakers (once called the antinomian Anabaptists of the English Revolution) who still believe in participatory democracy, went through a slow, steady decline in post-war America, and then boomed in the sixties as new meetings were founded around campus communities. The largest meeting in Massachusetts was right off Harvard Square.

One important thing about the counter-culture was its loss of faith in representative democracy in favor of participatory or demonstration democracy; the student New Left, led by Tom Hayden and other founders of Students for a Democratic Society (SDS), was determined to move political decision-making out of the halls of the legislature to the crowd-filled streets; the ballot was replaced by the bull-horn, the privacy of the voting booth by lonely crowds chanting simplistic solutions to complex political problems. The effectiveness of crowd politics depended on television which soon sent vivid audio-visual images round the "Global-Village" world, dramatizing the crowd behavior of 3,000 students gathered (for the Free Speech Movement) on Sproul Plaza, at the Berkeley Campus of the University of California, 1964; the crowd of 20,000 in the anti-Vietnam War March on Washington, in 1965; of 25,000 Hippies and New Leftists marching on the Pentagon, 1967, and finally, the angry, frightened student crowds battling the "pigs" (policemen) in Grant Park, and on the streets around the Democratic Convention in Chicago, in the summer of 1968, which demoralized the liberals (despised enemies of SDS).

James Miller described the end of that day in Chicago as follows: "The sun set. Klieg lights were switched on. Television cameras recorded the action.... Suddenly, without warning, the police attacked.... Fused by panic, rage and pride, the crowd began to chant: `The Whole World is Watching! The Whole World is Watching! The Whole World is Watching!'"

After Chicago the SDS fell apart, leaving a small remnant of Weatherman who were dedicated to violence. Their end was symbolized by two events in 1970; in May a splendid town house in New York City on 11th Street, right off Fifth Avenue, in the Village, was accidentally blown-up killing three Weathermen; the survivors including the owner's daughter, went underground; in May, National Guardsmen opened fire on demonstrating students, killing four. Bullets are real.

The rise and fall of the drug culture paralleled that of the student activists. The year following the Free Speech Movement in Berkeley, two hippies opened a psychedelic shop in the Haight-Ashbury district in San Francisco. By the "Summer of Love" in 1967, the Haight became the Mecca of hippie tribes from all over the nation who had tuned in, dropped out and been turned on by the religion of Timothy Leary who urged them to search for God in a pill. In this sad summer, as Leonard Wolf has said, "love had fixed itself in a place of excrement." These love children, who had left homes of stifling comfort and affluence, had no idea how to take care of themselves. Barefooted, longhaired, dressed in rags from thrift ships and grandmothers' attics, they lived on drugs and junk food, suffered from bad teeth, bad indigestion and lack of sleep, and were constantly stepping on rusty nails and broken glass; venereal disease flourished alongside sexual freedom. A free medical clinic treated some three thousand patients a month that summer.

The greatest event in the history of the counter-culture was the "Woodstock Festival of Life" when some 500,000 youths, left activists, drop-outs, and the just plain curious, found their way to a muddy farm in upstate New York, in August, 1968, just a month following the tragedy of the Democratic Convention in Chicago. For three days the stripped down, happily stoned crowd was orderly and friendly, even impressing the police and local farmers. If Woodstock was a success, the "Let it Bleed festival of Angels and Death," run by the Rolling Stones at the

Altemont Raceway, near San Francisco, in December, was a disaster. The Stones, to save money, hired a band of Hell's Angels (for $500 worth of beer) to keep order. The crowd of some 300,000 was far more stoned than at Woodstock. *Rolling Stone* magazine, a leading authority on Rock music, photographed Mick Jagger watching the Angels beating a young black man from Berkeley to death on stage, in front of the freaked-out crowd. Todd Gitlin, obsessed with the stench of death in the stoned crowd, asked himself: "Who could any longer harbor the illusion that these hundreds of thousands of spoiled, star-hungry children of the Lonely Crowd were harbingers of a good society?"

Note

This previously unpublished chapter was written in 1992.

References

Feuer, Lewis S. *The Conflict of Generations: The Character and Significance of Student Movements.* New York: Basic Books, 1969.

Fraser, Ronald. *1968: A Student Generation in Revolt.* New York: Pantheon Books, 1988.

Gitlin, Todd. *The Sixties: Years of Hope, Days of Rage.* New York: Bantam Books, 1987.

Hill, Christopher. *The World Turned Upside Down: Radical Ideas During the English Revolution.* Hamondsworth, Middlesex, England: Penguin Books, 1975.

Kennan, George F. *Democracy and the Student Left.* Boston: Little, Brown and Company, 1968.

Mailer, Norman. *Miami and the Siege of Chicago.* New York: Donald I. Fine, Inc., 1968.

Miller, James. *Democracy is in the Streets: From Port Huron to the Siege of Chicago.* New York: Simon and Schuster, Inc., 1987.

Newfield, Jack. *A Prophetic Minority.* New York: New American Library, 1967.

O'Neill, William L. *Coming Apart: An Informal History of America in the 1960s.* Chicago: Quadrangle Books, 1971.

Roszak, Theodore. *The Making of the Counter-Culture.* New York: Anchor Books, 1969.

Rothman, Stanley and Lichter, S. Robert. *Roots of Radicalism: Jews, Christians and the New Left.* New York: Oxford University Press, 1982.

Wolf, Leonard, ed. *Voices From the Love Generation.* Boston: Little Brown and Company, 1968.

Wolf, Tom. *The Purple Decade: A Reader.* New York: Berkeley Books, 1968.

Yinger, J. Milton. *Countercultures: The Promise and Peril of a World Turned Upside Down.* New York: The Free Press, 1982.

25

Habits of the Heart

Habits of the Heart: Individualism and Commitment in American Life[1] is a very, very modern and modish book. Its five authors are undoubtedly (to purloin their favorite adjectives) caring, sensitive, loving, friendly, tolerant and open members of the mobile middle classes which set the tone of our egalitarian, therapeutic, and alternative-life-style-encouraging culture: "We believe," they write in a methodological appendix, "for reasons argued earlier in the book, that the mobile middle classes define reality for most of us in the United States." *Habits of the Heart,* "based on conversations with ourselves, our ancestors, and several hundred of our fellow citizens," is an apparently objective and value-free study of values; having no agreed-on hierarchy of values themselves, as far as I can discover, the authors are unable to take moral stands on the superficial and often shallow values of the some two hundred men and women whose words, recorded in taped interviews, form the empirical backbone of the study. The tape-recorder is of course value-free and records with equal emphasis background static, words of wisdom, and just plain nonsense. Like the recorder, this book is full of objective information but hardly adds much to our understanding of causes and consequences. It is written in a tranquil and bland style, as Tocqueville might have predicted. The authors write, for example, that "the family is not so much 'fading,' as some have said, as changing." This is of course pretty conventional wisdom by now among the mobile middle classes, where "alternative forms of committed relationships long denied legitimacy, such as those between persons of the same sex, are becoming widely accepted." The authors add that "to the extent that this new atmosphere creates more sensitive, more open, more intense, more loving relationships, as it seems to have done, it is an achievement of which Americans can justly be proud." While most of their professional peers might be proud of such an achievement, it is my impression that the vast majority of Americans would definitely not be. In other words, this book tells us far more about the values of the parishioners of St. Stephen's Protestant Episcopal Church in the San Francisco Bay Area (surely, as approvingly described by our authors, a therapeutic, rather than a Christian, life-style enclave) than it does about the vast majority of American Christians, whether nominal, committed, or twice-born.

Actually, this book is far more biased than its bland tone would suggest. At its very outset, for example, the authors write as follows: "The central problem of our book concerns the American individualism that Tocqueville described with a mixture of admiration and anxiety. It seems to us that it is *individualism, and not equality, as Tocqueville thought,* that has marched inexorably through our history. We are concerned that this individualism may have grown cancerous—that it may be destroying those social integuments that Tocqueville saw as moderating its more destructive potentialities, that it may be threatening the survival of freedom itself" (italics mine). This shows a total misunderstanding of Tocqueville, whose brilliant contributions to our understanding of the totalitarian tendencies of our age (in both *Democracy in America* and in his *Ancient Regime*) depend on equality and individualism being, as it were, two sides of the same coin. Equality rather than individualism, moreover, is the independent variable: the more equality, the more individualism—not vice versa. How else are we to interpret the famous lines: "Men being no longer attached to one another by any tie of caste, of class, of corporation, of family, are not only too much inclined to be preoccupied only with their private interests, ever too much drawn to think only of themselves and to retire into a narrow individualism, in which every public virtue is stifled.... Despotism, far from struggling against this tendency, makes it irresistible." And every serious thinker from Walter Lippmann and Reinhold Niebuhr to Hannah Arendt has seen the causal links between egalitarianism, individualism, and totalitarianism.

But one must remember that the intellectual world inhabited by our five authors tends, at the moment, to sanction the rampant egalitarianism that has produced such thoroughly modern movements as feminism and gay liberation. Even Tocqueville would hardly have predicted the feminization of poverty, or the academic family with one partner in Buffalo and another in Milwaukee. All of this is not systematically discussed in this book, because to criticize egalitarianism (not even mentioned; the book has only a few lines about class) might lead to offending "significant others," as they say in the profession.

I found most of the interviews reported in this book rather stereotyped and boring, but I shall never forget dear Sheila Larson, of the therapeutic life-style enclave. She is a young nurse who describes her religious faith as "Sheilaism." "I believe in God," she tells the recorder. "I'm not a religious fanatic. I can't remember the last time I went to church. My faith has carried me a long way. It's Sheilaism. Just my own little voice." To have met Sheila is worth the whole book!

To get back to causes and consequences: "How," our authors ask, "did we get from the point where Anne Hutchinson, a seventeenth-century precursor of Sheila Larson, could be run out of the Massachusetts Bay Colony to a situation where Anne Hutchinson is close to the norm?" Although the battle between John Winthrop and Anne Hutchinson and her elite antinomian followers is mentioned in this book, any discussion of Winthrop's views on class and authority is conveniently avoided as uncongenial to the authors. At any rate, this is the most important unanswered question in this book.

Perhaps the real key to the great difference between *Democracy in America* and *Habits of the Heart* is that Tocqueville was a humanist amateur, while these five authors suffer from what Robert K. Merton has called the "trained incapacity" of their profession.

Notes

This chapter was first published in *Social Forces* 64, no. 3 (March 1986).

1. Robert N. Bellah, Richard Madsen, William M. Sullivan, Ann Swidler, and Stephen M. Tipton, *Habits of the Heart: Individualism and Commitment in American Life* (Berkeley: University of California Press, 1985).

26

An Exploration of Subculture in American Life

Things are apparently falling apart in modern America, or so it must seem to those who seek the truth about things, not in churches or Holy Books, but in the media world. Structured by the new priests of the press, that world thrives on reporting the unusual, the bizarre, the titillating and even the immoral—as opposed to the normal and often moral. Thus, as I write, the Mayflower Madam is visiting Philadelphia in the process of being made rich and famous by media people who, at the same time, must find Mayflower mothers mere bourgeois bores.

Similarly in *Cities on a Hill: A Journey Through Contemporary Cultures,*[1] a collection of fascinatingly written essays, all originally published in the *New Yorker,* journalist Frances FitzGerald, winner of a Pulitzer Prize for *Fire in the Lake,* has given us a study of four sometimes bizarre aspects of contemporary life—"the Castro," a gay community in San Francisco; Jerry Falwell's congregation of born again Christians in Lynchburg, Virginia; Sun City, a wealthy retirement community in Florida, and Rajneeshpuram, the utopian settlement in western Oregon that was built by wealthy Western disciples of an Indian guru before he was run out of the United States.

Fortunately, the vast majority of American men and women are still heterosexual, most Christians are birthright rather than born-again, most of the aged still live in the town and cities where they made their livings and raised their children, and finally, most of us cannot afford the spiritual-tourist bug that bit so many of our affluent and educated neighbors in the 1960s and 1970s and sent them west to the prophets of the Human Potential Movement in California, and east to the gurus of India. FitzGerald is, of course, aware that "journalists give more attention to the exceptional than of the run of the mill...."

At any rate, with a keen eye for what most titillates sophisticated modern readers, she placed her fine articles on the Castro first in this book. After all, the sex lives of the husbands and fathers who read the *New Yorker* are certainly tame and mundane when compared with those of the grown boys of the Castro who, in the 1970s, surely must have been the most active sexual athletes in American history.

"By 1978," according to FitzGerald, "the Castro had become the most active cruising strip in the city—and perhaps the country. Even in the daytime, there were hundreds of young men out cruising the bars, the bookshops, the restaurants and stores—even the vast supermarket.... At night, the bars were jammed—and cars had trouble getting through the crowd of men.... It was crazy, one gay activist told me, speaking on his first visit to the Castro: 'I belonged to the Yippies at home...but you know, we were still very sexually repressed. I came out here with my lover, and we couldn't believe it...We had dates at breakfast lunch and dinner.'"

As might have been expected, in the 1970s, the famous Kinsey Institute for Social Research of Bloomington, Indiana, opened a branch in San Francisco. In 1978, in a study of the city's gay community, Kinsey Institute researchers, according to FitzGerald, found that "about half the white males they had interviewed (about a third of the black males) said they had had over 500 sexual partners in the course of their careers; 28 percent said that they had over a thousand." No wonder "two thirds of the gay men interviewed had had VD at least once."

The gay rights and women's rights movements were both partly a product of the revolutionary, antinomian 1960s. Homosexuals and feminists were in revolt against the repressive patriarchal mores of heterosexual society. It came as a bit of a surprise that the male sexual free-for-all in the Castro "surprised gay women as much as anyone else."

FitzGerald's final summary of her brief but brilliant discussion of the differences between gay males and females must be one of the sharpest criticisms of her generation's efforts at constructing a new age of sexual similarity and equality: "If gay male society seemed in many ways impersonal and atomistic," she writes, "lesbian society seemed to be private and intimate to the point of claustrophobia. Liberated gay women, in other words, turned out to be archtypically women, and gay men in the Castro archtypally men—as if somehow the genders had been squared by isolation from the other sex."

FitzGerald covers many other aspects of the Castro community with thoroughness and great insight. Among other things, she does a fine job presenting the story Harvey Milk, who fled a square job on Wall Street, became a hippie at the age of 42 and settled in the Castro in its early days. While he had known of his homosexuality throughout most of his life and had long since come out of the closet, in the Castro he soon found out that he was a born politician.

To make a long story short, after unsuccessfully running for political office in 1972, when the Castro was a still a largely Irish, blue-collar neighborhood centering in the parish of the Most Holy Redeemer, Milk won a seat on San Francisco's Board of Supervisors in 1977. At the height of Milk's political influence, in November 1981, Dan White, an apparently clean-cut, all-American type, a former supervisor and opponent of Milk's, a good Catholic, former policeman and a resident of the last blue-collar neighborhood in the city, walked into City Hall and shot and killed Milk and Mayor George Moscone in cold blood.

Thus began a time of troubles which was to include the invasion of the Castro by AIDS. By the time of the Democratic National Convention in 1984, which was held in the city, the "gay capital" of California had moved to West Hollywood.

If the state of California is the center of present and future folly in America, the state of Virginia is inheritor of a proud past. Jerry Falwell, along with Anita Bryant a leading opponent of places like the Castro, has long sought to resurrect what he supposed to be our best traditions. FitzGerald, however, has hardly added much to the millions of words already written about the Moral Majority and Liberty Baptist Church. I even felt at times that she was bored by Falwell.

And so with the article on Sun City. In this case, while FitzGerald keeps up her charming enthusiasm, I myself was completely bored by the whole idea. Imagine living among white-haired contemporaries, all relatively affluent, mostly Protestant, all avidly participating in one or more of its 130 clubs! And all in a place so neat and clean that a stray piece of white paper, left lying on an impeccably manicured lawn, created a minor community crisis. After reading of the immaculate horrors of Sun City, how glad I am to be retired in filthy Philadelphia.

But FitzGerald offers us one more place. Sometime in 1981, Bhagwan Shree Rajneesh, an Indian guru brought his red-clad followers to Oregon, where he purchased one of the largest ranches in the state, a hundred square miles of dry hills and canyons surrounding the little town of Antelope—and collected 21 Rolls-Royces.

In many ways, this utopian community was a workaholic's paradise, and green pastures soon began to replace the driest land. "Work is our worship. We work 12 to 16 hours a day," one of the leaders told FitzGerald. "But it doesn't seem like work. It's our meditation. And Bhagwan taught us that work is play."

Work was combined with the Growth Movement hug as the ranch wallowed in the various therapies of the Human Potential Movement, rolfing, primal screaming, bioenergetics and so forth. Walking around the ranch one day, FitzGerald was particularly struck by the ubiquitous hugging and was amused to find "former Gestalt therapists working tractors, Langians in the kitchen crew, Reichians digging ditches, and post-Reichians in the A-frame factory."

She found no Freudians seeking to escape from the discontents of civilization, even though an Oregon University survey reported that "11 percent of the commune members had postgraduate degrees in psychology or psychiatry and another 11 percent had B.A.'s in the field."

FitzGerald not only does an excellent job, handling the Oregon experiment but nicely traces the highlights of the spiritual-tourist routs of the last three decades in America. As the guru put it: "Rich people are seekers. The poor are merely survivors. True religion is a luxury which can come only after one's survival needs are met."

And only the rich and the children of the rich could afford the Me generation's endless quest for perfection in escaping the duties of all rooted civilizations. But there is no permanent escape, and the ranch was breaking up by the time FitzGerald visited it again in 1986—it had lasted even fewer years than the Castro paradise.

One final word must be said about the fortunate title of this book, taken from the famous sermon that John Winthrop preached to his fellow passengers on the Arabella. His city up on a hill was no separatist community, but rather an authoritarian theocracy that was to include men and women of all ages, private opinions, even homosexuals, so long as they publicly obeyed a strict code of behavior backed by swift punishment. The deviant and vocal antinomians and separatists, such as Anne Hutchinson and Mary Dyer, however, were to be banished or hanged.

John Winthrop would have been horrified with the permissive paradise sought by the Me-people of the 1960s and their descendants. And just as feminists, homosexuals and the affluent seekers who supported the third-force values of the Human Potential movement were all in revolt against Freud, so they would have hated Puritanism and all John Winthrop stood for.

All of which suggests that FitzGerald would have done better, in her last summary chapter on comparative history, to relate her findings to the antinomian movement in 17th century New England and its affluent separatists, such as Anne Hutchinson, rather than to the leaders of the Second Great Awakening in upper New York state in the 1830s and 1840s. Charles Grandison Finney, John Humphrey Noyes and Joseph Smith were authoritarians who had hardly anything in common with the permissive dreamers of the Me generation. And today's radical feminists had more in common with Anne Hutchinson than with Susan B. Anthony or Elizabeth Cady Stanton, both upstate New Yorkers like Finney, Noyes and Smith.

Notes

This chapter was first published in *The Philadelphia Inquirer,* 19 October 1986.

1. Francis FitzGerald, *Cities on a Hill: A Journey Through Contemporary Cultures* (New York: Simon and Schuster, 1986).

27

Canon and Class

In the current debate between the mindless multi-culturalists and the rigid defenders of the "Great Books" canon, I tend to follow the Harvard philosopher George Santayana who once said that it was less important what particular books liberal arts students were required to read so long as they all read the same ones. In more than four decades of teaching undergraduates at University of Pennsylvania, I have constantly wished that all incoming students, at the time of admission, were given a list of some twenty books which they were required to read and be examined on by the end of their freshman year. All members of the faculty teaching undergraduates would be urged to read the same books and to refer to them as often as possible when illustrating ideas in their various courses.

Rather than discussing what the content of a liberal education should be, I should like to suggest how and why our best tradition of liberal democracy, and the liberally educated gentleman, which it valued so highly, have both been destroyed in post-Second World War America. McCarthyism in the 1950s, the counter-cultural revolution of the late 1960s, and the current victims revolution are all symptoms of the gradual and agonizing death of class authority and deference democracy in our time. It would be impossible for either Adlai Stevenson or John F. Kennedy, both graduates of the Choate School, in Wallingford, Connecticut, to understand the following confession of a recent graduate:

> I am a male WASP who attended and succeeded at Choate (preparatory) School, Yale College, Yale Law School and Princeton Graduate School. Slowly but surely, however, my lifelong habit of looking, listening, feeling, and thinking as honestly as possible has led me to see that white, male-dominated, Western European culture is the most destructive phenomenon in the known history of the planet....

Over three decades ago, a perceptive American political scientist, Andrew Hacker, wrote of the liberal democracy which prevailed in America for the century and a half between the generation of Averill Harriman, Dean Acheson, George Marshall, and George Kennan:

> Whether we like to admit it or not, a society which encourages the full flowering of individual liberty is, and can only be, a stratified society. It is only a secure class which can afford to set down the conditions which allow for non-conformist behavior.... Liberal democracy in America never had politics. It was essentially an upper-middle class creed. The class and not the ideology was accepted simply because the men who promulgated it were men who had deference automatically and unquestioningly accorded to them.

Hacker, much in the style of my own work in *The Protestant Establishment,* then goes on to show how the authority of a gentlemanly class establishment in a deference democracy was gradually replaced in the post-war decades, especially after the assassination of John F. Kennedy, by a classless establishment composed of human-engineering-oriented elites whose power depended on their ability to manipulate a new and defiant mass democracy in their own ideological interests. Liberal democracy gave way to ideological liberalism.

Liberal democrats applauded when Levi Jackson became the first black to captain Yale's football team and was tapped for *Skull and Bones* the next spring (1950); when a tired seamstress, Rosa Parks, refused to give up her seat in the front of a bus in Montgomery, Alabama, to a white man (1955); and when Ron Brown now chairman of the Democratic National Committee, became the first black to be elected to a fraternity at Middlebury College (1959).

While at first supportive, if somewhat ambivalent toward affirmative action, these same traditional liberals eventually opposed and resented the social-engineering liberalism which relentlessly supported affirmative action in college and professional school admissions and faculty hiring, as well as the feminization of traditional gentlemen's clubs at Harvard and Princeton (abolished at Yale) and in the downtown business centers of our cities from New York to Boston and from Philadelphia to San Francisco. The authority of gentleman liberals never approached the arrogant self-righteous power of modern, human-engineering liberals.

William Shakespeare lived through an age of change not unlike our own. One of his more interesting plays, *Troilus and Cressida,* has been more popular in the last three decades than at any other time since it was written (one critic had to caution enthusiasts that the play was not about the Vietnam War). At any rate Ulysses' famous speech surely anticipated Professor Hacker's and my own views of the reason for our defiant and oppugnacious democracy:

> O, when degree is shaked,
> Which is the ladder of all high designes,
> The enterprise is sick...
> Take but degree away, untune that string,
> And hark what discord follows.
> Each thing meets
> In mere oppugnancy.

According to Samuel Eliot Morison, the liberally educated, Anglo-American gentleman took root in Shakespeare's England. He write in his book on *The Founding of Harvard College:*

> A new upper class was arising. Enriched by the woolens trade or overseas commerce, glutted by the spoils of the abbeys, families like the Cecils, Russells, Greshams and Winthrops wished to educate their sons as gentlemen, and prepare them for active life. Oxford and Cambridge colleges were appropriate dwellings for such youths. They offered an opportunity, in luxurious surroundings and congenial company, to read the polite literature which Erasmus told them was necessary for a gentleman's education.

"One can hardly exaggerate the importance of this intrusion of 'young gentlemen' into the English universities, for there they remained, and to Harvard they have come," Morison continues. "This notion of a gentleman's education brought about an unwilling compromise between gentility and learning, a rubbing of shoulders between the poor scholar and the squire's son, has made the English and American college what it is today."

Although Morison was writing at the time of Harvard's three hundredth anniversary in 1936, the gentlemanly amateur ideal somehow survived at Harvard College down to the revolutionary 1960s. Until then, for example, all alumni of Harvard College whether the sons of ghetto Jews or Boston Brahmins, were considered to be "gentlemen" and were addressed appropriately by the Alumni Office with the title "Esquire" following their names: Robert Trail Spence Lowell, Jr. Esq., Theodore White, Esq., Norman Mailer, Esq., and so forth. Those were the days when the "Gentleman's C" was still legitimate.

One would hardly expect the present generation of Harvard men and women, all too many of them strivers for "pre-professional A's," to appreciate or approve being addressed in such an anachronistically polite manner. The more enlightened women among both students and faculty, moreover, are insulted by being referred to as ladies, all the while, not being averse to tacking an Esq, after their name, quite illegitimately, when becoming members of the bar. This gentry title was legitimately used in England by barristers (not solicitors) who were largely gentlemen anyway, and by leading members of the American Bar who were largely gentleman by birth and/or behavior before the Second World War.

The late Theodore White, who saw the 1960s as a tragic disaster and would be even more horrified at today's cult of multicultural victimology, wrote quite touchingly about his experiences with a Harvard that was both gentlemanly and meritocratic in his autobiographical book, *In Search of History* (1978). When he entered Harvard College in 1934, it still "combined the best of the old warmth and the new striving" but eventually became "the most competitive school in American scholarship, a meritocracy in which the students and professors vied for honors with little mercy or kindness."

He summed up his impression of modern Harvard as follows:

> I have served as an overseer of that majestic institution, Harvard University, a member of the Honorable and Reverend Board of the most ancient corporation in the Western world, the chosen thirty who tip their silk hats as they file, two by two, past the statue of John Harvard on Commencement Day in the Yard. But it was a better Harvard I entered in the 1930s than it was later, when I sat on the Board of Overseers, or than it is today.

Leo Marx, a distinguished professor of American cultural history at the Massachusetts Institute of Technology, graduated from Harvard College three years after White. Writing for the fiftieth anniversary yearbook of his Class of 1941, Marx, the first person in his family to attend college, contrasted gentlemanly and meritocratic Harvard in much the same way as White: "There, in that seductive ambience of affluence, erudition, status and well-heeled liberality, I made many of my most meaningful and lasting friendships and was the beneficiary of Harvard's rare capacity...for glamorizing the life of learning."

But, Professor Marx continued: "That quaint Harvard has been largely replaced by a much wealthier 'world class,' status-oriented research university whose faculty members' primary allegiances are to their professional peer groups around the world."

For over three centuries, until the 1960s, Harvard College had been molding a leadership class of gentlemanly scholars; while college leadership at Harvard today is less sure of its mission than it was before the Second World War, its graduate schools are training specialist elites just as they always have done. Unfortunately, the warmly liberal values of Harvard College have been swallowed up by the coldly universalistic and elitist values of Harvard University. How could one expect self-made and careerist-specialists to have time either for serious collegiality with undergraduates or for broadening their own cultural horizons through teaching in some sort of interdisciplinary, great books program?

Even more tragic is the fact that institutions of higher learning all over America now aspire to be like Harvard University rather than Harvard College. Thus the president of Dartmouth College, himself a graduate of post-war Harvard College, was alarmed from the first at Dartmouth's rustic, gentleman-sportsman values, so beloved by generations of graduates since Daniel Webster's day. President Freedman, according to Charles J. Sykes' recent study of the turmoil at Dartmouth, is now in the process of thoroughly revamping the college in the direction of what he calls a "Liberal Arts University," which sounds a bit oxymoronic to me. But his faculty is apparently behind his placing more emphasis on "research" at Dartmouth. A survey of the faculty, according to Sykes, found that 48 percent of them would leave Dartmouth if they had a chance, most preferring to go to research universities rather than teaching at liberal arts colleges. Having lost faith in the importance of individuals, many of whose lives have been changed by stimulating undergraduate teachers, modern academics have elevated 'research' into a God word. "Thank God this class is over, so I can get back to the important business of research," one of my undergraduate students not long ago reported of his instructor in another class.

The classical, Anglo-American, liberal education, I am bound to say in summary, will only be valued by a class society which places the ideal of the gentleman-amateur at the top of its hierarchy of values. Without a clearly articulated and deferential hierarchy of values, moreover, egalitarian (equality of values) societies are doomed to be eventually dominated by endlessly bickering "victims."

Reginald E. Zelnik, saw this as a member of the faculty at Berkeley in the 1960s: "When I was an undergraduate at Princeton ten years ago," he wrote in *Dissent* (May/June 1966), "things were just the opposite. Then the university subtly demanded of its students that they be like it, fashioning themselves in its image. The style of Princeton and many of its professors drew the students like a magnet. . . The present situation at Berkeley is that instead of the university setting standards for the students, the students are attempting to set standards for the university."

A brief look at the ten articles in a special issue of *The New Republic* (February 18, 1991) on "Race on Campus: Reports from Colleges around the Nation," tends to bear out the above views on class and liberal education. Eight of the ten articles deal with racism, affirmative action, diversity, multiculturalism, "P.C." ("political correctness") and so forth only on such high prestige campuses as Wisconsin, Yale, Harvard, Berkeley, Dartmouth, Duke, Smith, and Oberlin; all eight institutions were once class colleges whose leaders led because they knew what young ladies and gentlemen ought to be taught and how they ought to behave; by and large privileged members of clubs and fraternities (and sororities) set the style of life on the campuses and most students tried to conform.

"Growing up in Queens in the forties," writes Peter Schragg in *The Decline of the WASP* (1970), "I regarded myself simply as a New York Jew; thereafter, going to Amherst College, I tried (with less success than I imagined at the time) to become a WASP..."

Today, as all eight articles attest to, these once distinguished places are plagued with an egalitarian confusion of values; administrators (who have multiplied over the past decade far faster than either faculties or student bodies) are no longer educators but mediating human engineers, desperately trying to satisfy a continuing flow of unconditional demands by their various victim constituencies. Fraternities and sororities, anathema to the unstylish minds of most human engineers in student affairs offices, are slowly being banished from the campus scene.

Of course, this occurred largely at elite institutions where liberal learning is an issue. After all, most students at the some three thousand institutions of higher learning in America major in business administration or some utilitarian subject. Thus, while the eight *New Republic* articles on the problems of elite campuses leave the reader with deep sense of despair, the one article on higher education for under-privileged New

Yorkers by Jim Sleeper (who has also written a liberal stereotype-shattering book on the racial politics of New York), is hopeful and inspiring. The article is full of facts about City College of New York (38.5 percent black, 28.2 percent Hispanic, 14.5 percent Asian, and 18.5 percent white) and Baruch College (36 percent white, 26 percent black, 20 percent Asian and 18 percent Hispanic); in these natural, rather than engineered, conditions of multicultural diversity—the CCNY student body includes immigrants from eighty countries—the overwhelming drive for economic mobility has submerged the tensions described by the eight authors writing about privileged campuses.

Thus Sleeper quotes David Garrow, a biographer of Martin Luther King, Jr. who taught at City College for six years, as follows:

> It's really a first-rate student body. They're incredibly well-motivated and, among American-born blacks, far less damaged by the New York City public schools than one might expect. For these kids, City is still the personification of upward mobility. There is less ethnic tension and more interracial comradery here than anywhere else in New York.

Baruch College, incidentally, has the largest business school in the nation. Sleeper closes his article with the following telling anecdote. He asked Rafael Olmeda, editor of Baruch's student newspaper, if he had ever experienced racial discrimination? "Well, once, but it wasn't at Baruch; in fact, it explains why I'm here and not in the Ivy League. When I was a senior at Bronx Science, I sent for Harvard's admission materials. The package came to my house, and out came this Minority Student Information Request card for me to send in, and a leaflet saying, `Here are some of the things minority students experience at Harvard. And I thought: What is this...I want to know, what do students experience at Harvard? Like, what am I to them? Well, I knew what I was. I was a fulfillment of a quota. And I had no intention of being that."

Rafael surely got it right when he refused to be classified, and thus dehumanized, by the condescending human-engineers in the Harvard admissions office.

The final article in this special issue of *The New Republic* is a clearly argued and learned defense of the "canon" by the Marxist-bred literary critic Irving Howe. He shows that the opponents of the canon—feminists, black activists, Marxist, deconstructionists, and various mixtures of these—all tend to share the egalitarian, anti-elitist, and anti-hierarchical values so dear to the hearts of the "the left." Predictably, Howe is upset that his opponents have coopted "the left" especially the "Marxist left," and devotes the first part of his article to showing how his Marxist heroes, Leon Trotsky, Georg Lukacs, and Antonio Gramsci, were all strong defenders of the Western canon. Perhaps Howe protests too much here. At any rate, I fail to understand how Howe could write the following denial of any causal relationship between the class structure and the prevailing ideas and values in our society today:

> There is mischief and confusion in the frequent use of the term "hierarchy" by the academic insurgents, a conflation of social and intellectual uses. A social hierarchy may entail a (mal) distribution of income and power, open to the usual criticisms; a literary "hierarchy" signifies a judgment, often based on historical experience, that some works are of supreme or abiding value, while others are of lesser value, and still others quite without value. To prefer Elizabeth Bishop to Judith Krantz is not of the same order as sanctioning the inequality of wealth in the United States.

What Howe fails to see is that egalitarian social structures have always been breeders of greed—for power in socialist societies and for wealth in capitalist ones. Never has America been more classless and egalitarian and never have greedy leadership elites been more generous in rewarding themselves and more contemptuous of the poor. Howe, moreover, apparently has no understanding or sympathy for the class code of the gentleman which for some three hundred years has stood out against the naked money power and pure greed. Until intellectual leaders like Irving Howe come to see, in the style of Andrew Hacker, that freedom of intellect and liberal democracy are only possible in deferential and hierarchical societies, our forever bickering society will degenerate into the anarchy or tyranny that has marked so much of the third and Marxist worlds.

It must finally by observed that the stylish and snobbish Edwardian professor Henry Higgins could never land a job in modern American academia where proper diction is dismissed as elitist, and where modern pygmalions could not care less about polishing the "Pretty Woman's" accent but only want to teach her how to spend in the style of Beverly Hills, where everyone is shamefully affluent and socially placed by the prices of the cars they drive.

Note

This chapter was first published in *Society* 29, no. 1 (November-December 1991).

28

Bell Telephone's Experiment in Education

On June 23, 1954, thirty-one children and their parents were enjoying themselves at a picnic on the lawn in front of an old colonial farmhouse in Media, Pennsylvania, a suburb of Philadelphia. Many of the children were a long way from home: Melinda and Gayleen Woodruff lived in Palo Alto, California; Sally, Sue, and Cindy Hoverstock came from Houston, Texas; and Judy and Dick Asel had just driven up from Little Rock, Arkansas. They would all be driving home across America the next day. These children had come to visit their fathers, a carefully chosen group of businessmen from the Bell Telephone System, who were celebrating their completion of a novel experiment at the University of Pennsylvania. These young executives were, perhaps more than they knew, pioneers.

Many leaders in American business have been frankly worried about the supply of broadly educated executives for top management positions. Talented and conscientious young men who are now climbing the large corporation ladders too often exhibit the "trained incapacity" of the narrow expert, and for understandable reasons: many of them are recruited from business and engineering schools rather than liberal-arts colleges. Moreover, the pressure of their jobs narrows rather than expands their interests in the world about them.

The Bell system, with more than 700,000 employees, is the biggest industrial organization in America. To keep its tremendous daily traffic of calls, installations, and services humming requires, of course, a vast army of technically trained specialists. But there is nothing static about this business and at the policy levels executives are continually forced to solve new problems and find fresh answers to old ones. For some time the Bell system's top management has been worried about over-specialization among its younger executives, the very men who are ultimately going to have to be the system's imagination.

W. D. Gillen, President of the Bell Telephone Company of Pennsylvania and a trustee of The University of Pennsylvania, determined several years ago to find some way of broadening the educational background and expanding the point of view of Bell's most promising young men. In I952 he discussed with the representatives of the University of Pennsylvania a new kind of education for executive leadership—together they decided that in contrast to the usual executive *training* program, young executives needed a really firm grounding in the humanities or liberal arts. A well trained man knows *how* to answer questions, they reasoned; an educated man knows *what* questions are worth asking. At the policy level, Bell wants more of the latter.

Mr. Gillen took the plan to several other presidents of Bell companies and got their support. In the spring of 1953, as a consequence, the Institute of Humanistic Studies for Executives, sponsored by Pennsylvania Bell, came into existence on the campus of the University. Classrooms and administrative space were assigned, and Dr. Morse Peckham, an associate professor of English who had outlined a liberal-arts course for businessmen the previous autumn, took on the job of director.

The first group of Bell executives arrived the following September and, as a member of the faculty assigned to keep close tabs on the experiment, I got to know them and their problems well. There were seventeen of them, a carefully chosen lot from various sections of the country. But they were all from the middle levels of management. Eleven were between thirty-five and forty years of age, three were in their early thirties, and one was forty-eight; their average length of service with the Bell system was thirteen years; all were married and all, save one, were fathers; fifteen were college graduates, nine had B.S. degrees and six had B.A.'s

Each of them was granted a ten-months' leave of absence with full salary from his regular job in order to devote his full time to the Institute. The first nine months of the program included 550 hours of lectures, discussions, and seminars. The final four weeks of the program were set aside for a reading period during which the men were entirely on their own.

To jar the businessmen-students out of the job atmosphere from which they had come, the courses were deliberately arranged so as to proceed from unfamiliar ideas and material to those closer to their own lives and experiences. In the early months of the program the men received a highly concentrated dose of systematic logic, the study of Oriental history and art, and the reading of such works as the *Bhagavad Gita; Monkey* and the *Tale of Genji*—a far cry from the American suburban groove and business routine. By December many of the students were depressed—the "Bagdad Geisha," they felt, was a waste of time.

On the other hand, as the end of the program approached, the men were prepared to bring a wide-ranging intellectual experience to bear on problems much closer to home. In the final and most popular course, American Civilization, they spent twelve weeks discussing such problems as: the making of the Constitution; the Haymarket Riot and the industrialization of America; *Sister Carrie* and the revolution in American sex mores; *Main Street* and the disillusionment of the 1920s; and *The Lonely Crowd* and American character structure. The course was organized on the theory that one approached Carol Kennicott's struggles with Main Street from a broader point of view for having known something about Prince Genji in tenth-century Japan.

Through James Joyce's *Ulysses*

The study of James Joyce's *Ulysses* was the most controversial part of the curriculum. It was the director's pet idea, and he fought for it. To him it symbolized the function of a liberal-arts education-to provide a liberating experience and to stimulate the intellect. He believed that an intensive analysis of Bloom's day in Dublin, June 16, 1904, would do just that. (One of the students sent postcards to the other participants on June 16, 1954. On the card was written: "Happy Bloom's Day").

The *Ulysses* course consisted of eight three hour seminars for each of two groups of students. Fortified with the extensive "pony" literature on Joyce, dictionaries of mythology, encyclopedias, and Webster, each man prepared one or more reports for his seminar group.

They found it a challenging, and often exasperating, experience. At the close of each report, there was a sigh of relief from the man who had to report, and a wave of congratulations from the rest of the students: "I was proud of Gene! I never got half the stuff he saw in the chapter when I read it." And neither had anyone else, on even a careful first reading.

The final report in one of the *Ulysses* seminars suggests the tone of the whole program. The man who gave it was an accountant and, incidentally, a musician who had earned his way through college during the Depression by playing in dance bands. Patently cool toward the works of Mr. Joyce, he finally volunteered to report on Chapter XI, the "Sirens" section, in which Bloom's extreme loneliness is portrayed in a highly complicated and technical musical theme. His report took just forty-two hours to prepare. "You know, this man Joyce has something for everybody if he looks hard enough. I really got interested in that…chapter." The report was so thorough that the instructor had it mimeographed for distribution to the whole seminar group and for the use of his future graduate students.

The Institute courses were taught by several members of the faculty from the University, supplemented by two professors from Bryn Mawr and Swarthmore Colleges. In addition, to make sure the students came in contact with the best in the intellectual world, each instructor was asked to invite a series of guest lecturers. One hundred and sixty of America's leading intellectuals—including Lewis Mumford, Clyde Kluckhohn, W. H. Auden, Jaques Lipchitz, Delmore Schwartz, Henry S. Commager, Virgil Thomson, Ludwig Lewisohn, David Riesman, and Eric Goldman—visited West Philadelphia last winter.

The guest lecturers were interested both in the nature of the experiment and in the men who were participating in it. In a club room rented in a hotel near the University they had a chance to meet the students at the cocktail hour for informal discussion. "You mean," one of them said to me, "that this idea came from the Bell Telephone people!" Public relations cut both ways in these meetings. The distinguished visitors became acquainted with and, above all, were appreciated by the students.

For ten months the seventeen Bell men were kept busy. In addition to the regular classwork, they read constantly (more than the average graduate student); they went on formally planned trips to art galleries, museums, and historical sights in Washington, New York, and Philadelphia; a block of seats was reserved for them at the Philadelphia Orchestra; and they visited and studied in some of the distinguished examples of residential and institutional architecture in the city.

All of the men seemed determined to make the most of the experience. Not only did they want to justify the costs of the program to the Bell system, but they seemed to want to make up for what they had missed in their formal education. "College wasn't like this, or at least I never found it so," some of them said, and one graduate engineer told me: "It was the degree as a ticket to a job, not an education, that we were after in those Depression days."

Aspirin After Poetry

In Utopia, perhaps, men will be "trained" in their teens and "educated" in their thirties. While twenty may be the best age for learning mathematics, chemistry, or engineering, maybe *Hamlet* or *Faust* are better understood in maturity. To these students, a discussion of pragmatism was naturally related to their own anxieties about permissive education (one father, trained in a teachers' college, disciplined his child without feeling guilty about it for the first time during this period); *Babbitt* or C. Wright Mills' *White Collar* suggested disturbing insights into their own lives; and these men who had lived through the Depression knew what Walt Whitman was giving up when he left a well-paying editorship to devote his life to poetry, even if they could not quite understand his motives.

A real education is an emotional as well as an intellectual experience; and there were both pleasant and unpleasant experiences in this first year's experiment. Few of these students, for example, will ever forget the lecture on Leonardo da Vinci in the art class, or the reading of Ezra Pound's *Pisan Cantos*.

One morning in May a student described the slide-illustrated lecture on Leonardo to me over a cup of coffee at Horn and Hardart's restaurant. When the class was over, so his story went, the lights were turned on and the instructor walked out of the room with tears in his eyes; after several minutes of silence, the students filed out behind him. The eyes of this tall Lincolnesque executive, a Lieutenant Commander, USNR, who had seen the bomb damage at Nagasaki, were somewhat moist that morning as he described the lecture on Leonardo.

The poetry of Ezra Pound is still a controversial artistic fact. Whereas many young graduate students follow fashion, and either like Pound or not as the intellectual climate demands, his *Pisan Cantos* were an unpleasant emotional issue at the Institute. On a Wednesday evening in February, during a heated and somewhat tense discussion of Mr. Pound's poetry with a visiting expert from Harvard, there was very little sympathy for either the guest's admiration for the *Pisan Cantos* or his friendship for Mr. Pound. Driving home after the discussion, one of the students said: "You know I was so upset reading Pound last Monday night that I took two aspirins before going to bed and then got up at two in the morning to take a sedative before finally getting off to sleep. I could not, for the life of me, understand what the man was trying to say in those *Cantos.*"

"This is my one big opportunity," one of the men said to me after he had been in the course for several months, "and I mean to make the most of it." This sense of cramming into a short ten months what might have been for many men several years of education raised several questions. Were these men interested primarily in doing a good job in the Institute because it might mean later promotions in the Bell system for them? Having been exposed to an experience that would presumably change their attitudes toward their jobs and their leisure, was there a chance that they would never again be satisfied with the struggle up the corporate ladder? These were questions that those of us on the faculty asked ourselves, and some of the answers became apparent during the course of the year. Others will remain unanswered for some time.

The Lasting Effects

The Institute of Humanistic Studies for Executives, we were confident, introduced seventeen men of affairs to a new world of ideas, new values, new interests, and to a new type of personality, the intellectual; and the men of affairs changed considerably. They have taken to buying books and building their own libraries; they are collecting classical records; they think about replacing "wall-cover" with art in their homes; and they are more aware of the architectural cliches in American suburbs. One of them said to me: "When my brother-in-law recently gave his daughter a red Buick convertible for a graduation present, my wife and I thought how a trip abroad would have been a much more lasting gift. A year ago we would have taken the convertible for granted."

As the course was drawing to its close each of its members was asked to fill out an anonymous questionnaire in which he was to give his opinion of the course and the effect it had on him. A number of revealing, if not surprising, changes in attitude came to light. Reading habits, for one thing, had changed. "I'm taking more advantage of library facilities, reading two newspapers, and reviewing several good news magazines," one man said. Another reported, "I approach newspapers and periodicals with much more curiosity and speculation than before; politics make more sense; the art section in *Time* is not only readable but interesting; I read the book review section in the *New York Times;* questions concerning McCarthyism are thought through with some real attention to ultimate questions."

But perhaps more revealing comments were made by the men at a dinner held last May in a private dining room at the Philadelphia Racquet Club where Cleo Craig, the president of the American Telephone and Telegraph Company, was the guest of honor. After the entree Craig asked each of the men to summarize briefly what he had gotten out of the course. It was evident that the men had primarily learned something about themselves.

"When I first went to work for Bell during the Depression, I spent twelve to fourteen months collecting coin boxes," one of them said. "From that time on, I worked all the time and sacrificed everything to get ahead. Now things are different. I still want to get along in the company but I now realize that I owe something to myself, my family, and my community."

A second man said, "This course has given me a new interest in my status and my inheritance, and a mode of determining what they are." Another was, "less content with personal values than before," and went on to say that the course had "stimulated a creeping discontent and loss of complacency." Finally, one of them summed up his feelings about the program as follows: "Before this course, I was like a straw floating with the current down the stream. The stream was the Bell Telephone Company. I don't think I will ever be like that straw again."

The men all went back to their jobs in July. Almost six months later, during Christmas week, I talked with seven of them and had long letters from three others. Although the effects of such an educational program as this one cannot be measured with any precision, some interesting effects that it has had on the men are already apparent.

In the first place, it must be remembered they were chosen because of their demonstrated abilities and strong drives towards success in the Bell system. They are, they report, glad to be "in harness" again, and on the whole they have found the transition back to their jobs much easier than getting used to the program of the Institute. One theme runs through their comments on the effects of the program: they have considerably more confidence in themselves, which, in turn, has "created an even stronger desire for more and broader responsibility in the business."

This self-confidence has resulted, they feel, in a greater ability to make decisions: "I think the chief benefit from the program is a kind of emotional detachment. I don't feel the same personal involvement and emotional insecurity about business problems. This increase in objectivity adds to my confidence in taking the risk of decision. I get more sleep now too!" To find this confidence born of objectivity is all the more gratifying to those of us at the Institute because several of us visualized the successful business executive as someone who "flew by the seat of his pants," as the saying goes, and possessed some kind of intuitive "feel" for the right decision. Well aware of the archtypical intellectual's difficulty in arriving at decisions because of a tendency to see all sides of every question, we were afraid that the Institute's program might educate this intuitive feel out of these promising young men. The following comment seems to me a wise refutation of these fears:

> I have been much more efficient in organizing the relevant facts and placing alternative courses of action in sharp focus. Although I now see more angles and am less sure that any particular decision is *the* right one, I am aided in making it by the realization that there is probably no *one* right solution to many problems. I am now much less upset, and more able to learn, by mistakes.

Another man says of his new sense of perspective and objectivity: "This may sound contradictory, but I find myself to be much more critical than before and, at the same time, much more tolerant."

This confidence and assurance evidently has not been limited to their life in business. One man in a large Midwestern city, for example, talked about the Institute to a social club composed of professional people interested in the arts and literature: he was extremely gratified both by their response to his talk and because he got along with them so well in informal conversation afterwards.

These young men of affairs have not *become* intellectuals. They are not bringing bookish ideas from the program into their business and community life: rather, they have developed into sympathetic and informed listeners, or catalysts in drawing out other people's interests. As one writes: "A particularly well-read person in the company who used to interest me very little has become a fast friend of mine and is fostering my continued interest in ideas unwittingly. I of course do most of the listening."

Intellectual Know-How

What Americans proudly call "know-how" has produced many things: great corporations, great bombs, and a great many automobiles and refrigerators. In the Institute of Humanistic Studies for Executives, however, Bell's high managers are seeking to remedy a weakness in American democracy which Tocqueville discerned over one hundred years ago: "It would seem as if the rulers of our time," he said, "sought only to use men in order to make things great; I wish they would try a little more to make great men; that they set less value on the work, and more value upon the workman."

From the point of view of the Bell system, it is far too early to assess the value of their experiment. But it is perhaps significant that the wives, at the picnic celebrating the completion of the program, provided a large cake with one candle and this inscription:

With Love and Kisses to
"The Humans"
Class Of 1954.

Note

This chapter was first published in Robert Goldwin, ed. *Toward the Liberally Educated Executive* (White Plains, NY: Fund for Adult Education, 1957).

29

Soldiers and Civilians

When I was a graduate student in sociology at Columbia after World War II, the late C. Wright Mills once remarked to our class that a military interpretation of history might prove just as fruitful as the economic. Both Marx and Engels, of course, were extremely attentive to military development in history and were keen students of our Civil War. Modern sociologists, on the other hand, with such outstanding exceptions as Morris Janowitz, have largely ignored the military; so by and large have our historians. There seem to have been two main reasons for this neglect: in the first place, intellectuals in our day tend to be egalitarians and thus antipathetic to the hierarchical and authoritarian social organization of military life.

"Professional armies," as Marcus Cunliffe writes in *Soldiers and Civilians: The Martial Spirit in America, 1775–1865,*[1] "were undemocratic, un-American, and almost unnecessary: caste-ridden, cliquish, hidebound." In the second place, throughout a large part of our history we have enjoyed a security from invasion so complete that we have never had to maintain a military establishment of the size of European nations who have always lived with rival nations on their borders. It was not until after World War II that we became the major military and naval power in the world. Now that we are faced with the fact of a large and costly military establishment, it is quite natural that we should explore our traditional attitudes toward the military. The two books reviewed here are very useful introductions to the subject.

These are two very different books. The difference is far more than the fact that Peter Karsten, in *The Naval Aristocracy,*[2] is interested in the navy and Professor Cunliffe in the army. Professor Cunliffe, for instance, as the title of his book implies, is interested in the relationships between the professional army and civilian life in the United States. "I have assumed," he writes in his opening chapter, "that a nation's military attitudes may throw unfamiliar light upon its social order and its values. A second assumption is that the inquiry needs to be wide in scope.... The chapters that follow are therefore deliberately miscellaneous and discursive. If they seem to labor the obvious, to suggest implausible relationships, and to leave terminology vague, the reader is asked to share my view that something of value will emerge." As the author promises, his book is full of fascinating information. It begins with a description of the utter confusion of the militant amateurs who rushed into the battle of Bull Run. It then traces the role of the military in our national life from the time of the revolution, to Shays's Rebellion (which incidentally led to the calling of our Constitutional Convention), to the War of 1812, to the Mexican War, and finally to the surrender at Appomattox Court House. If the story is confusingly told, it is partly due to the fact that our attitudes toward the military were confused and ambivalent from the start. Although considered a militant nation, we have nevertheless been unusually anti-militaristic. Even West Point was largely justified in the years before the Civil War as an institution to train engineers, and a large proportion of its graduates, including George B. McClellan and U. S. Grant, resigned their commissions soon after graduation to engage in civil pursuits, successfully and unsuccessfully. West Point and the regular army were viewed with general antipathy because they were undemocratic, caste-ridden, and elitist. In this connection it is interesting that Andrew Jackson, who was beloved by the people for his defeat of the elitism of Nicholas Biddle and the Bank, also saved West Point by strongly supporting it. But the great democratizer was also a militarist, suggesting an apparent ambivalence that Tocqueville and many of his followers today would find not inconsistent.

If there is any theme to Professor Cunliffe's rather discursive and loosely organized book, it is that American attitudes toward the military may be divided into three points of view: that of the professional, the anti-professional, and the anti-militarist. He shows how the controversy over the existence of a professional military centered around the appropriateness, even the constitutionality, of West Point in a democracy. The opponents included Alden Partridge, an ex-superintendent of the academy, whose pamphlet *The Military Academy, At West Point, Unmasked* (1830) was widely read. Many members of Congress, such as Representative David Crockett of Tennessee and Senator Thomas Hart Benton

of Missouri, were also opposed. On the other hand, other politicians who had sons, nephews, and sons of constituents at the Point (Henry Clay had two sons there) were strong supporters. Representatives of grass-roots democracy opposed the professional school, while the Eastern upper classes were more inclined to support the need for a professional army. The more romantic and less acquisitive sons of the wealthy and powerful generally went to West Point where high ideals of service, duty, and patriotism were the rule.

The anti-professionals were strong supporters of the citizen-soldiers who served in the volunteer militia, on the one hand, and elitist volunteer regiments on the other. Most militia volunteers were militant and patriotic but suffered over the long haul from apathy and poor organization. Fashionable and gentlemanly regiments as the First Troop, Philadelphia City Cavalry, which was founded in 1774 and has fought in every war since the revolution, were better organized and adequately supported by their wealthy members.

With the exception of the South, finally, the anti-militarist tradition has been strong throughout our history. With no enemies on our borders and a great economic opportunity provided by the frontier, bourgeois and business values left no room for the military values of service and duty (with long periods of no promotion and low pay). Fortunately for America, all of the three traditions have survived: the professional at the two academies at West Point and Annapolis; the anti-professional in our army and naval reserve programs; and the anti-militarist in such religious sects as the Quakers, as well as in many sectors of civil society. A rich society needs its George Marshalls and George Pattons as well as its Quakers and brothers Berrigan.

While ex-generals have been called to the White House at regular intervals in our history, former admirals as yet have not. While Professor Cunliffe shows us the interplay between civilian life, politics, and the army, Professor Karsten has written a very different study of our Naval Aristocracy, as he calls our graduates of Annapolis. His is a more thoroughly researched and systematically argued book about a much narrower subject. It is a kind of collective biography of the men who have led our navy from the time of John Paul Jones to that of Admiral Mahan. It is an absorbing story of the Golden Age of Annapolis.

The subculture of our naval aristocracy was surely out of step with the democratic-business values of individualistic America. "If nineteenth-century America," writes Professor Karsten, "could in any sense be regarded as democratic, classless, anti-institutional, individualistic, pacifistic, or any of the foregoing, then the Naval Academy was out of step." Even more so than West Point, Annapolis in the nineteenth century was an extremely aristocratic oasis in the American desert of materialistic democracy. Professor Karsten carefully documents that not only were the candidates for Annapolis chosen from the higher levels of society in the first place, inbreeding and intermarriage made it a veritable consanguine caste. As befitted the "officers-as-gentlemen" ideal, Annapolis was no trade school but a place where the men of Alfred Thayer Mahan's generation were given a broad and liberal education. Honor, loyalty, and service to the navy and the nation came first and ran counter to the American ideal of individual advancement and mobility. And without these aristocratic ideals the peacetime navy would never have held together. The top twelve graduates of the class of 1868 at Annapolis, for instance, remained lieutentants for 21 years. In 1897 there were many capable ensigns with over fifteen years in grade (including Hugh Rudman who later rose to admiral rank). Even the conservative late-nineteenth-centry British navy, upon which our own was modeled, had captains and commanders who were a decade or two younger than our men of comparable rank.

It was no wonder that our naval leadership was on the whole more conservative than even our army. In his excellent chapter on Admiral Mahan, Professor Karsten shows how Mahan's famous book, *The Influence of Sea Power Upon History,* was more conservative than prophetic. All of his life Mahan preferred the romance of sails to the practicality of steam, the gentleman schooled in the arts, literature, and history to the narrowly trained engineer. In contemplating the technocratic minds who have seemed to be in control of our military establishment since the Second World War, perhaps Mahan was right after all, at least in his stand in favor of a broad and liberal education for leadership.

Both books are excellently written and the use of illustrations adds to the reader's enjoyment and edification.

Notes

This chapter was first published in *Armed Forces and Society* 1, no. 2 (Winter 1975).

1. Marcus Cunliffe, *Soldiers and Civilians: The Martial Spirit in America, 1775–1865* (Boston: Little, Brown, 1968).
2. Peter Karsten, *The Naval Aristocracy: The Golden Age of Annapolis and the Emergence of Modern American Navalism* (New York: Free Press, 1972).

30

Urbanization and Governmental Administration

This chapter analyzes the initial impact of urbanization and industrialization on the local governmental units of eighteen minor civil divisions in Lower Bucks County, Pennsylvania. This area is situated in the southeast corner of the County, on the west bank of the Delaware River just below the city of Trenton, capital of New Jersey, and approximately twenty miles northeast of Philadelphia.

Social change due to industrialization has been characteristic of Lower Bucks County for at least a decade. On the other hand, in December of 1950, when the United States Steel Company announced plans to build a $500,000,000 steel plant on a 4,000 acre site in Falls Township near Morrisville, this area was faced with the prospect of an appreciable increase in the rate of social change. The labor force employed in the construction of the steel mill, for example, precipitated an immediate, short-term, problem. Construction began in March, 1951, and the construction force reached a peak of over 10,000 employees in the summer of 1952. Eventually, the United States Steel Company and its subsidiary, National Tube, will employ around 6,000 at the new Fairless works, while other local industries will expand in size, and new concerns will be located in the area.

Population growth implies new housing. In the summer of 1952, the newly-formed County Planning Commission, in a report on Subdivision Developments in Bucks County, found that 11,000 single dwelling lots had either come into use or been proposed since 1950 (8,300 of these lots were recorded with the Commission in the first six months of 1952). These figures on completed and proposed subdivision development include 3,319 of the 16,000 lots planned for "Levittown", and 1,123 of the

4,000 planned for "Fairless Hills." Plans for these two large housing developments were announced soon after the announcement that United States Steel was coming to Bucks County. Construction at Fairless Hills commenced in May, 1951, and Levittown houses began to rise from the rural country-side in the late fall of the same year. Levittown is, of course, the largest housing project in the area and, due to the anticipated in-migration, it is welcomed by the community. However, as approximately one third or more of the present residents of the Levittown community are commuters from the Philadelphia area, this well-advertised development may not be an unmixed blessing as far as population pressure in the area is concerned. In addition, the fact that Levittown is situated within the political boundaries of Bristol, Falls, and Middletown townships as well as Tullytown Borough, further complicates, as will be shown below, the problem, of governmental administration.

The eighteen minor civil divisions in this area are, of course, differentially affected by both industrialization and new housing. At present, the pressures of social change are focused primarily on the townships of Falls and Bristol, and the borough of Tullytown (the minor civil divisions contiguous to the Steel Mill and Levittown). In the Bucks County Planning Commission report on subdivision development, mentioned above, 65% of the 11,000 lots proposed since 1950 were situated in Falls and Bristol townships. Another measure of the impact of "big industry" on these two minor civil divisions is the fact that, whereas the Fairless plant was assessed for tax purposes in 1952 at $14,000,000, the total assessed valuation of *all* property in Falls and Bristol townships in 1950 was only $2,335,401 and $6,776,930 respectively. Furthermore, little Tullytown Borough, with a total assessed valuation of only $418,838, no police force, one volunteer fire company, and only two small school houses (three rooms in all and valued at $30,000) in 1950, is, as it were, swallowed up by the rapid changes taking place in the area.

The boroughs of Morrisville and Bristol, although within the area of rapid growth, were relatively built over as of 1950 and consequently are not faced with many of the problems surrounding population increase. As the superintendent of schools in Morrisville remarked: "We school people have no real problems here; only the banks and bars are suffering from growing pains."[1] On the other hand, traffic and shopping problems are of major concern to both boroughs.

Lower Makefield Township, which includes an attractive upper middle class suburban area along the Delaware river, is growing rapidly but is not faced with pressing problems to the same extent as Falls and Bristol townships. Middletown Township, further removed from the steel plant, has grown in recent years as a result of commercial strip developments along U.S. Route 1. In the period under discussion, the township supervisors have been involved in a dispute with the Levitt firm over minimum zoning regulations in the proposed "Country Club" area of Levittown.

The boroughs of Langhorne, Langhorne Manor, Penndel, and Hulmeville, are growing due to the normal, post-war expansion of population and are also affected by the commercial strip developments along Route 1. Bensalem Township, Philadelphia-oriented, is growing rapidly as a result of the industrial growth in the northeastern part of that city.

Finally, the more rural townships of Upper Makefield, Newtown, Wrightstown, and Northampton, and the boroughs of Yardley and Newtown (the well known gentleman-farmer area of Bucks County) are, at present, relatively untouched by industrial expansion. In the discussion of governmental problems which follows, the emphasis will be placed on the minor civil divisions experiencing the most rapid social change.

For the sociologist, perhaps the central issue in Lower Bucks County today is whether "big industry" and "big housing" can be introduced into the area without an inevitable decline in laissez-faire individualism and local community autonomy. While this paper will be concerned primarily with a brief outline of selected, concrete developments in local government in the two year period when the United States Steel Company and Levittown first came to Lower Bucks, an exploratory attempt will be made to conceptualize these concrete developments by placing them within the framework of the underlying conflict of interest and sentiment between a traditional desire to retain individual and local community autonomy, on one hand, and a slowly emerging recognition of the need for more centralization and government regulation, on the other.

Following Max Weber, Louis Wirth has suggested that "the larger, the more densely populated, and the more heterogeneous a community, the more accentuated the characteristics associated with urbanism will be."[2] As Lower Bucks County increasingly acquires these characteristics associated with urbanism existing government units are called upon to provide additional community services and to participate in many more areas of community life as an agent of social control. For instance, an increase in the size of the population, especially an increase in young married couples with children, necessitates an increase in school facilities, while residential density requires a change from the private well and cesspool to the community operated and financed water and sewage system. Furthermore, an increasingly dense and heterogeneous population requires the addition of various municipal agencies of social control such as fire and police protection, zoning and subdivision regulations, and the introduction of community planning in general.

School Facilities

It is safe to say that the most pressing problem faced by the 18 minor civil divisions in Lower Bucks County in this period is that of providing school facilities for an ever-increasing number of pupils, especially at the elementary level.[3] As of February, 1953, for example, the county superintendent of schools estimates that an unprecedented 7,380 pupils were on a half-session schedule. In Falls Township elementary grades are on double or triple shift; eighteen houses in the Fairless Hill development were turned over to the Falls school board in order to provide temporary classrooms; and within three days in early February of 1953, fifty-three new pupils enrolled in one elementary school in the neighborhood.

The pressing school problem is largely one of finance and taxation. Although predominately conservative Republicans, the local residents would be inclined to agree with this conclusion. In the first place, the problem of financing new school construction is of major concern. As of 1950, for instance, the township of Falls had one school building worth less than $150,000. Since then, over three million dollars worth of new school construction has been planned by the Falls school board and should be completed in 1953 and 1954. Throughout the rest of the area, local school boards are engaged in unprecedented new school construction.[4]

In Lower Bucks County a major portion of the citizens' tax dollar goes to the local school board (whereas the average borough or township tax amounts to about 12 mills, the average school tax is over 30 mills). Needless to say, school taxes are increasing. Without going into details, of the eighteen local school boards, eleven have increased the school millage since 1950, three have added a "head tax" of between $5 and $10, six have added a 1% tax on all real property transfers which is, of course, tailored to raise funds in a rapidly developing community (Falls Township collected $484 in this way in 1950 as against some $29,000 in 1952) and finally, in response to the more mobile residents who have come into the area, Tullytown Borough and Bristol, Middletown, Falls, and Bensalem townships have added "trailer taxes" since 1950. As a revealing index of the mounting tax revenue in the area, the tax collector in Falls Township, who is paid a flat fee of 3% of all collections during the year, received $798.30 in 1950, $3,382.59 in 1952, and, much to the surprise of the local citizenry, it has been estimated that he will receive in the neighborhood of $15,000 in 1953. As a final index of centralization, in order to deal with the increasingly complex school problem especially at the high school level, four joint school districts have been created. Except for the independent districts of Bristol and Morrisville boroughs and Bensalem Township, all local school boards participate in these four joint districts which are in turn supervised by the county superintendent. Urbanization has resulted in both centralization of administration and increasing governmental costs in education.

Police Protection

The twin pathologies of modern urbanism are traffic and crime. In January, 1953, for example, the Chief of Police released the following statistics on crime and traffic violations in the township of Falls.

Most of the local municipalities have been forced to increase their police personnel and facilities in the past two years. Whereas the present Chief of Police in Falls Township was the sole member of the force in 1950, at present he has six full-time patrolmen and expects to add at least one more in 1953.[5]

	1950 No.	1952 No.	% Increase 1950–1952
Motor Vehicle Violations	178	844	370
Complaints Received by Police	60	482	700
Total Criminal Cases	6	44	600

At present the police situation in Tullytown and Bristol Township is of particular interest. "How have the combined police forces of these two minor civil divisions grown in the course of one year from two part-time employees to twenty-one full-time patrolmen and two chiefs? In January, 1953, this question was raised by a civic minded new resident of the Tullytown area of Levittown. This new resident, who was vice-president of the newly-formed Levittown Civic Association at the time, attended a meeting of the Tullytown Borough Council in which the forthcoming budget was under discussion. In the course of the meeting, he asked the president of council how six policemen (the size of the Tullytown force) were paid out of a budget of $1,500 set aside for police protection. The president replied that "moneys were donated by William J. Levitt, president of Levitt & Sons." When asked about the size of the donation, the borough secretary-treasurer replied, "that's immaterial." The vice president of the Levittown Civic Association, sensing the possible implications of this situation, then remarked that he had heard rumors to the effect that the Tullytown council had agreed to oppose the proposed incorporation of Levittown which would involve parts of Tullytown. A council spokesman replied that "Tullytown council has made no deals with Levitt or any other contractor."[6] The matter was not discussed any more that evening.[7]

At about this same time, two recently hired patrolmen in Bristol Township were dismissed. The controversy over this incident brought to light the fact that the combined police forces of Tullytown and Bristol had been operating under the direction of the "Levittown Coordinator of Police." This gentleman, president, incidentally, of the Bristol Township board of supervisors, was hired and paid for by Levitt rather than any local municipality. At the time the headquarters of the so-called "Levittown Police" were located in one of the Levittown sample homes with ten patrolmen from Bristol Township and five from Tullytown working out of this office. In other words, a private employee of the Levitt firm was directing the coordinated police forces of two minor civil divisions. The salaries of these men were in turn paid for partly by the taxpayers but mainly by funds supplied the local municipalities by Levitt.[8] Furthermore, due to the fact that Levittown spreads over four minor civil divisions, the police were often required to make arrests in civil divisions where they were not employed.

The briefly described police situation in the Levittown area is interesting for two reasons: in the first place, it illustrates the problem of urbanization and the concomitant need for centralized agents of social control; secondly it illustrates how big private enterprise, unavoidably and with no necessarily evil intentions, may be suspected of exerting pressure on small local governments.

Planning and Controls

Witnessing the rapid growth of Lower Bucks County, the local civic leaders finally saw the need for planning. Accordingly, in October of 1951 the Bucks County Planning Commission hired a full time executive director.[9] The Planning Commission has moved rapidly, if with cautious wisdom, into a very fluid situation. In December the new director announced a budget of $43,000 for 1952, and the employment of two technical assistants; in January the commission announced a set of minimum subdivision regulations for the county as a whole; in March, as a result of special state legislation designed to aid areas facing rapid growth or other planning problems, a planning consultant from State College entered into a two-year, $80,000 contract with the State Planning Board in order to furnish planning services to the Bucks County Planning Commission.

While planning has developed rather rapidly at the county and state level, planning by professionally trained staffs is non-existent at the minor civil division level, except for a part-time professional consultant in Morrisville. Recently, however, both Lower Makefield Township (upper middle class residential area) and Bristol Borough have announced their intentions of employing professional planning personnel.

In order to insure an orderly development of this area the work of the county planners should be supplemented at the local level by zoning and subdivision controls. In 1950 zoning regulations existed in only eight of the eighteen minor civil divisions; since that time, all except Falls, Bensalem, Wrightstown, and Tullytown, have enacted zoning ordinances. That no ordinances exist in Falls and Tullytown, while the Bristol Township ordinance was adopted only six months ago, suggests the reluctance of these traditionally independent citizens to agree to added controls.

In a growing community, where new housing developments are constantly being planned and constructed, subdivision regulations are essential. Although the county planning commission has the power to set minimum subdivision standards for the county as a whole, the professional staff is constantly cooperating with local officials and urging them to set up their own standards. At this writing, however, while the boroughs have an indirect control over subdividing through street opening, street lighting, and sidewalk ordinances, none of the townships in Lower Bucks has passed specific subdivision ordinances.

After describing several developments in local government over a two year period in Lower Bucks County, there remains the need to place these and other developments within a broader conceptual frame of reference. In other words, what is the underlying pattern of change? In agreement with Louis Wirth, as quoted above, it is our hypothesis that, as a result of the introduction of large scale industry and housing into an area such as Bucks County, centralization and increased regulation and control by government will gradually overcome the inertia of traditional beliefs in personal independence and small community autonomy. Having described the pattern of increased government regulations in zoning, police protection, subdivision regulation, and so forth, we shall now analyze the emerging pattern of government centralization.

In 1950, the base year for the present analysis of social change, Lower Bucks County not only lacked any sense of overall community solidarity, but in the early stages of urbanization there was a minimum of cooperation, even between contiguous minor civil divisions. The citizens and officials within each civil division were continually striving to remain independent of outside government influence, whether it was Federal, State, County, or other municipality. The two forces which tend to maintain this traditional independence and reluctance to cooperate are 1. the local citizens' and officials' self interest both real and supposed as the case may be, and 2. a provincial sentiment which tends to mistrust all "big city" or "large scale" influence. Time and again, in talking to local leaders and old established residents of the area, one hears the phrase, "You know, my private opinion is that we would be a lot better off if all this had never happened."

In this connection, the proposed incorporation of Levittown into one municipality (see below) is a focal point of controversy. In the fall of 1952, when the local officials of Falls and Bristol townships saw the possibility of this development, they temporarily halted all construction of new schools in the area: as one local official put it. "We have seen enough to know that Mr. Levitt has more power than we do." In contemplating this same incorporation proposal, the present residents of the Falls area of Levittown, which has the benefit of the large steel plant assessment for tax purposes, are quite understandably against it.

Reinforcing the desire for local independence which is motivated by self interest, the prevailing sentiment among established residents and officials is expressed by a cautious attitude towards any form of consolidation of local units of government or any interference from larger units such as the state or federal government. This was brought to light recently, for example, when the Philadelphia Housing Association, a liberal civic organization in Philadelphia, proposed that, in the logical interest of more efficient government, Lower Bucks County should be incorporated into one all-inclusive municipal unit. The secretary of one of the local school boards, in reply to this suggestion from the "big city," probably reflects local sentiment when he said, "With more and smaller communities we have a larger number of people directly participating either as municipal officials or actually helping to elect local citizens to local posts." After alluding to the dubious advantages of "controlled wards" and "boss rule" in the "big city," he went on to say that "there are fewer possibilities and less likelihood of graft and inefficiencies when it is possible for citizens to directly contact their officials who are also their neighbors." The desire to keep the locus of both social and political power from disappearing over the local horizon, as it were, is strong in this tradition bound part of the world. Six minor civil divisions in Bucks County celebrate their two hundredth anniversaries in 1953 while Falls and Bristol Townships have been in existence since the Seventeenth Century.

While the status quo is protected by a subtle blend of sentiment and hard-headed self interest, the need for more centralized administrative units is gradually becoming apparent to many civic leaders. As noted above, Levittown is situated in Falls, Bristol, and Middletown townships as well as Tullytown Borough. The incorporation of this whole development within one borough has been proposed by many civic groups in addition to Mr. Levitt himself. The complex situation as regards police protection mentioned above is only one aspect of a problem which has many ramifications.

The problems posed by the situation in Levittown suggest three alternative solutions to the problem of centralization in Lower Bucks County as a whole. First, the incorporation of Levittown might simplify certain administrative difficulties. There are, however, several objections to this proposal: this proposed municipality would be primarily residential with only a small area set aside for commercial and industrial development so the tax base might prove inadequate. Of course, the citizens and officials of Falls Township are against such a plan. In addition, the best professional opinion feels that an exclusively residential community, unless it is a fairly wealthy one, cannot support such expensive services as education. Finally, those who are in favor of the eventual consolidation of all of this area within one municipality naturally feel that this solution would only serve to divert attention away from this more inclusive solution.

A second alternative solution to this problem might be the annexation of the whole Levittown community to one minor civil division. Annexation to Falls Township, for example, would provide an industrial tax base which would include the steel company as well as other concerns coming into this area. (In 1951 Falls had more industrial employees than any other minor civil division in the area). This would undoubtedly be objected to by contiguous civil divisions which might feel weakened by this solution. Up to the present no one has publicly proposed such a move. Finally, this solution would be opposed by those desiring incorporation of the whole area.

Although there was much local criticism of the Philadelphia Housing Association's proposal to incorporate all of Lower Bucks County into one municipality, there are many arguments in favor of this solution. Among other things, a centralized governmental unit might be more efficient, especially in planning the development of the area as a whole. In addition, while part-time officials both legislate and administer governmental affairs in the existing minor civil divisions, a large municipality would be able to employ full-time, professionally trained personnel in administrative positions. Of course, local vested interests may be expected to work against this solution. Bristol and Morrisville boroughs, for instance, would hesitate to enter a municipality where they would conceivably be overpowered by the upstart Levittown community (the population in Morrisville was 7,000 and Bristol 13,000 in 1950 while Levittown is expected to contain over 60,000 residents by 1960).

In summary, incipient urbanization has introduced many new problems in local government. On the whole, government is playing a larger role in the life of each local community. Although the situation is, to say the least, a fluid one at this writing, there is an underlying trend towards some form of consolidation of existing local units. Although what eventual form consolidation will take is unpredictable at the present, inevitably a balance will be struck between a so-called rational solution on the one hand and conflicting local interests on the other.

Notes

This chapter was first published in *Social Problems,* July 1954.

1. Morrisville, with a population of approximately 7,000 in 1952, had eight tap rooms. Local Commissioners are apprehensive about the possibility of this quiet suburban town becoming "another Gary, Indiana, or South Pittsburgh." (*Delaware County Advance,* 10 April 1952).
2. Louis Wirth, "Urbanism as a Way of Life, *American Journal of Sociology* 44 (July 1938).
3. In an early census of 2,074 residents of Levittown in the winter of 1952-53, the following age distribution is quite revealing:

Age	Age
0-4 22%	30-34 43%
5-14 17%	35-64 16%
15-19 1.5%	Over 64 0.2%

4. Of course the problem of new school construction is nation-wide in scope and by no means peculiar to this area. In a recent survey of existing school facilities in this area, however, it was somewhat surprising to find no less than fifteen one room school houses.
5. The Falls Township annual financial statements include expenditures of $985.10 for police protection in 1950 as against $33,758.63 in 1952.
6. *Bristol Courier,* 22 January 1953.
7. The vice-president of the civic association referred to above was defeated at the next association election.
8. Since this paper was written Mr. Levitt has published the exact amounts contributed by him to the local governments for police protection purposes. Needless to say the "Levittown Police Force" is no longer in existence. *Levittown Advance,* 5 March 1953.
9. The new executive director, of old Quaker stock and the son of a local banker, has demonstrated the value of a thorough knowledge of local community folkways and prejudices in planning for social change.

31

Class and Scientism: America and England

I would like to elaborate on some of the ideas raised by the two previous speakers.[1] I was particularly interested in Mr. Melman's remarks about his study of the two factories, one in Detroit and the other in England. I would assume that the fact that one can purchase some 200 kilowatts of electric power for the price of one worker in America, as against only 50 Kilowatts per British worker, is at least partly a reflection of the less technocratic, and more humanistic, values of the British as compared with ourselves.

This, of course, raises the immediate question: why the contrasting values held by these two great industrial cultures? Before suggesting any answers to this question. Let me make some further observations on the contrasting values of these two cultures. In his book, *The End of Ideology,*[2] Daniel Bell gave us two different responses to similar situations. On the one hand, Bell observed that a turnpike was being routed down through New England to New York City; the most *technically* efficient route would have gone right through the center of an historic cemetery where some very distinguished Americans were buried. At about the same time in England, a new turnpike (still, by the way, referred to as a "carriageway") was being built out of London; the most *technically* efficient route would have gone through an historic Gothic arch which was too small to allow large modern buses and lorries to pass under it. As might be expected, the leaders of the two cultures made quite different decisions: In New England, the ancient graves were ripped up and the turnpike routed in the most technically efficient straight line; in Old England, the turnpike was routed around the ancient arch, tradition and historic continuity having triumphed over purely technical considerations, humane logic triumphed over technical logic.

One can find many other examples of the contrasts between the values of these two cultures. In a recent trip through England, for example, I kept asking myself why there were so few ugly telephone poles and wires cluttering up the beautiful countryside as in America? I discovered this was because they place them underground. Why no endless strip development and second-hand car lots which blight the outskirts of almost every town in America? Simply because the English leadership does not allow it and has instituted zoning laws against such consummate ugliness.

Our modern civilization, of course, is based on the automobile and various other means of rapid movement and communication. Telephone wires, turnpikes, and automobiles are here to stay. It is not a matter of doing away with them in the Luddite tradition; rather we must make them our servants rather than our masters.

There is, I think, a long tradition in America which has produced the particular set of values which include technology as master rather than as means. It undoubtedly has something to do with our well-known cult of efficiency, which is quite naturally the enemy of tradition. One recalls the brilliant and iconoclastic writings of Thorsten Veblen, who loved to ridicule the reactionary peculiarities of all sorts of "leisure-class" traditions which were forever holding us back from pursuing pure functional (or technical) efficiency. It was no wonder that Veblen was one of the patron saints of the "gray-suited" and "gray car" *Technocracy* Movement. Or take the case of the term "culture-lag," one of the most famous concepts in the jargon of American sociology, coined by William F. Ogburn in his book *Social Change*.[3] Like Veblen, and like Marx, Ogburn's term meant that the normative culture (or superstructure) had a reactionary way of lagging behind the rapid changes in technological efficiency, and technological progress. But why, we ought to be asking ourselves today, should cultural values chase after technological advances (innovations) rather than bending and shaping (or not even using) the technology to suit our traditional cultural values or social and political forms? Have the British necessarily "lagged" behind us just because they prefer the traditional drafty halls and open fireplaces to the central heating (and overheating) which is now considered a necessity for all Americans, from Maine to Florida, from the home of the slum-dweller to the millionaire's mansion?

What I have been trying to suggest, following Mr. Melman, is that British cultural values seem to include a more humanistic and less technocratic basis for making decisions than has been the case in America. I would further like to suggest the possibility that these contrasting sets of values are related to the different attitudes towards hierarchy and authority in these two cultures.

On the one hand, the English value system has been firmly and traditionally anchored in a strong sense of *deference* to a hegemonic set of upper-class values which include, among other things, (1) a sense of amateurism rather than professionalism, (2) an emphasis on stability rather than change, and (3) a general, classical or humanistic, rather than technical or scientific, education—at least for the sons of upper class members.

Our American values, on the other hand, are certainly not based on any deference to upper class authority; on the contrary, as foreign observers from Harriet Martineau and Tocqueville to James Bryce have found out, egalitarian ideals and disrespect for hierarchical authority have had a long tradition in this country. In contrast to the British, our values are to be found in the middle class ethic of mobility and change, in the values of the professional expert rather than the gentleman amateur, and in science rather than the humanities.

Now of course, the difference in values between the two countries is not a matter of kind, but degree. The deference or hierarchical set of values, for instance, are held in higher regard in the older communities along the eastern seaboard (and in the Old South in particular) than in the newer communities in the West, which are more geared towards the middle class values of mobility, equality, and change. The acceptance of sociology (in many ways an excellent index of the acceptance of a technical, scientistic and perhaps even dehumanizing view of man) was, for instance, much more rapid in the Middle West than in the eastern part of this country. In England, as might be expected, it was taken up by the newer, "Red Brick" universities rather than by the upper class strongholds at "Oxbridge." Following the same logic, both in England and America, sociologists have been far more likely to have originated in the lower-middle and lower classes than, for example, historians or students of literature and the arts. Nor is it any accident that those practicing sociologists who take a humanistic approach to their discipline are often called "soft," and are thus suspect (especially in America), while those who model their work on the natural sciences are called "hard" and, thus, good (for grants, at least, from both the government and the private foundations). Moreover, from a more inclusive point of view, is it not true that science and engineering, in both countries, tend to be middle rather than upper class vocations? The College of the City of New York, for instance, has produced far more graduates who have gone on to achieve Ph.D.'s in chemistry, physics, and engineering than have the graduates of Harvard College.

Now all of us, being all too human, are subject to the occupational hazard which Veblen nicely called "trained incapacity." Every profession or craft trains us to see in a certain way, to see things from a particular point of view, and thus, inadvertently due to our training, to fail to take other points of view into account. That is to say, the poet is likely to take a poetic view of the world and, at the same time, is likely to be blind to the point of view which sees tears of sorrow as merely H_2O following the laws of gravity. All of us have our point of view as well as our blind spots: psychologists are prone to psychologism, sociologists to sociologism and scientists to scientism. Which is to say we all are subject to the vices of our virtues, or the temptation to make legitimate means into ends. The poet or the philosopher is far more likely to see this sorry world as a tragic vale of tears, while his more scientifically-oriented friend may see it as a splendid opportunity for more perfect social engineering, dictatorship and violence eventually being abolished by the compulsory psychoanalysis of all candidates for leadership positions. Few of them would have read, or taken to heart, the great European humanist, Ignazio Silone's book *The School for Dictators,*[4] which shows how the values of a naive, American sociologist are, perhaps, just the ones which have led to the flight of freedom from our modern, disenchanted world.

What I am trying to suggest here is the simple proposition that a culture or subculture dominated by a middle class, scientistic, and technical set of values will be more likely to lead perfectly honorable and intelligent men into the trap of technocracy or scientism than would be the case of a culture where men still cling to upper class, hierarchical, and humanistic values. Again, it is not a matter of either/or, but of degree, more or less. In our society the scientistic subculture is more dominant than has been the case with England. And just as the former values led to ripping up the graveyard and the latter to routing around the arch, so one would predict that we would be more likely to make efficiency an end in itself rather than one factor in attaining more humanistic ends; to make the surgeon's knife, the psychiatrist's couch, the sociologist's survey, as well as the pill and the automobile, our masters rather than our servants.

Notes

This chapter is based on a transcript of E. Digby Baltzell's remarks as a panelist in a "Symposium on Technology and Authority," which was part of The National Conference on Technology and Social Change, held at the University of Pennsylvania in April 1971.

1. The other two panelists referred to here were Seymour Melman, professor of industrial engineering at Columbia University, and Melvin Tumin, professor of sociology at Princeton University.
2. Daniel Bell, *End of Ideology* (Glencoe: Free Press, 1960).
3. William F. Ogburn, *Social Change With Respect to Culture and Original Nature,* 2d ed. (New York: Viking, 1950).
4. Ignazio Silone, *School for Dictators* (New York: Harper, 1938).

32

Factory Folkways

In *Factory Folkways: A Study of Institutional Structure and Change,*[1] John S. Ellsworth, Jr., a sociologist at Yale University, attempts to apply certain concepts developed by anthropology and sociology in an analysis of a small factory in New England. In the author's own words, this book "intends to draw from the theoretical storehouse of social science some of the principles which seem to apply to industry in order to test and sharpen them by application and, equally, to suggest that they are principles by which social organization can best be comprehended."

Essentially this book does two things: In the first place, it is an historical study of the evolution of one particular factory from a partnership founded in the early nineteenth century to a modern corporation employing approximately 400 persons in 1950. After this excellent history of the firm, certain principles of social science are applied to the plant situation. Although the socio-anthropological analysis is, in the author's view, the most important part of the book, this reader found the historical material far more rewarding and certainly more interesting.

The author divides the history of the factory into six periods. The first period (1836–1866) was dominated by John Drew who came over from England in 1839. Drew had been a licensed preacher in England and continued to preach in America. In the words of one of his grandsons, he "hired, fired, advised, and helped, not only the workers but their families. He took a leading part in civic matters and religion." Drew and his employees, who were gathered in from the neighboring farms, worked side by side. Of Yankee stock, these independent employees considered work at the little factory (housed in converted farm buildings) as merely the complement to farming operations.

The second period (1866–1887) was marked by the growth in the number of employees from 50 to approximately 100 in 1887 when Drew died. As the business expanded, Drew found that he could no longer handle everything himself and eventually took three sons-in-law into the partnership. There were now two status levels—owner-managers and employees. "Interstatus contacts were frequent, face-to-face, and personal."

In the third period (1887–1907) Drew's three sons-in-law, with T. J. Shields as managing partner, ran the company. During this period, Shield's son (H. S. Shields) and two other members of the family joined the firm. Unlike the partners in the previous generation, the third generation were all college graduates. All the partners were familiar with and participated in all phases of the business; decisions were reached by mutual agreement; and the partners knew the employees personally as it was their custom to spend some time each week in the plant talking with the employees informally as well as to take Sunday walks through the working class districts of the town. In 1900, the first of the modern immigrant groups, a Pole, was hired at the factory. Hours were long (from 7:00 A.M. to 6:00 P.M.) and pay ranged from 75 cents to 2 dollars (a foreman's rate) per day. Older employees, however, remember leaving work to go swimming or play ball "two or three times a day" and there was plenty of time for "chasing the girls." There was a well understood, albeit informal, standard of what constituted a day's work.

The business was incorporated in 1907 and all six officers were members of the Drew family. Employment rose to 300 in 1914, and the changing ethnic background of the personnel is shown by the fact that in that year 122 employees had slavic names and 26 Italian. The author states that an informal and personal tone was still maintained between management and labor even though employment rose to 700 during the War. The continuing paternalistic policies of management were well suited to the cultural background of the new immigrants. As one of the Italians said when his son first went to work in the plant: "look up to the boss, honor the boss, and do exactly what he says because he is the boss." The most severe instance of friction between management and labor occurred shortly after the war and is still referred to as "the strike." It is interesting that although only a few employees participated in this incident, they were almost all "old Americans" or "old immigrants" rather than Poles or Italians.

In the fifth period (1918–1936) seeds were sown for a change away from a paternalistic, personal, and primary-group relationship between management and labor to one where impersonal, scientific standards of efficiency prevailed. The number of officials increased; the introduction of such administrative devices as double-entry bookkeeping and cost accounting resulted in a growth of salaried personnel (23 in 1922 and 39 in 1935); foremen and superintendents were introduced creating a hierarchy of positions between management and employees; hours spent by officials at the plant began to differ from the working hours of the labor force; finally, "it is probably safe to set the year 1928 as confirming the transition from personal to impersonal relationships between the officers and the factory workers. In that year a modified Bedaux incentive system was installed, and to the employees 'the system' symbolizes the change from one era to another." Although increasing social distance within the plant, the impersonal incentive system including time study men, and so forth, tended to break down the older, primary-group social system. H. S. Shields, now president and the dominant member of the firm, kept alive the dying forces of tradition until his retirement in 1935; he continued his customary Sunday walks through the labor class residential districts and knew most of his employees and their families: "you could talk to him."

The final period in the history of the factory began with the retirement of Harry Shields in 1935. At this time management felt that the company should no longer be dependent on the dominant personality of one man. Impersonalization and specialization of both authority and function characterized this period. Office personnel increased from 39 in 1935 to 71 in 1950; a highly recommended management engineer was employed in 1942 to reorganize the company along more "scientific" lines, and his plan, which included a modern management chart, was adopted in that year. The introduction of this management chart tends to symbolize the final stage in the trend toward an impersonal, scientifically managed social system within the factory. In 1944, on Valentine's Day, the plant was unionized (Textile Workers Union of America, C.I.O.).

Mr. Ellsworth has told an interesting and detailed story of one small factory in New England. Even the brief summary in this review contains many insights into the history of American industry as a whole as it has parallelled this New England factory's tale in so many respects.

Notes

This chapter was prepared from a manuscript; the original place of publication is not known.

1. John S. Ellsworth, Jr., *Factory Folkways: A Study of Institutional Structure and Change* (New Haven: Yale University Press, 1952).

33

The Illusions of Progress

The Idea of Progress, a French invention and a treasured American possession, lies at the very heart of the American Dream and the ethic of Anglo-Saxon Protestantism. Thus at the opening of our tragic century, in 1903, John R. Dos Passos (a successful New York lawyer and father of the famous novelist) quite naturally wrote that "the twentieth century is par excellence 'The Anglo-Saxon Century.'...It is now manifest that this great race is entrusted with the civilization and Christianization of the world." And the late Henry Luce, Calvinist Progressive par excellence, would have agreed with him, even as late as the 1950s.

Georges Sorel is best known to American readers for his book *Reflections on Violence*. He has been of particular interest to students of social change in recent years because of his emphasis on the creative role played by violence and myth in all social movements. As Sorel so well knew, men are moved to action by illusions rather than reality, by myths rather than facts. By and large, myths tend to be hortatory calls to action based on nonrational fables about heroes overcoming great obstacles, while ideologies tend to be rationalistic or pseudoscientific and abstract interpretations of history, often pejorative and debunking of traditional myths. In an age when myths are dying, ideologies come to the fore. Thus the bourgeois myths of Horatio Alger and all variations of the Protestant ethic of hard work, including the idea of progress, are now seen by our age of ideology as mere weapons of the bourgeois ruling classes. In *The Illusions of Progress*,[1] first published in France in 1908, Sorel used the method of ideology to debunk the myth of progress. It is no wonder that what moved our grandfathers to heroic achievements is now paralyzing those of our children who are not engaged either in revolutionary action or the making of new and countercultural myths.

Sorel was an unsystematic and difficult writer who, at the same time, possessed a great deal of insight and wisdom. There is no space here to cover the host of ideas spewed out on every page of this interesting book. I should like, however, to outline briefly Sorel's view of history which, I think, lies at the very core of his thought.

Now that God is dead, many thoughtful men in our time have sought for the meaning of life in one or another interpretation of history. They have, on the whole, tended to follow either the lineal or the cyclical interpretations. And the idea of progress, according to Sorel, is intimately bound up with the optimistic and activist view of history as a record of a lineal process leading to existential perfection, whether of the Hebraic, bourgeois, or Marxian variety. In its most optimistic and mythical form, everything is for the best in this best of all possible worlds. In striking contrast to this optimistic view, Sorel, much in the tradition of Tocqueville, Burkhardt, or even Max Weber, saw history as a cyclical process, more in accord with the philosophers of antiquity in the West and most of the Eastern religions. The idea of secular progress was of course antipathetical to the traditional tenets of Catholicism. Thus Sorel very perceptively shows how the French idea of progress can be traced back to the 17th century, even more concretely, to the publication of Descartes's *Discours de la méthode* in 1637, and Pascal's *Provinciales* in 1657. It was the members of high society, especially in the salons of witty women, who then supported the Cartesians as against the last-gasp Catholicism of Port-Royal and Pascal: "We might say," writes Sorel, "that the fear of sin, respect for chastity and pessimism all disappeared at about the same time at the end of the seventeenth century. Thus Christianity vanished from the scene." The faith in progress rather than Christianity, at first limited to the members of a decadent ruling class, eventually became the central myth of the whole bourgeois civilization in the 19th century. This 19th century myth was of course intimately bound up with the secular faith in science and technology. But while science progresses, art surely does not and instead is marked by cyclical fluctuations, as Sorel so clearly saw, between "Greatness and Decline" (the title of one of the best chapters in this book).

Much in the same vein as Roberto Michels in his famous "Iron Law of Oligarchy," Sorel saw history as eternally bound by an iron law of mediocrity. "Historical greatness," he writes, "is a condition against which humanity struggles." Just as Tocqueville took an extremely pessimistic view of his own providential law of "increasing equality" which he, in turn, equated with democracy, so Sorel saw democracy as meaning the increasing domination of mediocrity (he has been accused of sympathies with Fascism on this and other accounts, which cannot be discussed here). At any rate, he saw that many secular movements in every age, always sold to true believers in the name of progress, may well be simply indications of degeneration or cyclical recurrences in history. Thus he comments on Engels's *Origin of the Family* as follows:

> Engels does not think of announcing to us the reappearance of any of the old forms that he encountered in the books of Lewis Henry Morgan. His forecasts seem to me to have been carefully presented with a mind toward satisfying the tender sentiments of German women readers: "Monogamy, instead of being in jeopardy, will become a reality, even for men." Domination by the man and the indissolubility of marriage will disappear: "People will be spared the futile wading in the mud of a divorce trial" when love will have ceased to unite them. Thus socialism would end up by establishing a matrimonial system very analogous to that which existed in the Rome of the decadent period.

There are some true believers in our own day who would hardly approve of Sorel's philosophy of history as suggested in the above quotation. The 30-page translator's introduction is worth the price of the book and more. The foreword is written in Nisbet's usual learned style.

Notes

This chapter was first published in *The American Journal of Sociology* 79, no. 5 (March 1974).

1. George Sorel, *The Illusions of Progress,* translated by John and Charlotte Stanley with a foreword by Robert A. Nisbet and an introduction by John Stanley (Berkeley: University of California Press, 1972).

34

Changes in the Philadelphia Jewish Community

I was honored when my old friend, Murray Friedman, asked me to write a few lines by way of a preface to this volume[1] on the changes in the Philadelphia Jewish community during the almost half-century since 1940, the year John F. Kennedy graduated from Harvard and the year following my own graduation from the University of Pennsylvania. The essays in this book cover a period in Philadelphia Jewish history which exactly spans my own adult life.

I was raised in Chestnut Hill among a class of people who took anti-Semitism for granted. Several years of service in the armed forces, where privileges were based on functional rank rather than class or ethnic ancestry, were bound to challenge the traditional values of my generation. Both gentile and Jewish officers and gentlemen of the United States Navy, for the first time in their lives, shared leisurely intimacies in the wardroom as well as common dangers at their respective battle stations. Although country-club anti-Semitism was the overwhelming rule before the war, it would have seemed entirely out of place in the first class officers clubs at the Naval Air Stations at Norfolk, Quonset, or Corpus Christi, to say nothing of those more primitive bastions of privilege in the South Pacific, at Espietu Santo, Guadalcanal, or Guam. And many if not most of my fellow officers and friends returned to civilian life far less willing to tolerate the traditional, often dehumanizing, ethnic snobberies of our pre-war years. One of my South Pacific shipmates and a close friend, for instance, played an important role in eliminating the categorical exclusion of Jewish alumni from membership in the Harvard Club of New York City. I myself gave up a prewar business career to become a sociologist, receiving a Ph.D. from Columbia and then spending my entire academic career at the University of Pennsylvania. I did not join the Lenape Club, a private faculty club whose older members tended to be anti-Semitic. Instead I became an enthusiastic member of our present Faculty Club, whose membership by now is as heterogeneous in background as the United Nations. There was surely little or no anti-Semitism among my generation of faculty members at Penn, and the same was true of the Philadelphia College of Art, where my wife, Jane Piper, taught for three decades.

Outside of academic life, my wife and I confined our social life largely to the art and academic worlds, especially among a kind of countercultural elite of reform Democrats centering in the Americans for Democratic Action, who took the lead in bringing Joseph S. Clark and Richardson Dilworth into the mayor's office in the 1950s. Of importance here is the fact that the leading members of this reform counterculture were tacitly but emphatically agreed on the evils and destructiveness of anti-Semitism.

In the meantime, my writing and research interests parallelled my academic and social life. My first book, *Philadelphia Gentleman* (1958) examined the historical background and contemporary structure of Philadelphia's leadership class in 1940, a date purposely chosen because it preceded the post-war social changes such as those discussed in the essays in this volume. My second book, *The Protestant Establishment: Aristocracy and Caste in America* (1964), was an analysis of the history of anti-Semitism within the American WASP establishment in the years between the assassination of Czar Alexander of Russia in 1881, and the assassination of John F. Kennedy in 1963.

The first and most important thing to be said about elite anti-Semitism in the years since the end of World War II, especially since 1963, is that while Philadelphia was a familistic and class society in 1940, it is a relatively individualistic and bureaucratic society today. In 1940, a class of WASP gentlemen still dominated the business and cultural life of the city as their ancestors had since colonial days. For instance, Edward Hopkinson, Jr., the senior partner of Drexel and Company, was probably the most powerful man in the city. He had graduated from both the college and the law school of Penn; was a partner in one of the city's major law firms (100 percent WASP until the 1960s) for many years before going to the Drexel firm; was a descendant of a member of the first class to graduate from the College of Philadelphia; a great great great grandson of a founder of the American Philosophical Society, and a great great grandson of a signer of the Declaration of Independence. In that same year, Benjamin Rush, whose namesake was a signer of the Declaration and the city's most famous physician, was Chairman of the Board of the Insurance Company of North America (he had been president from 1916 to 1939). The Pennsylvania Railroad and the famous Baldwin Locomotive Works had a president and a majority of Board members who were listed in the *Social Register.* The University of Pennsylvania was entirely run by such proper Philadelphia gentlemen as Lippincotts, Cadwaladers, Merricks, Whartons and Peppers. Senator George Wharton Pepper, a life trustee, was Penn's most eminent alumnus and unofficial Dean of the Philadelphia Bar. Penn's president, Thomas S. Gates, the senior Drexel partner before Hopkinson and a birthright Quaker-turned-Episcopal Philadelphian, served without pay. And finally, the presidents of all the major banks in the city and a vast majority of their directors were listed in the *Social Register.*

At the same time, and most important, the class cohesion of the WASP leadership in 1940 was consolidated in an elaborate complex of city men's clubs and various exclusive cricket and golf clubs out in the suburbs, in all of which the anti-Semitic line was firmly drawn. In Center City, the members of the Philadelphia Club dominated the upper-class leadership in both business and culture. Like President Gates at Penn, most of the cultural institutions—the Art Museum, the Historical Society, the Academy of Fine Arts and the Philadelphia Orchestra and so forth—were headed by amateur volunteers (gentlemen of independent means) who served at minimal or no salaries.

All that has changed since the Second World War and especially since President Kennedy's assassination in 1963, and his brother's in 1968. One must always bear in mind that the Sixties, which peaked between 1968 and 1970, was the most egalitarian and atomizing era in American history. It was largely a revolt from the top: the 1969 "Bust" at Harvard was led, first by the sons of successful and even affluent Jewish intellectuals, and then by the WASP and preppy children of privilege who made up the majority of the 300 or so undergraduates who occupied University Hall on April 9, 1969.

The sixties accelerated a secular trend in America from a pre-war social structure dominated by a relatively open class system (despite ethnic barriers) to a more or less classless bureaucracy, based largely on educational achievement. John F. Kennedy's entering class at Princeton in 1935, for instance, ranked below the national average in IQ and included a handful of Jews (2-3%); the entering class today is at the very top levels of the nation academically and is composed of a third or more Jewish students. The school for gentlemen has been replaced by a school for pre-professional men and women. In those pre-war days, moreover, it was the colleges (especially Harvard, Yale and Princeton) which educated a class of leaders, whereas it is the graduate and professional schools which are now training bureaucrats; hence the pre-professional "A" has now replaced the upper-class "gentleman's C" of the old undergraduate days.

It is no accident that the revolutionary trend of the Sixties was centered on the prestige campuses of the nation such as Berkeley, Columbia and Harvard. For, as Max Weber observed in bureaucratic Germany before the First World War, the certificate of education finally replaced the test for ancestors after the Second World War, even in Philadelphia. Thus the largest private employer in the city today is the huge bureaucracy which is the University of Pennsylvania. Martin Myerson, quite unlike Thomas Gates, was not only the first Jewish president of a major American university, but had spent a lifetime as an agile academic bureaucrat of the first rank. The trustees were no longer primarily high born Philadelphia Gentlemen, but persons of merit from all over the nation—Jew and gentile, black and white, female or male.

The Drexel firm, always allied with the Pennsylvania Railroad and the heavy industries such as the Baldwin Locomotive Works which marked the pre-war city, is no longer a major Proper Philadelphia institution; the prestigious and traditional name has been retained by the largely Jewish and very successful New York firm of Drexel Burnham Lambert Incorporated (and Mr. I. W. Burnham, II, became a Penn trustee under the Meyerson regime). Today, there is no man or woman of informal and traditional dominance in the city's life to compare with Edward Hopkinson, Jr. Nor is there an unofficial dean of the bar to compare with Senator Pepper. The official position as head of the Philadelphia Bar Association, moreover, is no longer a mark of personal prestige but is more likely to be rotated from firm to firm as a duty to be discharged rather than strictly an honor. While the most prestigious law firms in the city in 1940 were small and homogeneous partnerships (all save the German Jewish firm of Wolf, Block, Schorr & Solis-Cohen), entirely old-stock and Protestant in membership, they are today becoming larger and larger bureaucracies with partners—men and women—of varying ethnic backgrounds, including Jewish. Some would also say that the law is increasingly becoming a business rather than a profession (just as Penn is now in the "education business," as members of the administration are so fond of saying).

While the traditional class authority of men like Hopkinson and Gates in 1940 emanated from the halls of the Philadelphia Club (the oldest of its kind in the nation), the elite Union League club, far more likely to include the big industrial and financial leaders of newly achieved status, has now become the focus of most of the important bureaucratic power struggles in the city. While the members of the League were almost entirely WASP and supporters of the Republican party in 1940, today one meets men of mannerly power and often new money, of all races and ethnic backgrounds (and convictions, even including confessed supporters of the Democratic party). As I write, the League has just voted to accept women members, after years of threats from City Hall and prodding from the media. Similarly, the Philadelphia, Racquet and Rittenhouse clubs, more upper class than the League, have recently let down anti-Semitic barriers to membership and presumably will soon accept women (the Racquet already has).

What I have been saying here is that, in the three post-war decades, elite anti-Semitism and ethnic prejudice has declined to a considerable degree. But what are the prospects for the future in an atomistic and elitist, bureaucratic society as against the traditional class society which marked pre-war America and Philadelphia? In the first place, the present Philadelphia (and American) leadership structure has never been so justly chosen and meritocratically based; at the same time, it is my contention that it has never been so prone to atomization and disorder. There is, for example, no organic and historically rooted center of authority or responsibility in Philadelphia or in America today. A WASP establishment such as we had in Philadelphia in 1940 is no longer possible or desirable today. Some sort of authoritative establishment, however, may be a prerequisite for the ordered freedom which we and the British have enjoyed to a greater extent than any other nation in modern times.

This is especially so in contrast to post-Bismark and pre-Hitler Germany which was extremely bureaucratic compared with the Anglo-American class systems of that period. There were no upper-class educational institutions in Germany which melded the sons of the old nobilities, such as the agricultural and militaristic Junkers, and the sons of the rising upper-bourgeois into one coherent class ethic. There has never been anything to compare to the colleges of Oxford and Cambridge in England or the undergraduate colleges at Harvard, Yale and Princeton in this country, where the sons of the aristocracy, gentry and high middle-classes in England or of the old professional gentry and the new industrialists here were molded in a single gentlemanly ethic. On the contrary, the great universities such as Heidelberg, Bonn, or Berlin have always been engaged in educating scholars and scientists and in training professional bureaucrats. We imported the Ph.D. from Germany and the Bachelor of Arts from Oxbridge. Similarly with secondary education: in Germany, the Gymnasium, a total community school run by the state, was much like our public high school or the British grammar school. There have never been national class schools in Germany, such as Eton, Harrow or Rugby in England or Groton, St. Paul's, Exeter and Andover in America. Organized games and the gentlemanly sportsmanship ethic which they once stood for, have never been a part of either Gymnasium or university education in Germany. There are no class rituals to compare with the Eton-Harrow cricket matches at Lords each Spring or the Harvard-Yale football games at the end of each Fall. I have often thought, how different modern history might have been had Karl Marx captained his (non-existent) college football team at Bonn or Berlin, or had the Nazi leadership been schooled in some German equivalent of the playing fields of Eton. All this is not to say that the positive values of the Anglo-American sportsmanship ethic were not correlated with a gentlemanly anti-Semitism. But on the other hand, there have been no Dreyfus cases or concentration camps, and ultimately no permanent barriers, as the current Jewish experience makes clear.

At any rate, just as the shallow forms of socially humiliating anti-Semitism did not exist in liberal and permissive Weimar Germany to anywhere near the extent it did in America during that era, so today our permissive society has never seen so little manifest anti-Semitism. And yet...perhaps it has never been so structurally weak at the top levels of leadership and consequently, so I contend, never so vulnerable should some new anti-Semitic movement take hold in America. Nothing in this life comes without a price, and our atomized age of total (even intolerant) tolerance must pay the price of weakened authority and social cohesion. The decline of anti-Semitism is, of course, all to the good. Let us hope that my reflections here on the unanticipated consequences of undoubted progress will never be tested.

Notes

This chapter was first published as a preface written by E. Digby Baltzell to *Philadelphia Jewish Life, 1940–1985,* edited by Murray Friedman.

1. Murray Friedman, ed., *Philadelphia Jewish Life, 1940–1985* (Philadelphia: Seth Press, 1986).

35

The Jewish Communities of Philadelphia and Boston, 1740–1940: A Tale of Two Cities

(With Allen Glicksman and Jacquelyn Litt)

> New York's Jewry...generated an uncontainable dynamic of its own which helped to reshape both New York's and the nation's culture. All other Jewish communities in America absorbed the ideas of their host cities....
>
> —Theodore H. White,
> *In Search of History*

As institutions are but shadows of great men, as Emerson once remarked, so are cities largely, if not entirely, the lengthened shadows of their founders. The authoritarian Puritans dominated New England; and Pennsylvania was of course the center of left-wing sectarianism from its very founding by the Quakers. In my book, *Puritan Boston and Quaker Philadelphia,* I contrasted the origins, subcultural values and leadership structures of the political and cultural centers of these two regions:

> Just as our whole post-Christian and secular world today is still living, as a kind of cultural rentier, on the spiritual and moral capital built up in the more religious periods of the Judeo-Christian tradition, so the citizens of modern Massachusetts and Pennsylvania, whether they are professing Jews, Catholics, Presbyterians, Episcopalians, or just plain agnostics or atheists, are still marked, to a greater or lesser degree, by the original ethics of Puritanism and Quakerism. There is, for instance, a great difference between the Puritan Catholicism of Boston and the much milder Quaker Catholicism of Philadelphia. If immigrants absorb some of the values of the host society, one would predict that the Irish-Catholics of Boston would be more driven to leadership and excellence than their countrymen who settled into the milder and more egalitarian culture of Philadelphia. Whereas the first Irish-Catholic mayor of Boston took office in the 1880s, the first Irish-Catholic mayor of Philadelphia came into office in the 1960s. Philadelphia has produced no leaders of the quality of Curley, Fitzgerald, or the Kennedys, nor incidentally has it ever had an Irish-Catholic Democratic machine in the classic style of New York,

> Jersey City, or Chicago. It is indeed symbolic that the most famous Irish-Catholic families of the two cities should have produced in this generation a President and two U.S. senators, on the one hand, and on the other, a charming expatriate socialite and sometime actress (Grace Kelly).[1]

With regard to the Jewish families of the two cities, this contrast also is apparent. Boston's (and America's) most widely known Jew was the crusading lawyer, Zionist and Associate Justice of the Supreme Court of the United States, Louis D. Brandeis, while probably the most famous Philadelphia Jew was the 19th century beauty and philanthropist, Rebecca Gratz, subject of four Thomas Sully portraits and no doubt best known for the tradition that she was the original of Rebecca, heroine of Walter Scott's Ivanhoe. A study of how the contrast in aspirations and accomplishments between these two Jewish communities developed must begin with their quite different histories.

The first Jewish community in what is now the United States was founded in 1654 when 23 Jewish refugees from Brazil aboard the bark *St. Charles* landed in New Amsterdam. Though the authoritarian Peter Stuyvesant was hardly receptive to this alien group, they were allowed to remain largely because of the influence of the powerful Dutch West India Company, which included among its stockholders a number of wealthy Sephardic Jews who, after having been expelled from the Iberian Peninsula, settled in Amsterdam, then the financial and cultural capital of Europe. "With Jews," wrote Jacob R. Marcus in his definitive study, *The Colonial American Jew,*[2] "what motivated settlement was nearly always, if not always, economic opportunity." By the end of the colonial period, in addition to the settlement in New Amsterdam, Jewish communities had also been established in Philadelphia, Newport, Charleston, Savannah, and Richmond—but not in Boston. "That Boston," continued Marcus, "the largest city in the British provinces of North America during the first half of the eighteenth century, was not to shelter a formally organized Jewish community until about 1849 was surely an anomaly."[3] And this anomaly was largely to be explained by the intolerant and hierarchical values of the Puritan ethic. That thriving Jewish communities existed in Philadelphia and Newport, in contrast, testified to the egalitarian and tolerant Quaker ethic that dominated these two cities.

Thus part of the contrast between the present-day Jewish communities—as well as Catholic—of Boston and Philadelphia can be attributed directly to the fact that Philadelphia had settlements of these two groups from colonial times, while Boston had none until almost the middle of the 19th century.[4] Philadelphia's first Catholic Church, St. Joseph's, was built in 1732 in an inconspicuous spot in Willing's Alley; and though early records are inadequate, it is believed that in the 1740s a small group of Jews began holding divine services in a house on Sterling Alley. It was not until 1782, soon after the nation's founding, that the formal Jewish community was organized with the construction of the first synagogue, Mikveh Israel.

The early Jews in Philadelphia, without a synagogue or visible Jewish community, participated for the most part in the social and economic life of the city as individuals. Two Jews, David Franks and Samson Levy, were among the original subscribers to the exclusive Dancing Assembly, the oldest organization of its kind in America today, when it was formed in 1748 by 59 of the city's most prominent families. And Rebecca Franks was one of the most popular belles of Revolutionary society in the city.[5]

With the construction of Mikveh Israel and hence the formation of a more unified Jewish community, came the first overt, if mild, antisemitism in Philadelphia. The original plans called for the synagogue to be built in Sterling Alley. However, the lot was contiguous to that of a German Reformed congregation, and such vigorous protests were made by the Protestant community that the Jewish leaders finally built the synagogue on Cherry Alley, north of High (now Market) Street, between Third and Fourth Streets. This location was in the Plain Quaker part of colonial Philadelphia, rather than in the fashionable Anglican neighborhood south of High Street. The congregation thrived, and in 1810 a second synagogue, Rodelph Shalom, was built.

The Philadelphia Jewish community reached a kind of high-water mark in the 1830's. Even though there was now a definite, coherent and visible Jewish community, there was little antisemitism, and the families who had made their money and consolidated their position by that time participated extensively in the Gentile world. Five members of the Gratz family, for instance, were taken in the exclusive Philadelphia Club (founded 1834); and Hyman Gratz, wealthy merchant and member of Mikveh Israel, was so popular in Gentile circles that he served as temporary president of the Philadelphia Club while Commodore James Biddle was fighting in the Mexican War.[6]

Another excellent example of the absence of antisemitic prejudice in Philadelphia before the Civil War was the election to the United States Congress in 1857 of Henry Meyer Phillips, a Democrat.[7] One of the city's leading lawyers, Henry Meyer Phillips was an active member of Mikveh Israel (both his father and grandfather had served as President of the Congregation), and in his younger years was active in Jewish affairs, serving as president of the Society for Visitation of Sick and Mutual Assistance. A measure of his stature in the city as a whole was his leadership in such coveted Proper Philadelphia institutions as the Board of City Trusts (president), the Academy of Music (president), the Pennsylvania Company for Insurance on Lives and Granting Annuities (director), and the Pennsylvania Railroad (director). Unlike most members of Mikveh Israel, who lived north of Market Street, Phillips—and most of the Gratz family, as well—lived at the heart of fashionable Philadelphia. His magnificent house at 1325 Walnut Street was a fitting residence for one of the city's leading patrons of the fine arts. He was not reelected to Congress, and while never returning to governmental service, was active in the cultural and business life of Philadelphia until his death in 1884. His father, Zalegman Phillips, also a leader of the Philadelphia bar, was the first member of the local Jewish community to graduate (in 1797) from the College at the University of Pennsylvania.

Because of this admixture of Jewish as well as Catholic and other components, Philadelphia's upper class was quite different from Boston's WASP establishment. While Boston upper class families were almost entirely British in origin, with no clear cases of Jewish (nor Catholic) ancestry, the traditional Quaker-turned-Episcopal gentry in Philadelphia were quite heterogeneous in origins. By 1850 and ever since, the Philadelphia Gentleman was far closer to the "promiscuous breed" which J. Hector St. John Crevecoeur called "the race now called Americans," than were his homogeneously British-stock peers of Proper Boston. Thus, the historian of the Philadelphia Assembly Balls could write in the 1940's that subscribers then "included families of the following racial strains: English, Welsh, Irish, French, German, Dutch, Swiss, Italian, Spanish, Portuguese, Swedish, and Polish."[8] (What he meant, but did not spell out, was that the impeccable elite establishment in the city was composed of families whose ancestors included Spanish, Portuguese, German and Polish Jews; Irish, French and Italian Catholics; and Protestants from many nations, if predominantly from the British Isles.)

These striking differences between the ethnic and religious compositions of the Boston and Philadelphia upper classes of course were reflections of the two communities as a whole. Thus, while Pennsylvania was settled first by English Quakers, they were soon joined by German and Dutch Protestants; in addition, there were Anglican, Baptist and Presbyterian congregations in Philadelphia by 1700. By the end of the colonial period, Pennsylvania was the most ethnically and religiously heterogeneous of all the colonies. On the other hand, between the founding of the Massachusetts Bay colony in 1630 and the final disestablishment of religion there in the 1830's, Boston was surely the most homogeneous community in British North America. In contrast to the mild and tolerant Quaker oligarchy of early Philadelphia, the early generations of Boston clergymen, while highly moral and learned men (Tocqueville thought them the best educated in world history), were at the same time bigoted and to the last degree intolerant. The stiff-necked prejudice of the Pilgrim Fathers was directed toward all outsiders, as well as non-conformists in their own ranks. The dissenters Roger Williams and Anne Hutchinson were turned out in the winter wilderness; and in the springtime of 1660, the Quaker Mary Dyer was hanged by her neck on the Boston Common. The arrival of the first Jew in the colony sparked a similar, if slightly more humane, reaction. In 1649, one Solomon Franco came to Boston with a cargo assigned to the Major General of the colony. Not only was Franco disallowed his claim for a commission, but he was ordered to return to Holland by the Great and General Court, who assigned "said Solomon Franco, the Jew, six shillings per week out of the treasury for ten weeks for his subsistence till be could get his passage into Holland."[9]

After Solomon Franco's banishment, few Jews came to colonial Boston. The only notable one was Judah Monis, who came to the colonies via Jamaica, finally settling in Cambridge, where he combined peddling with the writing of a Hebrew grammar. In 1720, he submitted his manuscript to Harvard College, who in return awarded him the Master of Arts degree and thus made him the first Jew to receive a college degree in America. But the laissez-faire cultural pluralism which characterizes Harvard Yard today was intolerable in colonial Massachusetts. So, at a ceremony in the Common Hall of Harvard before "as numerous an assembly as the place could admit," "Rabbi" Monis converted to Christianity. Upon his conversion, he was appointed instructor in Hebrew, a post he occupied for nearly 40 years.[10]

The rejection by the Calvinist Puritans of the Jews is indeed one of the ironies of American history, especially since there was such a close affinity between Judaism and early Puritanism, whose creed and communal structure were deeply rooted in the Old Testament. As Edmund Wilson wrote:

> The Puritans of New England were a kind of New Judaism, a Judaism transposed into Anglo-Saxon terms. When the Puritans came to America, they identified George III with Pharaoh and themselves with the Israelites and their search for the promised land... Winthrop and Bradford were Moses and Joshua; Ann Hutchinson was pilloried as Jezebel.[11]

At Harvard College, Hebrew was taught as a second language; and not only there, but in the schools also. Yet the people of the law and the book were turned away by the Old Testament Puritans, while in Philadelphia, they were accepted from the very beginning by the Quakers, who favored, not the ancient law, but the new spirit of the Gospels, and whose inner-light doctrine of love was an extreme form of New Testament Christianity.

In terms of the sociological theories of ethnic relations in American, then, the histories of these two cities have been excellent examples of, on the one hand (Philadelphia), cultural pluralism; and on the other (Boston), what has been termed the Anglo-ideal, assimilation.[12] And these two contrasting attitudes toward ethnic diversity have been particularly relevant to the histories of the Jewish communities in each of the two cities.

Between 1776 and 1815, when immigration had slowed to a virtual standstill, America went through its longest period of undisturbed cultural consolidation.[13] After the defeat of Napoleon, however, immigration increased and Jews came along with large numbers of their fellow Germans. The American Jewish population was almost entirely German. Those not from Germany proper were from areas under the German cultural hegemony, such as Austria, Hungary, Bohemia and western Poland. Their numbers, estimated at 15,000 in 1840, increased to 150,000 by 1860. A characteristic of this German Jewish immigration, in contrast to the earlier more individualistic migration, was that they came as families, groups of families, and even whole communities of Jews from the same town in the old country.

Another difference between these later immigrants and the Jews of the eighteenth century was that, while the earlier ones were largely merchants, the German immigrants almost invariably began as itinerant peddlers. William Filene, father of the founder of the famous Boston department store, began as a New England peddler before settling down as a small storekeeper in Salem. And Meyer Guggenheim, founder of the wealthiest Jewish dynasty in America, came here at the age of 18 in 1848 and began his way to wealth as a peddler of shoelaces on the streets of Philadelphia.

As the Civil War approached, then, both Philadelphia and Boston had clearly defined Jewish communities. While Boston's was small and only beginning to take shape, Philadelphia's, more than a hundred years old and the most intellectually and religiously vigorous in the nation, played the leadership role for nineteenth-century American Jewry that New York eventually assumed in the twentieth. There were five pre-Civil War synagogues in Philadelphia and three in Boston, and it was the synagogue leadership in each city which set, and reflected, the style and tone of the Jewish communities as a whole. This was especially true of the two elite synagogues, Mikveh Israel in Philadelphia, and Temple Israel (Adath Israel) in Boston. Just as Isaac Leeser (1806–1868), *hazan* of Mikveh Israel between 1829 and 1850, put his conservative and orthodox stamp on Philadelphia's Jews, so Solomon Schindler (1842–1915) rabbi at Boston's Temple Israel between 1874 and 1894, prepared that city's Jewry for cultural pluralism and reform. This is borne out by the fact that as of this writing, the major center city synagogue in Philadelphia is a Conservative congregation, Beth Israel Beth Zion, while Boston's elite synagogue, also located in center-city, is the Reform congregation of Temple Israel.

The Development of Philadelphia's Jewish Community: The Hegemony of Mikveh Israel, 1829–1940

Mikveh Israel, Philadelphia's oldest synagogue, was Sephardic in ritual and definitely the home of the majority of elite Jews from the beginning of the Jewish settlement until well into the twentieth century. When Isaac Leeser was appointed its *hazan* at the age of 23 in 1829, nobody realized that by the time of his death in 1868 he was to make Philadelphia the creative center of Jewry in American.[14]

Isaac Leeser came to Richmond, Virginia from Westphalia, in Prussia, in 1824. He learned English while working in his uncle's store there, and after his appointment at Mikveh Israel, became a true Renaissance man—or, more properly for Philadelphia, the Jewish Benjamin Franklin. Among his accomplishments, which had their influence not only on Philadelphia's Jewish community, but American Jewry as a whole, were:

- Editing and translating the first American edition of the Sephardic prayer book (1837)
- Writing the first American Hebrew primer for children (1838)
- Founding editor of the first successful American Jewish periodical, *The Occident and American Jewish Advocate* (1843)
- Establishing the first American Jewish publication society (1845)
- Compiling a Hebrew-English Torah, the first to be edited and translated by an American Jew (1845)
- Translating the first complete English edition of the Ashkenazic prayer book (1848)
- Translating the entire Bible into English, the first such translation by an American Jew (1853)
- Founding the first Jewish defense agency—the Board of Delegates of American Israelites (1858)

In addition to these notable firsts, Isaac Leeser was a leading force in Jewish philanthropy; perhaps his most lasting monument was his founding, along with Abraham Sulzberger, of the Jewish Hospital in 1865. Seeing the chaos produced by too many charitable agencies competing for support, he was a major force behind the United Hebrew Charities, founded in 1869, a year after his death. He also committed much of his energy and drive to Jewish education, prodding the philanthropist Rebecca Gratz to found the Hebrew Sunday School Society (1838). He also played a major part in the founding of the Hebrew Education Society in 1849. Finally, just before his death, he was a major founder and the first president of Maimonides College (1864), the first Jewish theological seminary in America.

All these activities, combined with his vast correspondence with Jews throughout the country who contributed to his publication, *The Occident,* made Isaac Leeser perhaps the most widely known Jew in American during the ante-bellum period. Further, with the founding of Maimonides College in 1864 (even though it lasted only until 1873), Philadelphia became firmly established as the intellectual and institutional leader of Jewish America.

Partly in response to Philadelphia's influence, America's Jews at the time when Isaac Leeser's brilliantly creative career was coming to a close were conservatively Orthodox as well as German to the core. In most synagogues, German was used along with Hebrew, and German was spoken within the family. German music was preferred. Wealthy Jews went abroad on the Hamburg-American line and relaxed at such German watering places as Baden, Carlesbad and Marienbad. At the Harmonie Gesellshaft in New York, the oldest and most distinguished Jewish club in America, German remained the official language; and as late as the 1890s the Kaiser's portrait hung in the hall.[15]

Isaac Leeser's conservative and creative influence on the Philadelphia Jewish community, as well as on American Jewry as a whole, was carried on after his death by two remarkable successors, Moses Aaron Dropsie (1821–1905) and Mayer Sulzberger (1843–1923). Both were members of Mikveh Israel, and both were lawyers. Like their mentor Leeser, they were bachelors and hence able to devote a great deal of their time to the welfare of their community. These two leaders were strongly influenced by Leeser's teaching and example.

Moses Dropsie was brought to Philadelphia from Amsterdam by his parents in 1819. His mother was a Christian, but his parents encouraged their children to choose their own religion. After a thorough training at Mikveh Israel under Leeser, Moses at the age of fourteen chose Judaism. He built up a large fortune as a lawyer and as founder and president of several street railway companies. An ardent Whig, he was eventually one of the founders of the Republican Party in Pennsylvania. He served on the original board of trustees of Maimonides College and also served on the first board of Gratz College (1895), the first Hebrew teachers' college in America. After his death, his fortune went to found Dropsie College for Hebrew and Cognate Learning (1908).

Serving with Moses Dropsie on the boards of Maimonides and Gratz Colleges was Mayer Sulzberger, a younger man who had once served as apprentice in Dropsie's law office. Sulzberger was also on the first board of governors of Dropsie College, attesting to his close relationship with his senior colleague.

Born in Baden, Germany of a family of rabbinical scholars, Mayer Sulzberger was brought to Philadelphia in 1848. He graduated with an A.B. from Central High School, and after his apprenticeship in Dropsie's office, was a member of the Philadelphia bar for thirty years. Then, between 1895 and his retirement in 1916, he served as a judge in the Court of Common Pleas, the first Jewish member of the Philadelphia bench. Like Dropsie, Sulzberger grew up in the Mikveh Israel congregation, and was greatly influenced by Isaac Leeser. In addition to serving on the board of directors of the three Jewish colleges, he was the first president of the Philadelphia YMHA when it was founded (1875), and also first president of the American Jewish Committee, serving between 1906 and 1912. Further, he was a founder and enthusiastic leader of the Oriental Club of Philadelphia.

But while the leadership of American Jewry in Philadelphia was still orthodox and conservative, changes were going on elsewhere. The Reform movement was gaining strength in many areas of the country. The most important index of the attempt to shift the intellectual center of American Jewry was the founding (1875) of the Hebrew Union College in Cincinnati by Isaac Mayer Wise (1819–1900). Wise, who was more than a decade younger than Isaac Leeser, came from Bohemia to America in 1846, serving a congregation in Albany, New York before going to Cincinnati in 1854.[16] Almost immediately he founded a weekly, in English, the *American Israelite,* to oppose the conservative ideas of Leeser's *Occident.*

When Wise founded the Hebrew Union College in 1875, Reform Judaism seemed to be the wave of the future. That so few walked out when shrimp was served at the dinner celebrating the graduation of the first class of the new college in 1883 was a confirmation that changes were already becoming acceptable.

In 1861, while Isaac Mayer Wise was organizing Reform Judaism in Cincinnati, Temple Keneseth Israel, Philadelphia's fourth oldest Jewish congregation, appointed as its rabbi a brilliant and radical native of Germany, David Einhorn. More intellectual and perhaps even more radical than Wise, Einhorn stayed in Philadelphia for only five years before going to New York. In 1869, his successor, Rabbi Samuel Hirsch (1815–1889), who had come to the city from Germany only three years before, chaired a meeting held at Keneseth Israel of Einhorn and other rabbis of radical views. This was the first conference on Reform Judaism in American. The discussions were to continue for sixteen years, and in 1885 the finished platform of Reform Judaism was adopted at the well-known Pittsburgh Conference. The Reform position can be nicely summed up in the following sentence taken from the full document:

> We consider ourselves no longer a nation, but a religious community, and therefore expect neither a return to Palestine, nor sacrificial worship under the sons of Aaron, nor the restoration of any laws concerning the Jewish state.[17]

There was an almost immediate counterreaction to the Pittsburgh platform, led by Sabato Morais (1823–1897), who had followed Isaac Leeser in 1851 as rabbi of Mikveh Israel.[18] Morais had the support of about a dozen congregations, including Rodeph Shalom in Philadelphia, which was then led by a very distinguished Talmudic scholar, Marcus Jastrow (1829–1903). Jastrow had been on the faculty of Maimonides College with Morais and was himself a leading conservative force in Philadelphia. But more important was the support of Henry Pereira Mendes (1852–1937), rabbi for almost half a century of New York's fashionable Sephardic Congregation, Shearith Israel. It was at Shearith Israel that the fledgling Jewish Theological Seminary, founded in 1885 under the leadership of Sabato Morais, held its first classes, beginning in 1887. Morais was president of the seminary until his death in 1897.

Sabato Morais was the last rabbi at Mikveh Israel to pay a major leadership role in either the Philadelphia or national Jewish communities; but his student and younger friend, Cyrus Adler (1863–1940), was to become a key lay force in both areas in the first four decades of the twentieth century.[19] Adler was not only a pupil of Morais at Mikveh Israel, he was bred in the conservative atmosphere of the Sulzbergers and other leading Philadelphia Jewish families. He was concerned about the ever increasing numbers of devoutly Orthodox Jews who were coming to America from eastern Europe, and, according to Nathan Glazer, felt that "the Jewish Theological Seminary might serve to turn young East European Jews into modern English-speaking rabbis for the East European Orthodox masses."[20] Toward this end, Adler persuaded Jacob Schiff to put up money to revive the Seminary, which was on its last legs at the time of the death of its founder and president, Sabato Morais. Though a Reform Jew himself, Schiff had more sympathy for the East European masses flooding our shores at the time than many of his conservative and snobbish German Jewish peers. So he along with a group of like-minded friends put up half a million dollars towards rejuvenating the Seminary. Among other things, this gift allowed the Seminary to bring Solomon Schechter (1874–1915) from England as president.[21]

Cyrus Adler was born in Arkansas and, after his father's death, was raised by his mother (nee Sulzberger) and her brother. After graduating from the University of Pennsylvania in 1883, Adler obtained a Ph.D. at

Johns Hopkins, where he taught in the Department of Semitics. Later, he became assistant secretary of the Smithsonian Institute, a position from which he resigned in 1908 to become the first president of Dropsie College for Hebrew and Cognate Learning in Philadelphia, a non-theological graduate school leading to the Ph.D. degree.

Adler was now the generally recognized leader of American Judaism. He was a major force in the production of the first Jewish Encyclopedia (1901-06); and a founder of the American Jewish Historical Society (1888) and its president from 1898 to 1922. In 1910 he brought the Jewish Quarterly Review from England to Philadelphia, editing it until his death in 1940. At the death of Solomon Schecter in 1915, he was appointed acting president of the Jewish Theological Seminary, and, in spite of having no theological training or degree, served as its permanent president between 1924 and his death. He had organized Conservative Judaism in America in 1913, when he founded and took the presidency of the United Synagogue of America. (He resigned in 1917 because of its Zionist platform.) He served as president of the American Jewish Committee from 1929 until his death. Though a great many of the organizations in which Adler was a leading force were located in New York, it is a significant tribute to the distinctiveness of the Philadelphia Jewish character that he chose to remain a resident here.

Cyrus Adler was more than a leader in the Jewish community. His contribution to wider public service included terms as president of the board of the Free Library, president of the American Oriental Society, and vice-president of the nation's most distinguished scientific body, the American Philosophical Society. He was also a member of the Philadelphia Board of Education.

Following in the footsteps of his beloved mentor, Sabato Morais, who in 1887 was the first Jew to receive an honorary degree from the University of Pennsylvania, Adler was awarded an honorary Litt.D. degree from his Alma Mater in 1933, fifty years after his graduation. In the spring of 1940, Adler died at his home in Philadelphia and was interred in the cemetery of Congregation Mikveh Israel.

Cyrus Adler's death in 1940, the bicentennial year of the founding of Mikveh Israel which he had served as president, marked both the end of the unchallenged German hegemony within American Jewry and the final passing of national Jewish leadership from Philadelphia to New York.

The winds of change from Conservative to Reform had begun blowing as early as 1861, with the appointment of David Einhorn as rabbi at Keneseth Israel. The movement gained momentum in 1887 when Keneseth Israel chose as its rabbi the brilliant Prussian, Joseph Krauskopf, who had been in the first graduating class of Cincinnati's Hebrew Union College, and a vice-president of the Pittsburgh Conference of 1885. With the retirement of the traditionalist Marcus Jastrow from Rodeph Shalom in 1892, and the death in 1897 of his ally at Mikveh Israel, Sabato Morais, the major spokesmen for Philadelphia Jewry became Krauskopf and other Reform rabbis.[22]

While such older-stock Brahmins within the Jewish community as the Binswangers, Wolfs and Rosenbachs moved in Conservative Mikveh Israel circles with their greatly distinguished peer, Mayer Sulzberger, elite Jews of new wealth and distinction moved "uptown" as it were, and joined Reform temples. Thus, Keneseth Israel became one of the Jewish community's leading congregations in the first two decades of the twentieth century, counting among its members the great merchants Ellis Gimbel and Lessing Rosenwald, the real estate tycoon Albert M. Greenfield, and the first Jewish member of the Supreme Court of Pennsylvania, Judge Horace Stern. During the same time, Rodeph Shalom, founded in 1795 as the first Ashkenazi synagogue in America and a bastion of conservatism, was gradually brought into the Reform movement by Henry Berkowitz, who had been appointed its rabbi in 1892 and where he served for the next three decades. Berkowitz's sister had married Joseph Krauskopf, and the two rabbis worked closely together, eventually establishing "joint services, joint Sunday Schools and joint efforts in behalf of Reform Judaism."[23] Reform Judaism continued predominant in Philadelphia at least until the Holocaust when larger and larger numbers of descendants of eastern European immigrants rose to elite status after World War II.

The Development of Boston's Jewish Community: Temple Israel and Reform

The formal organization of Boston's Jewry dates from the founding of Congregation Ohabei Shalom ("Lovers of Peace"), chartered by the Massachusetts legislature in 1845. The previous year, the first Jewish cemetery in Boston was created by a vote of the Board of Alderman, and in 1852 the first synagogue was built, on Warrenton Street in the South End. Moses Ehrlich was elected the first president of the new congregation.

Prior to the consolidation of Boston Jews into an established ethnic entity, some of the more successful were assimilated into the social and civic life of the city. One of these early leaders was Moses Michael Hays (1729–1805), a wealthy merchant who had come to Boston from Newport soon after the nation's founding. He frequented the best of society in the style of the Gratzes and Franks in Philadelphia, was a friend of Senator Harrison Gray Otis, had his portrait painted by Gilbert Stuart, and was a benefactor of Harvard. His son Judah was also active in community leadership, being, among other things, one of the founders of the Boston Athenaeum. They are both buried in the family plot in the Jewish cemetery in Newport, since there was no Jewish community to establish a cemetery in early nineteenth-century Boston.

In 1854, the same year that Isaac Mayer Wise had gone to Cincinnati's Congregation B'nai Jeshurun and initiated the Reform movement there,[24] foment for change began in Boston's Ohabei Shalom congregation. Twenty-five of its more prosperous members, including president Moses Ehrlich, formed a new congregation, Adath Israel (soon changed to Temple Israel), which first met in an old wooden building on Pleasant Street. Two years later, a small group of east Europeans separated from Ohabei Shalom and combined with another temple to found Temple Mishkan Tefila, the first synagogue in Boston to join the Conservative Movement. Of these new congregations, it was Congregation Temple Israel that has been most closely associated with the leadership of Boston's Jewish community, from the time of its founding in 1854 down to the present day. In fact, it was more influential in shaping the Jewish character in Boston than Mikveh Israel was in shaping Philadelphia's.

Temple Israel was founded at the height of New England's first literary renaissance. William Dean Howells once spoke of the flowering of literary Boston as "the Unitarian harvest-time of the old Puritan seed time."[25] Similarly, perhaps Reform Judaism was the fruit of the seeds sown by the puritanical orthodoxy of Isaac Leeser's generation.

Yet for two decades after its founding, Temple Israel remained Orthodox—men and women were seated separately, men with their heads covered; the ritual was in Hebrew, the vernacular in German; all prayed for the restoration of the Holy Land; there was no sermon and the Hebrew Sabbath was still sacred.

In the meantime, the congregation included more and more rapidly rising shopkeepers and merchants in a business community still dominated by Boston Brahmins who exemplified the Anglo-ideal in culture and education. "These merchants of Orthodox background," wrote a historian of Temple Israel, "wanted to acquire the Boston speech, the Boston dress, the Boston religion: they wanted to be like unto others. More than that, they feared that their American children would embrace Christianity if the *shul* were not Americanized...."[26] And from Cincinnati, Wise warned in his *Israelite* that "unless Judaism assimilates the American way, we will have no Jews left in this country in half a century."[27]

When the leaders of Temple Israel appointed German-born Solomon Schindler (1842–1915) as their rabbi in 1874, they were getting far more than they bargained for.[28] In the twenty years of his leadership, the congregation shed most of its Orthodox traditions and became the leading Reform synagogue in New England. Schindler had come to Boston after three miserable years as rabbi of an Orthodox synagogue in Hoboken, New Jersey. He was determined to Americanize his new congregation, and from his first days in this thinking city, he seemed to be more at home with non-Jews than with Jews. He was especially attracted to intellectuals, radicals, and Unitarian ministers who had done to traditional Christianity what he planned to do at Temple Israel with traditional Judaism. His first sermons, later published as *Messianic Expectations and Modern Judaism* (1885), were delivered to large audiences which were "more than half Christian," according to his close friend, the Darwinist-Christian Minot Savage. In the preface to Schindler's book of sermons, Savage hailed the popular rabbi as true to the spirit of an age in which "Christians were ceasing to be Christians and Jews ceasing to be Jews." The Channing Club rejoiced in the fact that Reform Judaism and Unitarianism had "few if any...theological differences." Both of course were casting out the Old Testament traditions and values of their Puritan and Orthodox ancestors.

By the middle of the 1880s, Temple Israel had tripled its membership, which included "100 of the richest and most influential Hebrews in the city." In 1885, in an attractive section of the South End, a new temple was built, in the Romanesque style of H. H. Richardson's celebrated Trinity Church on Copley Square. The dedication address was delivered by the Reverend Dr. Gustav Gottheil, rabbi of Temple Emanuel in New York (the "Canterbury of American Judaism"), who charmed his listeners with his impeccable Anglo-American diction. Other speakers were Minot Savage, Edward Everett Hale, and Phillips Brooks himself. By now the prosperous congregation was thoroughly Americanized. Soon after the move into the new synagogue, the sermons delivered at Sunday services were in English rather than German. Already in place were family pews, an organ, a choir with hymns, and the Reform prayer book containing no reference to a future return to Palestine.

But Schindler was moving away from traditional roots too fast and too far for all but the most liberal of his congregants. Though they wanted to Americanize, they still wanted to retain the Jewish identity which Schindler wanted to destroy. The Sunday services he had introduced too fast, and they were soon done away with. He outraged his congregants again in the early 1890's, when he advocated intermarriage with liberal Christians. But above all, they failed to follow him when he preached the socialism of Edward Bellamy, which he embraced with the idea of creating a society free of class, race, and religious differences. (He had befriended Bellamy and had translated into German his classic, *Looking Backward.*) Though the Jews of Temple Israel aspired to the rational religion of their liberal Christian peers, the Unitarians, they had no wish to revolutionize society or to convert their temple into a community church. Finally, in 1893, Schindler and his congregants agreed to part, and Charles Fleischer, assistant to Rabbi Berkowitz of Philadelphia's Rodeph Shalom, was called to Temple Israel as rabbi.

Charles Fleischer (1871–1942) was an even more ardent Americanist, if possible, than his predecessor. He was pleased when he was welcomed to Boston at the railroad station by Dr. Edward Everett Hale, the incarnation of the liberal spirit of the city in the following words: "Now my son, you too are one of the preachers of New England."[29] German born but educated in New York, Fleischer was a hauntingly handsome bachelor during his years at Temple Israel, and he soon became a star in the intellectual and artistic circles of Boston. Referred to as the "Beau Brummel of the Back Bay," his portrait was done in black and white by his good friend, John Singer Sargent. He was admired and was friends with liberals like Charles W. Eliot of Harvard and Robert A. Woods of South End House, in addition to his many Unitarian minister friends.

Fleischer had been appointed rabbi of Temple Israel in order to preserve the Jewish identity of the congregation, and, for at least a dozen years, he did not, in the pulpit, go beyond the limit of Reform Judaism or the Unitarianism upon which it had been modeled. He was a "cultural pluralist" long before the Harvard-trained philosopher, Horace Kallen, first used the term. "The strength of a community," Fleischer once told a congregationalist men's club, "is measured by the variety within it."

That the Jew should maintain his traditional identity was confirmed in the architecture of the new temple built in 1907. Instead of following the example of the old synagogue, which was modeled after the Romanesque type of the Episcopalian Trinity Church, the new temple, erected on Commonwealth Avenue, was a modern Moorish-style tabernacle referred to by the press as "Solomon's Temple." The dedication ceremonies of the new building were attended by a host of community leaders, including Edward Everett Hale, "The Grand Old Man of Boston," now an octogenarian. The main address, delivered by Rabbi Stephen S. Wise, an early Zionist, evoked a spontaneous ovation.

After the Temple Israel congregation moved into its new temple on Commonwealth Avenue, Charles Fleischer reintroduced Sunday services, preaching to audiences made up of almost as many non-Jews as Jews. He was, in fact, making Temple Israel into a veritable civic forum, and was beginning to spend more time with non-Jews than with Jews. He was soon a popular preacher in pulpits once occupied by Cotton Mather and Ralph Waldo Emerson. In 1908 he publicly noted that he admired Emerson more than he did Moses, and felt it was time for him to leave Temple Israel. A year later, President Eliot of Harvard, who had been a firm believer in the melting-pot in his youth, came out squarely against assimilation and uniformity, stressing the desirability of a diversity of races and ethnic groups living side by side. He also acknowledged his philosophic kinship with Charles Fleischer in recognizing the need for a new religion which reverenced truth, science, the individual, and social service.

The end came in 1911, when Temple Israel's Rabbi Emeritus, Solomon Schindler, preached a sermon there on "Mistakes I have made." His chief mistake, he noted, was "in trying to make the Jew like the Gentile." The effort failed because "the Jew will never succumb to the melting pot." Fleischer replied by preaching on "Some Mistakes I have Gladly Made." He did not want to make Jews like Gentiles, he said, but hoped to fuse all Americans into a new people. Shortly after, Fleischer left Temple Israel to found Boston's first community church, the Sunday Commons, a nonsectarian religion for persons of all backgrounds, stocks and traditions. In 1919 he married a gifted and intellectual Vermonter of Scotch descent and Presbyterian upbringing who shared his liberal views.

Both Schindler and Fleischer were German-born intellectuals and marginal men in America, and served Temple Israel during the Indian Summer of Boston's intellectual leadership of the nation. Until William Dean Howells moved to New York in 1891, Boston was still the literary capital of America; and in the election of 1884, Boston Brahmins led the nation's Mugwumps—Republicans who refused to support the party's ticket in that election. In the same year, young Josiah Quincy graduated from Harvard, became a Democrat, and then went on to become Mayor of Boston (1896), the third of his family to do so, to make his city "the cutting edge of reform in America."[30]

At that time, local politics in Boston were following a dialectical pattern of reform and reaction. The very Brahmin class which adopted Howells and produced Quincy and the liberal Unitarian ministers who welcomed both Schindler and Fleischer to Boston, also produced the leaders of a newly rising tide of antisemitic and anti-immigrant sentiment. This bias gradually infected much of old-stock America between 1881, when the pogroms against the Jews began in Russia, and the final closing of the gates of unrestricted immigration in America in 1924. For instance, Phillips Brooks, the barometer of the Brahmin mind, who in the early 1880s had prayed for the newer Americans in our "strange meeting place of races," in 1891 joined the Sons of the Revolution, saying he felt it was well to "go in for the assertion that our dear land at least used to be American."[31] Similarly, Henry Adams, in his 1880 novel, *Democracy*, wrote of Jews as upper-class Americans with no ethnic stigma; yet by the time of the Dreyfus Affair (1894), he was becoming a pretty rigid antisemite.

An even more overt confirmation of this reactionary sentiment was the founding in Boston in 1894 of the Immigration Restriction League by three Brahmin graduates of Noble's Country Day School and Harvard's Class of 1889—Robert DeCourcy Ward, Prescott Farnsworth Hall, and Charles Warren. (Ironically enough, young Warren was the son of Winslow Warren, a Brahmin Mugwump and later a Democratic ally of the reforming Josiah Quincy.) Another major advocate of the restriction of immigration while a supporter of the League of Nations from its beginning was Henry Cabot Lodge, as was A. Lawrence Lowell of Harvard. Among those opposed, as might be expected, were Charles W. Eliot and William James. Others, like John Murray Forbes, stood on the sidelines but privately were pleased with the League's work.

It was in this climate of opinion that young Louis D. Brandeis practiced law between 1879 and 1897 with his closest Yankee friend, Samuel D. Warren. We shall return to the fascinating story of how Brandeis, an assimilationist and philo-Puritan who stood socially aloof from the conservative German-Jewish community at Temple Israel, eventually became an ardent Zionist and, by the time he went on to the United States Supreme Court in 1916, the most famous Jew in America.

We have emphasized here the articulate, bigoted, ambivalent nature of the Boston community in the days when Schindler and Fleischer led their congregation at Temple Israel. There was no such ferment in Philadelphia. Mugwumpery was hardly a real issue among Philadelphia gentlemen, who preferred to enjoy their privileges in a tolerant, live-and-let-live atmosphere. While Justice Brandeis of Boston had led a lonely life of ostracism for the thirty years before he went on the Supreme Court, his counterpart in Philadelphia, Judge Mayer Sulzberger, was warmly rooted in the conservative Jewish community there; and while Brandeis was always a controversial intellectual, Sulzberger was the secluded scholar at heart who avoided a controversial issue if it was at all possible.

Philadelphia and Boston Jewish Communities: Comparative Institutions

Table 35.1 shows the major Jewish secular institutions in Philadelphia and Boston, in addition to the synagogues already discussed. On inspecting Table 35.1, one is immediately impressed how institutions that are essentially similar developed in each city. Though they were often established earlier in the far older community of Philadelphia, there were two exceptions: centrally organized charities, and hospitals. These exceptions may be of crucial importance in understanding the differences between the two communities.

Organized Charities

Second only to the synagogue, the organization and leadership of charitable giving has been a central motif of Jewish life in America. It

TABLE 35.1: Philadelphia and Boston Jewish Communities: Institutional Structures

Philadelphia	Boston
Pre-Civil War Synagogues	
Mikveh Israel (1782)	Ohabei Shalom (1852)
Rodoph Shalom (1810)	Adeth Israel (1854)
Beth Israel (1840)	Mishkan Israel (1858)
Keneseth Israel (1847)	
Adath Jeshurun (1859)	
Charitable Organizations	
United Hebrew Charities (1869)	United Hebrew Benevolent Association (1864)
Hebrew Charity Balls (1843)	Purim Balls (1869)
Federation of Jewish Charities (1901)	Federation of Jewish Charities (1895)
Hospitals	
Jewish Hospital Association (1865)	Jewish Dispensary
56th & Haverford (1865)	North End (1892)
Old York & Tabor Roads (1873)	
Mt. Sinai (1899-1905)	Mt. Sinai Hospital Association (1902)
2nd & Pine; 5th & Wilder	North & West End
Lebenon Hospital, N. 4th (1907)	South End & Roxbury
Northern Liberties (1920)	Beth Israel Hospital
Albert Einstein Medical Center (1951)	Roxbury (1916)
York & Tabor; Daroff Division, 5th & Reed	Brookline Avenue (1928)
Educational Institutions	
Hebrew Education Society (1848)	Hebrew Education Society (1868)
Maimonides College (1867-1873)	Hebrew Teachers College (1920)
Gratz College (1895)	
Dropsie College (1908)	Brandeis University (1948)
Newspapers	
Jewish Exponent (1887)	Jewish Advocate (1902)
Social Clubs	
Mercantile Club (1853)	Elysium Club (1880)
Philmont Country Club (1906)	New Century Club (1900)
Locust Club (1920)	Kernwood Country Club (1914)
	Belmont Country Club (1940)
NEIGHBORHOODS	
German Middle Class (19th early 20th century)	
Franklin Square—Green Street	South End—Brookline
East European Ghetto (19th early 20th century)	
Delaware River—Front to 6th	West End—North End
Girard to Rasker	Chelsea
Lower Middle Class	
Strawberry Mansion—Logan	Roxbury—Dorchester
Upper Middle Class	
Old York Road—Wynnefield	Brookline—Newton
Upper Class	
Rittenhouse Square (Chestnut Hill)	Back Bay (Cambridge)

became even more important as more and more Jews became financially successful in the American, Horatio Alger tradition. It is our thesis here that the reason Jews did so well was largely because equality of opportunity (if not equality of condition) was deeply embedded in their own culture, along with a definitely hierarchical society, centralization of leadership, and a powerful tradition of charitable giving. By ancient religious law and long social habit, both the rights of the poor and the obligations of the rich and successful were implied in the Hebrew concept of *Tzedakah.*[32] Charity has always been central to the Christian religion, too, of course; but fund-raising affairs such as charity balls have never been of first importance in Christian society as were the early Hebrew charity balls (1843) in Philadelphia, or the Purim balls (1869) in Boston. (That charitable giving in both religions should be so intimately connected to such an elite event as a Society ball in these cities would incline a cynic to remark that perhaps their idea of charity was not necessarily to relieve the bitterness of the poor by correcting the abuses of inequality and other conditions leading to poverty, but mainly to soften differences and ease the conscience of the rich.)

Organized Christian philanthropy in America has been, from the beginning, more characteristic of the Puritan ethic than that of other Protestants. Thus, the Boston establishment, as in all its institutions, favored an efficient system of charity that was highly organized and managed by a hierarchy of leadership, while in Philadelphia, the less structured Quakers clung to the more catholic idea of spontaneous giving. As might be expected, the two rather different climates of opinion had their effect on the newer Jewish communities in these two cities. Boston's Jewry centralized its charitable fund-raising by the creation of the United Hebrew Benevolent Association in 1864, a good five years ahead of Philadelphia's United Hebrew Charities. Similarly, the founding of the Federation of Jewish Charities in Boston, the first of its kind in the nation, came six years before a similar consolidation in Philadelphia in 1901.

It is almost a truism to say that business success, community leadership and charitable giving are closely linked, and this was apparent in the Jewish communities of Philadelphia and Boston no less than anywhere else. Thus, a comparative analysis of the Jewish charitable institutions in the two cities gives a parallel glimpse into the lives, families and successful careers of their civic and business leaders.

In Philadelphia,[33] an important element that helped to unify and strengthen the Jewish community was the city's "neighborhood spirit," a phenomenon which still exists today, and which, along with benign, laissez-faire Quakerism, made Philadelphia an ideal experimental seedbed for the formulation of Jewish culture and institutions. So favorable was this environment that by the decade just prior to the Civil War, the Jewish community was large and stable enough to produce a coherent and familistic upper class which stood at the forefront of community leadership right down to the 1940s.

The patriarch of this emerging class was Hyman Polock. He was born in Amsterdam in 1786, coming to Philadelphia in 1813 where he was moderately successful in business, and a civic leader for many years. A member of Mikveh Israel, he was among the founders of the Hebrew Society for Visitation of Sick and Mutual Assistance (1813) and the Hebrew Education Society (1848). But Hyman Polock's major achievement was having three daughters who married men who were to become three of Philadelphia Jewry's most outstanding leaders: Isadore Binswanger, Abraham Simon Wolf, and Morris Rosenbach. The influence of these three men was felt in most areas of Jewish accomplishment in Philadelphia. When the Mikveh Israel congregation built a new synagogue in the Franklin Square vicinity at Seventh and Arch Streets just before the Civil War (1858), Abraham S. Wolf was among those on the building committee. Just down the street at Sixth and Arch, upper-class social life now centered at the new (1853) Mercantile Club, among whose eighteen charter members were Abraham S. Wolf, Morris Rosenbach, and Isadore Binswanger. After the Civil War, when the Jewish Hospital Association (1865) and the United Hebrew Charities (1869) were organized, Messrs. Wolf, Rosenbach and Binswanger were among the founders of both.

As might be expected, these three family-founders and civic leaders were also the richest members of the Jewish community. (In 1865, a report entitled "Rich Men of Philadelphia," showed that, wealthy as these men were, the income of R. H. Gratz was as much as that of the three combined, but by this time, Gratz and his family were largely assimilated, and no longer active members of the Jewish community.)

At the turn of the century, while the Wolf-Binswanger-Rosenbach clan still remained at the apex of the Jewish class structure in Philadelphia, newer families, such as the Fleishers, the Guggenheims, the Loebs and the Gimbels, were coming to the fore as community leaders. And many of these new leaders were members of Reform congregations. Two major Reform synagogues, Rodeph Shalom and Keneseth Israel, were on Broad Street, near the center of gravity of the Jewish elite, now located to the west of Broad Street in the newly fashionable Jewish neighborhood along Broad, 15th and 16th Streets, between Spring Garden Street and Columbia Avenue, with Green Street as the hub. Halfway between the Reform synagogues was the new Mercantile Club (built in 1895), at 1422 North Broad. All the leading Jewish families of the city lived within a few blocks of one another.

Just as the Green Street neighborhood was becoming firmly established as the most fashionable Jewish area of the city, a few prominent Jewish families started to move out to the northern suburbs along the Old York Road. One outgrowth of this trend was the founding, in 1906, of the Philmont Country Club by members of the Gimbel, Snellenberg, Loeb and Wolf families; it was the original Jewish country club in Philadelphia, and is still the most exclusive. Its first president, Ellis Gimbel, remained in office for forty years; after his retirement in 1946, he served as president emeritus until his death.

This, then, is the background of the great Jewish families who had the money, prestige and position necessary to bring about the establishment of organized philanthropy in Philadelphia's Jewish community. Boston's organizers, while of backgrounds quite similar, were influenced in addition, by the Yankee values of aggressiveness, ambition, and, above all, competitive leadership, characteristics that even today still mark the Puritan "City upon a Hill."

In the last quarter of the 19th century, Jacob Hecht was the acknowledged leader of a close-knit group of prosperous German-Jewish businessmen in Boston who had founded family firms such as the Leopold Morse Company, Lehman Pickert and Company, Charles Weil and Company, Jacob Dreyfus and Sons, Conrad and Company, and William Filene's Sons Company. Hecht himself was an enormously successful member of the family-owned Hecht Brothers, a national boot and shoe firm. Born in Bavaria in 1834, Jacob Hecht had come to America in 1848, peddling shoe laces and other notions before making his way to San Francisco. There the family business was founded by Hecht and his father and four brothers. In 1867 he married Lina Franks, a native of Baltimore and the daughter of well-to-do immigrants, also from Bavaria. Hecht and his bride moved to Boston where for almost a quarter of a century, they led almost every do-good endeavor in the local Jewish community. In 1876, Hecht was named president of Temple Israel's United Hebrew Association, an organization which belied its name in that it was virtually the exclusive charity project of Temple Israel. It had been founded by twenty-six of the congregation's more prosperous businessmen within a decade of the founding of Temple Israel in 1854, when the entire Jewish community numbered only about four hundred families. Hecht immediately changed the leadership structure of the Association so as to include members of the Ohabei Shalom congregation, and streamlined the operating procedures so that the United Hebrew Association became the Jewish counterpart of the Yankee-dominated Provident Association, a pioneer in the nation.

Charles Weil was second only to Jacob Hecht in influence in the early Jewish community; his wife Carrie worked closely in many charitable undertakings with Lina Hecht. He was a class progenitor in much the same style as Hyman Pollack of Philadelphia. Like Pollack, he had three daughters who married three of the Jewish community's most promising businessmen—A. Lincoln Filene, Jacob Dreyfus and Ludwig Eisemann. Lincoln Filene headed William Filene's Sons Company, which eventually became Boston's most famous department store; he was childless and was never an active member of Boston's Jewish community. Jacob Dreyfus was a leading shirt manufacturer; his son, Carl Dreyfus, was listed in the 1940 Who's Who as a publisher and capitalist. Ludwig Eisemann was a wool merchant, along with his two brothers. His son, Philip Eisemann, graduated from Exeter Academy and Harvard, and rose to be the president of the Old Colony Trust Company, a distinguished and ancient Yankee institution.

Leopold Morse was a member of Temple Israel and a leader in Jewish charitable affairs in the style of the Hechts; among other things, he was the founder of the Boston Home for Infirm Hebrews and Orphanage. After becoming one of New England's leading men's clothing manufacturers and dealers in the post-Civil War years, Morse ran for Congress in 1872 as a Democrat in an overwhelmingly Republican district. He lost that election, but four years later he became the first Jew in Boston to serve in Washington (six sessions: the 43rd, 45th, 46th, 48th, and 50th). (The first Philadelphia Jew to go to Congress, Henry Mayer Phillips, served only one term, the 35th Congress. He was elected in 1850).

Leopold's younger brother, Godfrey Morse, was the first Boston Jew to graduate from Harvard (1870). While there, he was an editor of the *Advocate* as well as manager of the first Harvard crew to row at Henley against Oxford. After graduation, he went on to the Law School and had a distinguished career at the local bar, representing the major Jewish firms in the city (along with Louis D. Brandeis). He later went to Washington as an assistant counsel of the United States in the settlement of the Alabama claims.

This close-knit German-Jewish elite consolidated itself in the 1880s in the fashionable South End of Boston, and there Temple Israel erected its handsome Romanesque synagogue (at Columbus Avenue and Northampton Street) in 1885. The center of this upper-class Jewish society was the Elysium Club, located nearby on Concord Street.

For five decades before its eventual demise in about 1930, the Elysium Club, with its receptions, weddings, formal dinners and private dances, defined the standards of the Jewish elite in Boston. Founded in 1880, Jacob Hecht was its first president, and most of the German-Jewish leaders of the city, from Godfrey Morse, Esq., to Louis Kirstein, have served in that office since.

By the time of World War I, there was a gradual movement out of the South End to the Back Bay and Brookline. The Hechts were the first Jewish family to move to the Back Bay, followed by Henry Ehrlich, who had married a niece of Jacob Hecht and who had been the first Boston-born Jew to graduate from the Harvard Medical School (1886). Ehrlich had first practiced in the South End, and had lived in the heart of the Back Bay, at 172 Commonwealth Avenue, for many years before he died in 1926. According to the 1940 *Who's Who,* the following prominent Boston Jews were residents of the Back Bay in that year: Isadore Henry Coriat, friend of Sigmund Freud and founder of the Boston Psychoanalytic Society; Abraham Ratshesky, chairman of the Board and founder of the United States Trust Company, a civic leader of great distinction, and president of the Federation of Jewish Charities between 1909 and 1919; and finally, Louis Kirstein, vice president of Filene's since 1911 and a business leader of national distinction as well as the successor of Jacob Hecht in the leadership of Boston Jewry between the two wars (he was president of the Federation of Jewish Charities in 1922–24 and 1930–42).

Although the Back Bay was the elite Jewish address in 1940, Brookline became the center of upper-middle class Jewry in the inter-war years;

Harvard Street, especially Coolidge corner where it intersects with Beacon Street, remains today as a reminder of a glorious Jewish past in Brookline. Before the first World War, a few elite Jewish facilities began to summer on the North Shore, in the Swampscott area. A select group of them had bought the old Peabody estate in North Salem in 1914, where they founded the Kernwood Country Club, the first of its kind in Greater Boston, with Louis Kirstein as its first president. The club remained the exclusive preserve of the German-Jewish elite until after the second World War.

It was thus that the solid and successful German-Jewish communities settled comfortably into their prosperous and elite life-styles, originally in the Green Street neighborhood in Philadelphia and in the South End of Boston. Their social life centered around their favorite synagogue, their exclusive clubs, and, not least, their charitable organizations.

But an alarming disruption in the two communities was in the offing. Beginning around 1881 and continuing for several decades, wave upon wave of Orthodox Jewish immigrants from Eastern Europe (so-called "Russian Jews" landed on our shores, flocking in the small "East Side" ghettos in most of America's major cities. This immigration was set off when the Russian government in 1881 encouraged and directed a series of anti-Jewish riots in St. Petersburg. These pogroms shocked the whole Western world. In Paris, Victor Hugo led a meeting of protest; and on March 4, 1882, Philadelphia's civic and religious leaders, Gentile and Jew alike, gathered at the staid Academy of Music to discuss the Russian atrocities.

Though they were outraged at the merciless persecutions suffered by their fellow Jews in eastern Europe, many of America's German-Jews were appalled at the hordes of alien "Russians" who were flooding their cities. Themselves successful, conservative, Republican and Reform, they were taken aback by the ideological passions of the new immigrants, who were desperately poor, fiercely Orthodox, and forever arguing over socialism, anarchism, territorialism and Zionism. Reform Judaism in American has no interest in any isms (especially Zionism), nor in promoting a separate Yiddish culture. Having become thoroughly assimilated and Americanized, these Jews were horrified when signs in resort hotels reading "No Jews or dogs allowed" appeared for the first time in 1880s, denoting a new and unbending kind of anti-Semitism within the Protestant establishment.

Fortunately, the wisest of the "uptown" Jews in America realized that, in spite of their vast cultural differences, both the "Germans" and the "Russians" were basically one people—Jews in a Gentile world. It was partly as a response to the need for helping these new immigrants that Boston's Federation of Jewish Charities was founded by the German Jews in 1895, followed by Philadelphia's six years later.

In Boston, the first real Eastern European Jewish ghetto was a small area in the North End bounded by Hanover, Prince, Endicott and Bennett Streets. With unbounded energy and thrift, these poor immigrants, under the leadership of Rabbi Morish Margolies, had accumulated $50,000 with which to build themselves a new synagogue, Congregation Beth Israel.[34] (Two small congregations already existed in the area.) The new synagogue soon became the center of social and religious life for North End Jews, and it was here that the idea of a federation of Jewish Charities got its start. Beth Israel allowed Lina Hecht to start a Sunday School for girls on the premises. The next year she founded the Hebrew Industrial School for girls, which began with twenty pupils in rooms on Hanover Street in the heart of the North End. Two years later, it moved to the West End (Chambers Street) and welcomed boys. Many of these boys went to Hebrew School in the afternoons, and in the evenings to the Jacob Hecht Boys Club, where they listened to lectures on such varied topics as "Character Building," "Jewish History," "Personal Cleanliness," and "The Evils of Alcohol and Tobacco." One of the pioneers of American social work and vocational guidance, Mayer Bloomfield, an immigrant himself, was a guide at the Hecht Club while an undergraduate at Harvard. He was also the first director of the Civic Service House, in the North End, which was founded and financed by the Yankee philanthropist Pauline Agassiz Shaw, a good friend of Lina Hecht.

During the five years following the founding of the first of these schools and clubs, twelve-hundred Jewish children were taught to be wage-earners and self-respecting, intelligent citizens.

The first paid superintendent of the resultant Federation of Jewish Charities was Solomon Shindler, who had introduced Reform Judaism to Boston's Temple Israel, and who had stepped down as rabbi in 1893. His appointment in the new Federation was the culmination of a dream he had long had of a more centralized and professional system of charitable giving. Among the lay officers of the organization were Jacob Hecht, president; and Godfrey Morse and Lehman Pickert, vice-presidents.

Consonant with Schindler's pioneering views on women's equality, the original board also included Mrs. Jacob Hecht, Mrs. Charles Weil, and Mrs. Abraham Spitz.

Solomon Schindler recommended Yankee techniques of philanthropy, "Participating in a study of urban poverty with native spokesmen of social reform," wrote Barbara Miller Solomon, "Rabbi Schindler transmitted to the Hecht coterie contemporary approaches to immigrants' problems."[35]

Jacob Hecht remained as president of the Federation until just before his death in 1902. He was followed for brief periods by Godfrey Morse and Lehman Pickert before Abraham C. Ratshesky, the next leader of first-rate stature, took over the presidency in 1909 and served until 1918. Ratshesky was succeeded as president by Louis Kirstein, who became the number-one Jew in Boston during the inter-war years. In addition to his presidency of the Federated Jewish Charities (1922–24), he was also president of the new Associated Jewish Philanthropies (1930–42).

Thus, for three-quarters of a century—from 1867, when Jacob and Lina Hecht first came to Boston, until Kirstein stepped down from the presidency of the Associated Jewish Philanthropies in 1942—Jacob Hecht, Abraham Ratshesky and Louis Kirstein dominated the leadership of the small Boston Jewish community. Since Kirstein there has been no single leader there of major influence.

The development of federated Jewish charities in Philadelphia came later (1901) and was not so direct or clear cut. Unlike the Boston Federation, where three important leaders of the community served in turn for three decades between them, the presidency of Philadelphia's Federated Jewish Charities was less central to the city's Jewish leadership as a whole, and more of a temporary honor and a chore to be rotated. The two Federations were also different in that Boston hired a paid full-time executive from the beginning, while Philadelphia's Federation was run by a small nucleus of German-Jewish laymen who were allied by marriage and social ties, with the first executive director not hired until 1918.

Federation came to Philadelphia Jewry, as it did to Boston's, in response to the flood of immigrants from Eastern Europe. This began on February 23, 1882 in Philadelphia, when the SS. *Illinois* landed at the Delaware River pier with 222 Jewish refugees from Russia. Since their plight had been well publicized by the affair at the Academy of Music, the immigrants were given a municipal reception, and some $20,000 was raised to help them settle. These Jews congregated along the Delaware riverfront area, and by 1900, six Orthodox synagogues had been built within the two city blocks founded by Fourth, Fifth, Pine and South Streets.

Because this influx of Eastern Jews immigrants was causing such a drain on Philadelphia's organization for charitable giving, the United Hebrew Charities, it steadily increased its fund-raising efforts. However, its methods became increasingly inadequate. In 1891, for example, the Hebrew Education Society built a new facility near the new South Philadelphia ghettos, and within the first year, 1,345 pupils crowded into its Hebrew, English and vocational courses. Such needs were multiplying.

Then, in 1899, at the first meeting of the newly formed National Conference of Jewish Charities, a major topic for discussion was the so-called Liverpool Plan for federating charities, already adopted in Boston, Chicago and Cincinnati. The president of Philadelphia's United Hebrew Charities, Max Herzberg, had attended this conference, and he came back to Philadelphia determined to follow Boston and other cities in some sort of federated system. So, along with his close associate at the United, Louis Wolf, a local box manufacturer, together with a solid nucleus of Sulzbergers, Loebs, Fleishers, Wolfs, Lits, Gimbels, and Fels, the Federation of Jewish Charities was organized in 1901, with Jacob Gimbel as its first president. Gimbel had played no part in the leadership of Philadelphia Jewry, and his being chosen to lead the new Federation was to imply the spirit of non-partisanship between the nine agencies which made up the original Federation.

After the first decade, Louis Wolf, who had devoted a great deal of his time to membership and money-raising activities, succeeded Jacob Gimbel as president (1912–1924). Though Wolf served a dozen years as president, no one who followed him in that office served for more than a three-year term. In 1918, when the Federation had expanded to thirty-nine constituent agencies, recognition was given for the first time to leaders of East European ("Russian") origins.

Hospitals

Jewish communities all over urban American are justifiably proud of their support of medicine and hospitals. In both Philadelphia and Boston, hospitals were founded by the German-Jewish leadership as a response to the Orthodox immigrants, who needed hospital care by people who understood and sympathized with their special dietary and other requirements and needs. Thus, the Jewish Dispensary was founded in Boston's North End in 1892 (see Table 35.1), and the Mt. Sinai Hospital Association founded hospitals both in the ghettos of the North and West Ends as well as in the South End of Roxbury, where German Jews had long been settled (by 1902), and Russian Jews were rising more and more to middle-class status. Philadelphia Jews located their hospitals along the same pattern; except for the original German-Jewish hospital founded after the Civil War, the Lebanon Hospital on North Fourth Street 1907) and branches of Mt. Sinai Hospital at Second and Pine and Fifth and Wilder, were all in the heart of the Russian ghetto.[36]

While the needs and patterns of hospital founding in the two cities were more or less parallel in the early days of the Eastern European immigration (from 1880 to World War I), the final consolidation of the Albert Einstein Medical Center in Philadelphia and the Beth Israel Hospital in Boston were, I think, significantly different. Boston had consolidated its major hospital effort in Beth Israel, in Roxbury, in 1916, moving to its present site on Brookline Avenue, in the heart of medical and educational Boston, in 1928. The relocation of Beth Israel Hospital next to the Harvard Medical School was done at the insistence and leadership of Louis Kirstein, who would have only the very best, and he held that Harvard University in general, and its Medical School in particular, were the best in the nation, if not in the world. For over a quarter of a century, Beth Israel was the only teaching Jewish hospital in the nation.

In Philadelphia, on the other hand, though the first Jewish hospital was opened soon after the Civil War, and the present site of the Albert Einstein Medical Center at Old York and Tabor Roads was purchased in 1873,[37] the Jewish community did not centralize its hospital facilities in the Einstein Medical Center (see Table 35.1) until 1951, and is even now located in two places: the Daroff Center in South Philadelphia as well as the original location on Old York Road. Only recently have these two branches been recognized as teaching hospitals: in the north affiliated with Temple University Medical School, and in South Philadelphia associated with Thomas Jefferson University Medical School. The original building of the Center (the called the Jewish Hospital) was built in 1873. By 1901, the annual budget of the hospital was more than the total cost of the building, and as such was Philadelphia Jewry's proudest institution. But that it took the Jewish community over seventy-five years to organize its hospital system into one cohesive center illustrates again the Philadelphia/Quaker pattern of letting institutions and people do their own thing, contrasted with the Boston/Puritan emphasis on quality leadership and organization.

Educational Institutions

A glance at Table 35.1 shows that the older Philadelphia community's institutions of learning were founded earlier than Boston's. The first Hebrew teachers' college in the nation was Philadelphia's Simon Gratz College. Dropsie College concentrated on a non-theological graduate school leading to a Ph.D. in Hebrew and related studies, and was unique and fitting to conservative and orthodox Philadelphia; while Brandeis University, the only non-sectarian institution of higher learning in America to be founded and supported by Jews, was located at its founding in 1948, appropriately enough, in the Boston area.

Perhaps nothing better symbolizes or sums up the difference between Quaker Philadelphia and Puritan Boston than the attitudes of the University of Pennsylvania and Harvard towards Jews. The egalitarian tolerance of Quakerism was characteristic of Penn, from which developed a laissez-faire cultural pluralism. At Harvard, on the other had, the hierarchical intolerance of Puritanism, ambivalent at first, eventually produced a kind of Brahmin hegemony highly conducive to assimilation. Philadelphia Jews have been students at Penn ever since the eighteenth century, whereas it was not until 1870 that the first Jew, Boston's Godfrey Morse, graduated from Harvard College.[38]

More indicative of their differences, however, were the reactions of Harvard and Penn to the rising tide of anti-Semitism in America in the first part of the twentieth century, especially as it reached the college level in the inter-war years. At Harvard, its two presidents during this era, Eliot and Lowell, both Brahmin-bred to the core, held very different views of the masses of immigrants from southern and eastern Europe who came to America in the years before the first World War. Eliot, as a reaction to his Puritan heritage and upbringing, was an extreme Unitarian liberal, while Lowell acted more in accord with his Puritan roots. Eliot vigorously opposed the ideals of the Immigration Restriction

League, while Lowell supported the League and its vice-president after 1912. While Eliot once said that, as a Unitarian, he would be glad to be followed in the Harvard presidency by Brandeis, a Jew, Lowell wrote to Woodrow Wilson after the election in 1912 that Brandeis "did not stand very high in the opinion of the best judges in Massachusetts."

In brief, Eliot, who built the finest graduate school in the nation at Harvard, at the same time atomizing life at the College with his famous elective system, believed in individualism, diversity and cultural pluralism. Conversely, Lowell believed in paternalism, hierarchy and community, and concentrated his energies on the College, where he built new halls for freshmen in 1914, and in 1928, after the Harkness gifts, constructed colleges for upper-classmen, all in an effort to create an atmosphere of "intellectual and social cohesion."

Above all, Lowell believed in assimilation to some sort of traditional Harvard ideal. What he once wrote of the Irish, who were coming increasingly to Harvard in his day, applied to all minorities:

> What we need is not to dominate... but to absorb... Their best interests and ours are, indeed, the same in this matter. We want them to become rich, and send their sons to our colleges, to share our prosperity and our sentiments. We do not want to feel that they are among us and not really a part of us.[39]

These assimilationist sentiments Lowell tried to apply to limiting the Jewish population at Harvard, whose numbers had grown from less than 10 percent of the student body when he took office to more than 20 percent by the early twenties. Lowell's proposal to establish a formal quota for Jews was turned down by the Overseers ("howled down by men who preferred hypocrisy"). Bruce Kuklick, in his judicial discussion of anti-Semitic sentiments in Harvard's philosophy department,wrote of Eliot's position:

> In the early 1920's, when he tried to establish a formal quota for Jews, he did so not because he felt any prejudice against the Jew per se, but because Harvard could not assimilate the Jews if their number became too large. One of Harvard's goals was to produce the "pure American" Jew. Harvard had to give "special consideration" to the Jews just as it did to alumni children: the nation would be strong only if both groups received Harvard socialization.[40]

The University of Pennsylvania had none of this soul-agonizing conflict. The long tradition of cultural pluralism which marked the university as well as the city carried into the inter-war years. All during the twenties and thirties, when many other of the leading Eastern institutions were becoming more and more restrictive, Penn tended to accept any student, regardless of ethnicity or race, and especially if their parents could afford to foot the tuition bills. As Lawrence R. Vesey wrote in his book, *The Emergence of the American University,* "the University of Pennsylvania welcomed commuters, immigrants,and socialites alike; it was said to have "the democracy of the street car."[41]

However, even though Jews were acceptable at Penn as students in the classroom, they were not integrated into the campus social life. Penn, with perhaps the largest proportion of Jews in what is now called the Ivy League, was dominated socially by a large number of fraternities, rigidly divided into "A" ones (Gentile), and "B" (Jewish).

One wonders whether Jewish alumni have been more loyal to democratic but segregated Penn, or to discriminating but assimilating Harvard. Theodore H. White, who entered Harvard as a freshman from the Jewish ghetto of Dorchester a year after Lowell's retirement in 1933, has made some interesting observations on this point. White noted that when he entered Harvard, it still "combined the best of the old warmth and the new strivings."[42] He also noted that Conant, of New England lineage as ancient as Lowell's, had more of Eliot's values and "made Harvard the most competitive school in American scholarship, a meritocracy in which students and professors vied for honors with little mercy or kindness."[43]

White wrote these words in the late 1970's, when Penn as well as Harvard was a highly competitive, intellectual meritocracy, and both were far more democratic than ever before in their histories. And White's reaction to this was as follows:

> I have, in the years since, served as an overseer of that majestic institution, Harvard University, a member of the Honorable and Reverend Board of the most ancient corporation in the Western world, the chosen thirty who tip their silk hats as they file, two by two, past the statue of John Harvard on Commencement Day in the yard. But it was a better Harvard I entered in the 1930's than it was later, when I sat on the Board of Overseers, or than it is today."[44]

Louis D. Brandeis: America's Most Famous Jew

The central difference between Jewish Boston and Jewish Philadelphia, at least in the early part of this century, is well illustrated by the life and career of Louis D Brandeis. If Theodore White is one of the more distinguished American Jews of this generation, surely Louis D. Brandeis was the most distinguished Jew in American history. Both men shared a loving admiration for the values of Old New England Puritanism, and for Harvard University. Brandeis once said that his years at Harvard Law School were "the happiest of my life...For me the world's center was Cambridge."[45] Though he admired Charles W. Eliot, the optimistic liberal, and Oliver Wendell Holmes, Jr., the skeptical aristocrat, Brandeis idealized the traditions of Puritan New England. His Brahmin law partner, Samuel D. Warren, once told him: "In many ways you are a better example of New England virtues than the natives."[46] And Brandeis finally embraced Zionism only when he came to feel that his own generation of Boston Brahmins had betrayed their Puritan heritage by, among other things, surrendering their independence to the New York monopolists. For him, the Zionists among his own people, the Jews, were the "New Puritans."[47]

Nowhere are the ambivalent attitudes of the Brahmin Bostonian towards the Jew more sharply delineated than in the life and career of Louis Brandeis. Although Jacob Hecht had gone surety for his tuition at the Law School, and Lina Hecht had invited him to her Sunday afternoon at-homes on Commonwealth Avenue, young Brandeis preferred to avoid active membership in the Jewish society centered around Temple Israel and the Elysium Club.[48] This was especially so after he was asked to form a law partnership by his best Yankee friend, Samuel D. Warren, in 1879. Warren, a prosperous paper manufacturer's son and a member of Porcellian at Harvard, provided an ideal entree into Boston Society, where Brandeis was listed in the *Blue Book*, and later in the *Social Register* when it first appeared in the 1890's. Though he was not a member of the Country Club in Brookline nor the Somerset in Boston, he was a member of the respectable Union Club in the city and the suburban Dedham Club, of which his partner Sam Warren was a founder and president.

Even though overtly accepted in Boston's best social circles, Brandeis soon realized that it was through Warren's social and family connections that most of the State Street clients came to the partnership; consequently, he turned to a small group of prosperous Jewish firms, such as Hecht Bros. and Co., in order to contribute his share of clients.

Unfortunately, the relationship between Brandeis and Warren cooled somewhat after Warren married in 1883 and his caste-conscious bride refused to include Brandeis among the 100 or so invited guests. When Brandeis married Alice Goldmarks in 1891, the wedding, held in New York, was a small and very private family affair. And when the newly-weds settled in Boston, only a few of the prominent clients of the law firm sent wedding gifts or left calling cards.

Brandeis bought a country place in Dedham in 1900; a few of the neighbors were friendly, according to his daughter. She remembers solitary walks and canoeing with her father. At the Polo Club, Brandeis was allowed to "flock by himself," as a member once rather callously put it.

At any rate, by 1910, the doors of high society were pretty firmly closed to elite Jews in Boston. In reaction, the eccentric bachelor and reformer, Edward Filene, in a bitter battle to avoid being classified as a Jew, founded the Boston City Club, where liberal businessmen, gentile and Jew alike, have lunched together to this day. Edward's more conservative brother, Lincoln Filene, even after becoming a Congregationalist to please his wife, finally joined the Kernwood Country Club in order to play golf.

For Brandeis, the final turning point in his relationship with Yankee Boston was probably the suicide of his friend Warren in February 1910. Though hardly intimate with the family, it was Brandeis who took charge and prevented the scandal reaching the press. Then, within a week of the suicide, the Dedham Polo Club partially burned and the membership merged with the Norfolk Country Club in Weston to form the present Dedham Country and Polo Club. Members of the Brandeis family were not asked to join the new club.

In the meantime, Brandeis was gradually rediscovering his Jewish heritage. First publicly identifying himself as a Jew in 1905, his movement back to Judaism was quite complicated. It was during Woodrow Wilson's campaign for the presidency that Brandeis came to know Jacob De Haas, later his biographer and at one time the secretary (and forever a hero-worshiper) of Theodore Herzl. De Haas had taken over the editorship of Boston's *Jewish Advocate,* which vigorously supported Wilson in 1912. After the Democratic victory, the *Advocate* reported that Wilson had received an unusual amount of Jewish financial and political support, especially from such prominent Jews as Henry Morganthau and the well-known lawyer, Samuel Untermyer. Brandeis now worked closely with De Haas in ethnic politics, finally making him his private secretary and "instructor in the history of Zionism."

It is indicative of the mind and heart of Louis D. Brandeis that he made his first public statement on Zionism at the New Century Club rather than at the stolid and conservative Elysium Club. The New Century Club in Boston was founded in 1900 by a rapidly rising group of Russian-Jewish professional men, many of whom had gone to the Boston University Law School where they had been members of the Century Club. So, on March 22, 1913, according to De Haas, "in the privacy of the monthly dinner... Brandeis made his first serious utterance on Zionism. He... unfolded his deep solicitude for the spiritual welfare of the Jews. He explained his interest in Zionism and identified himself in unqualified terms with the cause.[49]

Notes

This chapter appears here in this form for the first time. An earlier, much abbreviated version was published in Murray Friedman, ed. *Jewish Life in Philadelphia, 1830–1940* (Philadelphia: ISHI, 1983).

1. E. Digby Baltzell, *Puritan Boston and Quaker Philadelphia: Two Protestant Ethics and the Spirit of Class Authority and Leadership* (New York: Free Press, 1979), 7.
2. Jacob R. Marcus, *The Colonial American Jew: 1492–1776*, vol. 1 (Detroit: Wayne State University Press, 1970), 299.
3. Marcus, *The Colonial American Jew* 297.
4. Baltzell, *Puritan Boston and Quaker Philadelphia* p. 419.
5. E. Digby Baltzell, *Philadelphia Gentlemen: The Making of a National Upper Class* (Glencoe, Il: The Free Press, 1958), 277.
6. Baltzell, *Philadelphia Gentlemen,* 277-99.
7. Henry Samuel Morais, *The Jews of Philadelphia: Their History from the Earliest Settlement to the Present Time* (Philadelphia: The Levytype Co., 1894), 402-04, 427-29.
8. Joseph P. Sims, ed., *The Philadelphia Assemblies,* 1748-1948 (Privately printed, n.d.).
9. Isaac M. Fein, *Boston—Where It all Began: A Historical Perspective of the Boston Jewish Community* (Boston: Boston Jewish Bicentennial Committee, 1976), 1.
10. Fein, *Boston—Where It all Began,* 7-8.
11. Edmund Wilson, "*A Piece of My Mind* (New York: Anchor Books, 1958), 88-89
12. See Milton M. Gordon, *Assimilation in American Life* (New York: Oxford University Press, 1964), chaps. 4, 5, and 6.
13. Nathan Glazer, *American Judaism* (Chicago: University of Chicago Press, 1957), 22.
14. Bertram Wallace Korn, "Isaac Leeser: Centennial Reflections," *American Jewish Archives,* November 1967, pp. 127-41.
15. Stephen Birmingham, *"Our Crowd": The Great Jewish Families of New York* (New York: Harper & Row, 1967), 131.

16. See Glazer, *American Judaism,* 36; and *Dictionary of American Biography,* vol. 20, pp 426–27.
17. Glazer, *American Judaism,* 42.
18. Glazer, *American Judaism,* 57; see also, *Dictionary of American Biography,* "Sabato Marais," vol. 13, pp. 149–50; and "Marcus Jastrow," vol. 10, p. 102.
19. See Adler biography in *Dictionary of American Biography,* supp. II, 5–6.
20. Glazer, *American Judaism,* 75.
21. Ibid., 75–78.
22. *Reform Congregation Keneseth Israel, Its First 100 Years 1847–1957* (Philadelphia: Drake Press, 1950).
23. Esther M. Klein, *A Guidebook to Jewish Philadelphia* (Philadelphia: Jewish Times Institute, 1965), 102.
24. Arthur Mann, ed., *Growth and Achievement: Temple Israel 1854–1954* (Cambridge: Riverside Press, 1954), 7.
25. M. A. DeWolfe Howe, *Boston: The Place and Its People* (New York: Macmillan, 1924), 225.
26. Mann, *Growth and Achievement,* 46.
27. Ibid., 46.
28. For facts about Schindler, see Mann, *Growth and Achievement,* chap. 4; and *Dictionary of American Biography,* vol. 16, pp. 433–34.
29. Mann, *Growth and Achievement,* chap. 5.
30. For an excellent discussion of Solomon Schindler and the Yankee and Irish reformers in late 19th-century Boston, see Arthur Mann, *Yankee Reformers in an Urban Age* (Cambridge: Harvard University Press, 1954).
31. Barbara Miller Solomon, *Ancestors and Immigrants: A Changing New England Tradition* (Cambridge: Harvard University Press, 1957) is a brilliant discussion of the founding of the Immigration Restriction League.
32. Barbara Miller Solomon, *Pioneers in Service: The History of the Associated Jewish Philanthropies of Boston* (Boston: Associated Jewish Philanthropies, 1956), 4.
33. For Jewish community leadership, see Baltzell, *Philadelphia Gentlemen,* chap. 11.
34. Solomon, *Pioneers in Service,* 21.
35. Ibid., 10.
36. Baltzell, *Philadelphia Gentlemen,* 284.
37. Maxwell Whiteman, *Mankind and Medicine* (Philadelphia: Albert Einstein Medical Center, 1960); and Solomon, *Pioneers in Service.*
38. For the University of Pennsylvania, see Morais, *The Jews of Philadelphia,* 431–43; and for Harvard, see Albert Ehrenfreid, *A Chronicle of Boston Jewry: From the Colonial Settlement to 1900* (Copyright 1963 by Irving Bernstein). See also Samuel Eliot Morison, *Three Centuries of Harvard* (Cambridge: Harvard University Press, 1963), 57, 198, 203, 417, 422.
39. Bruce Kuklick, *The Rise of American Philosophy: Cambridge, Massachusetts, 1860–1930* (New Haven: Yale University Press, 1977), 407.
40. Kuklick, *The Rise of American Philosophy,* 407.
41. Lawrence R. Vesey, *The Emergence of the American University* (Chicago: University of Chicago Press, 1965), 288.
42. Theodore H. White, *In Search of History* (New York: Harper & Row, 1978), 41.
43. Ibid., 41.
44. Ibid., 40.

45. *Dictionary of American Biography,* supp. III, 94.
46. Allon Gal, *Brandeis of Boston* (Cambridge: Harvard University Press, 1980) 83.
47. Ibid., 180.
48. Ibid., chap. 5.
49. Ibid., 186.

36

The Ordeal of Civility

In our age of the rude, the crude, and nude, and the decline of table manners—to paraphrase a colorful chapter heading in John Murray Cuddihy's *The Ordeal of Civility: Freud, Marx, Levi-Strauss and the Jewish Struggle With Modernity*[1]—it is hardly surprising that a subtly rude book such as this one should have appeared on the shelves of my favorite campus bookstore last September. I purchased it at the proprietor's suggestion and read it with keen interest. Conspiracy theories of historical or intellectual causation are always fascinating.

Some time after reading this book I was asked to review it. My impulse was to decline the invitation. I felt much like Tocqueville, who delayed for some time before answering his friend Gobineau, who had sent him an advance copy of his book *Essai sur l'inégalité des races* for his comments. I too heartily dislike what Tocqueville called those "useless battles waged by the pen." At any rate, partly becuase my reactions to this book were so strong and unsympathetic, I eventually decided that I was duty-bound to have brief say.

The sociology of knowledge seeks the social roots of cultural values and ideas in order to make their content more understandable. This book is a brilliant example of the sociology of knowledge-gone-wild, or the crudest kind of sociological reductionism. For it is, I think, far less interested in contributing to our understanding of the ideas of Freud and Marx, for example, than in dismissing them as impolite products of Jewish resentment.

The central theme of *The Ordeal of Civility* is that diaspora Jews in Europe and America, from the giant generation of Marx and Freud, through the puny but successful American generation of Norman Podhoretz, Norman Mailer, and Saul Bellow, down to the outrageously impolite generation of Abbie Hoffman, have all been afflicted with what the author sees as the particularly Jewish disease of bad manners, or lack of civility, brought on by their "sociocultural status-humiliation" at the hands of the *goyim*. The theme, relentlessly illustrated and elaborated in endless metaphors, is thus summed up by Mr. Cuddihy:

> There is a respectable tradition that views great works of art as issuing from the psychological traumata of their creators (this is the view of Edmund Wilson's *Wound and the Bow,* for example). Socio-cultural wounds, it is my hypothesis, lie behind the ideological creations of the giants of the Jewish Diaspora. In Freud and Marx, as we have seen, the "inferior" Jew loses his inferiority and the mighty *goyim* are brought low. The "final triumph" of the Freudian hermaneutic, with its remedial reading of social delicts as medical symptoms, is its transvaluation—"the implication," Goffman tells us, "that *socially improper* behavior can be *psychologically normal*...and *socially proper* behavior can be *truly sick*" [my emphases]. The "final triumph" of Marxism is Marx's refusal to give a remedial and apologetic reading of the economic behavior of the Jews, describing it with unembarrassed bluntness, only to turn around and make this crude *Judentum* the very stuff (*Unterbau*) of the bourgeois civilization of the *goyim*.

This hypothesis is surely plausible and hardly one to quarrel with. On the other hand, the author is so obsessed with the "wound and the bow" that he tends to forget the arrows. Reading this book is very much like sitting in the Sistine Chapel endlessly discussing Michelangelo's social origins or physical deformities without ever looking up at the ceiling.

Almost half the book is devoted to unmasking what Mr. Cuddihy calls Freud's "modernization complex." And Marx suffered from the same complex. This means that the generation of Marx and Freud felt strongly that the warm, *shtetl gemeinschaft* had been displaced by modern society's cold, *goy gesellschaft.* (The tone of this book is revealed in the author's curiously continuous use of such terms as *goy, shtetl, shiksa, Agunah, Schadchen, goyisherkop,* and so forth.) According to Mr. Cuddihy, in order to unmask the gentility of Gentile society "Freud installed an id-'Yid' in the personality system of each of its members.... Europe's social pariah, the 'Yid,' becomes in this way everybody's psychological pariah, the id.... In one stroke, Freud, a new 'Moses' in his own fantasy, 'passes' his Jews into the Gentile *Gesellschaft* and 'converts' his Gentiles into 'honorary Jews.'"

According to Mr. Cuddihy's methodology, then, if we only look behind the scientific concepts of id and superego, of *gemeinschaft* and *gesellschaft,* we shall find the Yiddish id and the Jewish *gemeinschaft* at war with the *goy* superego and the Gentile *gesellschaft.* All very interesting, but a bit bizarre. Surely Gentiles have shown no less longing for *gemeinschaft* than Jews.

This volume, of course, has a lot to say about Freud's "unforgiving and uncivil" treatment of the various defectors from the psychoanalytic movement. Thus, for example, he dismissed the ideas of Adler as merely the products of a "Jew boy from a Viennese suburb" who made good among the *goyim*. Cuddihy shows how Phillip Rieff "handles this 'scandal' (Freud's coarseness must always be cleaned up) by saying that 'Freud would not suffer the false civility of separating ideas from men.'" But, in contradiction to Rieff and to the whole tone of this book, Mr. Cuddihy says in the next sentence that "just such a differentiation of men themselves from the ideas they hold is exactly what civility is, true civility." With this I should heartily agree. But the author seems to have no ability or inclination to separate ideas from the Jewish men who hold them, for he sees their ideas really as plots to unmask the shams of *goy* gentility.

Mr. Cuddihy and I would probably agree that all civilizations are based on what Yeats called a commonly agreed-upon "ceremony of innocence." As Mr. Cuddihy nicely puts it, Western civilization has been based on "the ancient idea of 'charity,' feudalized into 'chivalry' in the Middle Ages, secularized into 'courtesy' (and 'curtsy') in the seventeenth and eighteenth centuries, undergoing a final metamorphosis in the nineteenth century into the 'civility' of the emergent civil societies in the nation-states of the West." I would agree too with one of the major assumptions of this book—as Freud and Herzl, among many others, have put it—that all of us are anti-Semites. But there are two kinds of anti-Semitism: the pogrom and the polite variety. In America, from the generation of Edmund Wilson (a "WASP philo-Semite," according to Cuddihy) to our own, liberal intellectuals have taken the polite position. This position is, of course, opposite that of Marx, whose position, according to Mr. Cuddihy, "looks like anti-Semitism, but it isn't. It is anti-philo-Semitic."

At the moment there are an infinite number of signs that liberalism and polite anti-Semitism too are in retreat in America. In his self-assigned role as the unmasker of the unmasking ideologies of Freud and Marx, Mr. Cuddihy, in my opinion, is obsessively opposed to the liberal "ceremony of innocence." Between every line of this book lurks a kind of ill-mannered obsession with exposing the unreality of liberal philo-Semitism. He is, for instance, bound to expose the Jewish "eleventh commandment": "Thou shalt not reveal in-group secrets to the *goyim*."

And of course this is exactly what Hannah Arendt did, Mr. Cuddihy is pleased to tell us, in her well-known series of articles in the *New Yorker* on the Eichmann trial.

But (or so it seems to me) there is all the difference in the world between a Jew telling an anti-Semitic joke and his Gentile friend doing the same thing. This distinction is at the very heart of the liberal code, as opposed to the code of the members of the Racquet Club. And it has not been due to the *innocence* of liberals (most of the revelations about the Jewishness of Marx and Freud here have been covered, if in different and more judicious ways, by others), but rather to their observing an agreed-upon code of civility, or *ceremony,* of innocence. And ironically, John Murray Cuddihy, in exposing the weaknesses of polite philo-Semitism, has placed himself in the same impolite and tactless position he attributes to Marx and Freud. In other words, if one reserves impoliteness for the Jew, how is one to explain this very impolite book by a Gentile? Freud was free to admit his own impoliteness in "saying in public" what others of his circle, such as Breuer, Charcot, and Chrobak, saw but dared not say. By the same token, there is no doubt that Mr. Cuddihy has cleverly revealed, in a colorful style, what others of his turn of mind have seen but preferred not to say. I suppose that now all those whom Merton once called "fair-weather liberals" will feel more free to speak out.

What I am saying is that the clever and colorful parts of this book add up to an appalling lack of civility. Though Mr. Cuddihy may have the gift of prophecy and an understanding of all mysteries, he surely has not charity. Which, as Corinthians I:13 has taught us, is to have nothing—or, in any highly serious sense, to have not even the truth. All of which brings me back to Tocqueville and Gobineau. On January 8, 1856, Tocqueville wrote to his friend as follows: "What I disapprove of in the book I have told you before: it is less the work itself than its tendency, which I consider dangerous...." Tocqueville's observation is pertinent to this book.

Notes

This chapter was first published in *Worldview* 18, no. 2 (1975).

1. John Murray Cuddihy, *The Ordeal of Civility* (New York: Basic Books, 1974).

37

Drunk as a Lord, Sober as a Judge: The English Reformation and the Puritans

The new philosophy calls for all in doubt;
'Tis all in pieces, all coherence gone;
All just supply and all relation.
Prince, subject, father, son, are things forgot,
For every man alone thinks he has got
To be a Phoenix, and that he can be
None of that kind of which he is but he.
—John Donne

Virtue makes power, as the soul does sense,
And merit far exceeds inheritance.
George Chapman
The core of the Rebellion...are the universities.
—Thomas Hobbes

Walk worthy of the calling, wherewith ye are called.
—Ephesians IV:20

Charles Horton Cooley, in his brilliant essay, "Genius, Fame and the Comparison of Races," attempted to refute Galton's *Hereditary Genius* by arguing that the three most creative periods in western history—Periclean Athens, the Italy of Leonardo and Michelangelo, and the England of Shakespeare and Milton—could hardly have been produced by sudden genetic changes in the respective races but rather, must have been due to some particular kind of cultural conditions which demanded greatness and produced leadership.[1]

The American colonies were founded by Englishmen during this third creative period, in the century which began with the defeat of the Spanish Armada (and John Winthrop's birth) in 1588, and ended with the Glorious Revolution in 1688. It was a turbulent, violent and revolutionary age of change when such giants as Elizabeth, Cromwell, Raleigh, Sidney, Shakespeare, Ben Jonson, Donne, Spenser, Milton, Bunyan, Dryden, Hobbes, Locke, and such pioneers in science as Harvey, Bacon, Boyle and Newton walked onto the stage of history.

In understanding the roots of American traditions, it is extremely important, I think, to always bear in mind that, in the three and a half centuries of our history (1607–1967), more than a third was lived under British Colonial rule, and well over half by a population predominately British in origins. In spite of the modifying effect of a frontier environment, it was English cultural norms—in the family, in religion, education, law and government—which dominated the Colonial Period and retained their influence on the young nation throughout the nineteenth century. At the upper class and leadership level, moreover, the largely English ideal of the Christian Gentleman held sway until at least the beginning of the First World War. Finally, of course, it was the turbulent history of sixteenth and seventeenth century England which brought forth the Puritan ethic which we shall explore, along with the rise of Puritanism, in the following pages.

The English Reformation

The Reformation officially came to England under the Tudors who brought the country out of feudal anarchy, after the devastating Wars of the Roses, in order to produce a unified nation and state machine, more than a century before the centralization of France by Louis XIV, and more than three centuries before Bismarck unified Germany. Henry VII came to the throne in 1509, the year of Calvin's birth, and broke with Rome in 1534, the year of Calvin's conversion. Henry broke with Rome for political rather than theological reasons, in fact, he was hostile to the teachings of Luther and was awarded the title "Defender of the Faith" by the Pope in 1521 for his *Defensis Septem Sacramentorum.* At no time did he admit that in creed he was anything but an orthodox Catholic. As he needed a male heir in the interests of Tudor continuity, his desire for a divorce was for reasons of politics rather than passion. Nor was he theologically against the principles of monasticism; the great problem of the New Monarchy was one of financing a centralized state; thus he sold the monasteries (many of them in a state of corruption and decay anyway) to his friends and allies in order to raise revenue for the Crown and to consolidate his political position. His brilliant but much maligned public servant, Thomas Cromwell, moreover, took charge of the dissolution of the monasteries as part of his attempt to rationalize, even bureaucratize, the state machine, and spent much of the money received from their sale in strengthening the working hierarchies of the Church and state, as well as in improving education. When Henry VIII founded Trinity College and the first Regius professorships at Cambridge (1546), sufficiently endowed with the spoils of the monasteries, he in fact sowed a seed which was to eventually grow into the founding of Harvard College in the New World: the first head of Harvard College (Nathaniel Eaton) and the second president (Charles Chauncy) were Trinity men; and at Trinity were educated five of the first twelve Overseers of the College: Governor Winthrop, John Cotton, Hugh Peter, Thomas Weld and John Humfrey.[2]

As with so many other institutions in English history, the church followed the comprehensive and middle way: Canterbury stood squarely between the traditions of Rome and the innovations of Wittenberg and Geneva, following the views of the gentle Erasmus rather than those of Luther or Calvin. At the two universities, to which Henry appealed for the justification of his break with Rome, it was mostly those who belonged to the Erasmian and humanist groups who became leaders in the Church hierarchy.

In doctrine and worship, the English Church remained essentially Catholic throughout Henry's reign, and was only purged of its Catholicism during the brief reign of Edward VI where the Anglican Church did away with confession and the celibacy of the clergy; replaced Latin with the superb English prose of the *Book of Common Prayer;* replaced the mystical doctrine of the real presence of Christ at the Mass by a more Zwenglian interpretation of the Communion as a spiritual commemoration of the last supper ("Take and eat this in remembrance that Christ died for thee..."); and finally, in the Lutheran tradition, the wine and bread were given to the laity. In the meantime, the *Bible,* translated into English during Henry's reign, was being read by more and more Englishmen.

It seems to be the nature of man that all political and religious movements eventually split into right, left and center parties or groups. At first, the English Reformation divided into the moderate Anglican center which stood for a traditional church hierarchy established by law and backed, and eventually dominated, by the state; on the right were the unregenerate Roman Catholics, composed largely of the wealthy and conservative landed nobility; and on the left were those who came to be called "Puritans," originally a derogatory term applied to various types of extremists who all agreed on the need for purging the Church of all vestiges of Catholicism.

During the reign of Mary Tudor, right wing Catholicism came back into power and many of the more ardent Puritans exiled themselves on the Continent. These Marian Exiles were a dedicated group of sociologically successful men, including five bishops and five deans of the English church, and more than fifty doctors of divinity; eighty-seven of the exiles were graduates of Trinity College, Cambridge.[3] After the death of Mary, the Marian Exiles returned to England and Puritanism became a definite movement within the Church; it was against all formalisms such as the keeping of holy days, making the sign of the cross, elaborate vestments and stained glass windows; it stood for simplicity of worship and more rigid moral standards, determinism rather than free will, and a more rational approach to religion which centered on pulpit and preacher rather than altar and priest; truth was, above all, to be sought in the *Bible* rather than in the pronouncements of a sacred hierarchy.

Queen Elizabeth, devoid of strong religious convictions herself, sought to solve the religious question on the basis of political expediency. Though the Thirty-Nine Articles were more Calvinist than she would have liked, the Elizabethan settlement was an attempt to hold to the middle way. It was "not so much concerned to have everyone *think* alike as to *act* alike. Eternal salvation through correct belief was left to God and the individual, whereas the public aspects of religion were relegated to the state. All of this pointed towards a latitudinarianism in belief and uniformity in practice.[4]

In spite of her tolerance, Elizabeth was forced by the course of political events to finally outlaw Catholicism. Along with her excommunication by the Pope in 1570, and the twin threats from her Catholic cousin and legitimate heir, Mary, Queen of Scots, on the one hand, and of the possible invasion by powerful and Catholic Spain on the other, Elizabethan Englishmen began to see all native Catholics, and especially Jesuits (much like modern America's fear of Communists in their midst) as potential traitors plotting to overthrow their government.

At the same time, the Puritan movement on the left gradually split into three groups, Presbyterians, Independents and Separatists. Both the

Presbyterians and the Independents were content to remain within the established church; the Presbyterians hoped to reorganize the hierarchy along the lines of the Presbyterian *Book of Discipline*, while the Independents wanted the church to give more local autonomy to preachers and congregations. Both of these more conservative groups of Puritans were made up primarily of sociologically successful men of the kind that went into exile under Mary and who were, as we shall see, rapidly coming to the fore in law, medicine and science in the city of London, in the expanding universities and in the leadership of the countries as Justices of the Peace and members of Parliament; as Michael Walzer has put it, "the initial Puritan effort had been to turn gentlemen and magistrates into saints, to convert great men, so that hundreds would follow their example.[5] We are mostly interested in the Independents who, at first, a minority compared to the Presbyterians, rapidly came to the fore in the 1620s and led the way to Massachusetts Bay as well as the Rebellion under Cromwell, especially after the Presbyterians have been purged from the Long Parliament, just before Charles II was brought to trial in 1648.

While the Presbyterians and Independents were the heirs of Calvin and Geneva, where many of the more influential Marian exiles had settled, the Separatists were more in accord with the left-wing of the Continental Reformation. The Separatists, in the egalitarian, Anabaptist tradition, saw the established Church as an example of Anti-Christ or the Whore of Babylon and beyond all hope of reform; made up of more radical and less successful men, they met in small groups outside the Church and tended to congregate in the rootless urban environments such as London. Though Elizabeth more or less tolerated the Presbyterians and Independents, she was largely successful in suppressing the Separatist movement by the end of her reign. One small group of them, however, remained intact at Scrooby Manor in Nottinghamshire, eventually fleeing to Holland, and thence to the New World where they landed at Plymouth Rock. The ideal of Separatism did not die with its prosecution under either Elizabeth or the Stuarts but eventually led to the various left-wing sects, both political, such as the Levellers and Diggers, and religious, such as the Fifth Monarchy Men, Seekers and Quakers, all of whom came to the fore during the Rebellion.

In the meantime, under the first two Stuarts, the Court grew in size and became increasingly extravagant and corrupt. London, the seat of both the Court and the City, for example, tripled in size between the accession of Elizabeth and the death of James I (to some 300,000 souls, in spite of plagues in 1603 and 1624 which took the lives of more than 65,000 Londoners). It was during the reign of James I that the Puritans began to emphasize the need for a more rigid moral code in reaction to the dissolute, and even perverted, lives of so many Jacobean courtiers.

While Elizabeth had been able to control both Parliament and the Puritan movement, James I and then Charles I alienated both. Soon after coming to the throne, at the Hampton Court Conference in 1604, James tactlessly told the Puritan leaders that he would make them conform or "harry them out of the land." While James' arrogance and political indolence alienated the Puritans and parliamentarians, it was thought that the son of the Catholic, Mary Queen of Scots would be more tolerant, even favorable, towards Catholics. After the infamous Gunpowder Plot (1605) was uncovered, however, anti-Catholic sentiment rose to fever proportions and anti-Catholic legislation became increasingly severe. In this climate of opinion, a Catholic gentlemen, Sir George Calvert, later Lord Baltimore, obtained a charter for the establishment of a colony in Newfoundland (later exchanged for a Maryland charter in 1632).

If the arrogant and centralized Jacobean Court alienated, and thereby strengthened, both the Puritan and parliamentarian movements for decentralization of both church and state, James' successor, Charles I, along with his Archbishop, William Laud, finally provoked the exodus to Massachusetts and the Rebellion. Before discussing the Laudian reaction, however, it is important to see how the Puritan movement was deeply involved in the momentous secular changes which brought English society out of Feudalism and into the modern world in the century preceding the execution of Charles I in 1649.

Noble Anarchy

The problem of power, which always comes to the fore in ages of transition, is that of translating anarchical violence and coercion into new forms of social order or legal authority. No society of men has ever done away with violence; successful societies have been those which were able to control violence through its monopoly by a sovereign authority, whether it be the tribal chief or noble lord, the city state, empire or nation state—and, in our age of national and even local anarchy, in some system of world sovereignty. The anarchists within the emerging national community in sixteenth century England were the noble magnates whose power rested in their control of violence (as with anarchy in the present world community which results from the national control of violence.) Just as the United Nations today is still dependent on the nation state for its control of violence, so Tudor England still had to depend on the private military forces of the noble magnates. This was even so through the reign of Elizabeth. Though national armies had been assembled by the nation state by the time of the Armada, some 1,000 footmen and 1,600 horses were still supplied by the nobility and leading gentry. In 1588, for instance, the Earl of Pembroke wrote the following profession of loyalty to his Queen: "I will, whensoever it shall like you to command, attend your service with 300 horse and 500 foot at the least of my followers, armed at my own cost and with my own store."[6]

The rise of the New Monarchy under the Tudors, much like our own day, was quite naturally marked by violence. After all, Henry VIII did away with wives, relatives and trusted associates in the interest of the national (often his) will. Thus he beheaded Anne Boleyn and Catherine Howard, his cousin Exeter, rivals Buckingham, Suffolk and the Countess of Salisbury, along with once trusted advisors like Thomas More and Thomas Cromwell. Under the reign of Henry's son, the young Protector, Edward VI, the Duke of Somerset executed his own brother who wanted to marry Elizabeth and then was himself executed by Warwick, Duke of Northumberland. Bloody Mary, essentially a mild and sincere Catholic, was nevertheless forced by reasons of state to burn some 300 Protestants at the stake, including such leaders as the Cambridge reformers Cranmer, Ridley and Latimer. Elizabeth, a master politician of consensus who cared little for ideological or religious issues, was forced to less brutality than the rest of her family (though officially sanctioning it, she wept upon hearing of the beheading of her cousin, Mary Queen of Scots). The personal politics of assassination, however, continued throughout her reign.

As late as the 1570s, for example, the Earl of Oxford ventured forth from his castle with an armed following of client gentry, a retinue of personal servants, and a bodyguard of 100 "Tall Yeomen" dressed in distinctive livery with a Blue Boar on their left shoulders. Thanks to the studied neutrality of the Queen, he and many of his peers were allowed to commit murder after murder with complete impunity: "Both the brutality of their tactics and in their impunity from the law," writes Lawrence

Stone, "the nearest parallels to the Earl of Oxford...in the London of Queen Elizabeth are Al Capone and Dien O'Banion, Bugs Moran and Johnny Torrie in the Chicago in the 1920s."[7]

It is difficult for us to imagine the difference between the brawling Tudor nobility and the "quiet self-control" which Max Weber found in "the best type of English or American gentlemen" in his day (see below).[8] For it would not be far from the truth to say that the social character of the Tudor nobility had more in common with the innocent and brave Ulysses of Homer's heroic age than with the Eton-Oxford trained, public servants of the nineteenth century. Among the Earl of Oxford's peers, tempers were short, weapons to hand, impulsive and childish ferocity the norm and, of course, loyalty above the law. In personal relations, direct action was the rule: "In 1578 Edward Windham," writes Professor Stone, "was attacked on Fleet Street in broad daylight by twenty-five retainers of the 2nd Lord Rick, urged on by their master with blood thirsty cries of 'Draw Villains, draw,' 'Cut off his legs', and 'kill him,' an assault that Windham met by firing a pistol at his Lordship and then fleeing into the French ambassador's house."[9] Such stories could be repeated endlessly in that day of anarchy on the streets and in the countryside.

From Brawl and Duel to Law

The noble sport of lawless private brawling, along with the noble sport of war, declined after the turn of the sixteenth to the seventeenth centuries as English society moved from the Tudors to the Stuarts. Technological factors were of course important. We shall discuss war in a moment. Brawling declined as the deadly rapier and the pistol replaced the clumsy sword. Dueling, with its rigid code of rules, replaced the brawl, and then itself died down under the Stuarts. James I made strenuous efforts to curb the duel which seriously threatened the workings of his court. But it was the steadily increasing Puritan sentiments in England which partly explain why the duel never reached the heights that it did in France. Both the duel and the assassination, to the rational Puritan mind, were impulsive and irrational ways of handling private disputes. Gradually, even among the leisured nobility, law replaced violence in the settling of private disputes. "In the late sixteenth and early seventeenth centuries," writes Lawrence Stone, "more nobles and landed gentlemen acquired a smattering of legal education than at any time before or possibly since."[10] Like the members of Cafe Society or the Jet Set today, long drawn out law suits became the time-consuming sport of the leisured members of the nobility: When a well-known diarist of the period came up to London, "he looked forward to three pleasures, good food and drink, the society of pretty women and entertaining mornings at the law courts, watching the cases there."[11]

But the nobility were only taking part in the more general increase in the importance of the law. The legal profession, according to R. H. Tawney, increased by two-thirds between the decades of 1591–1600 and 1631–1640.[12] The increasing importance of lawyers in the increasingly rational-contractual society was, of course, followed by their rapid rise in wealth and the buying of land as an indication of social advancement. Thus E. W. Ives has noted that "between James I's accession and the calling of the Long Parliament, fourteen men presided over the courts of King's Beach and Common Pleas at Westminster: of these chief justices, two were created earls and one a baron, the families of five more were later raised into the peerage, and another four established dynasties of landed gentry which endured into the nineteenth century."[13]

The Rise of the Gentry

The rise of the lawyer was intimately related to the rise of the gentry. For it was the gentry, according to A. L. Rowse, who "essentially changed things, who launched out along new paths whether at home, or overseas, they achieved what was achieved, they gave what all societies need—leadership."[14] In many ways it was both those who rose into this class—from the yeomanry in the country or the lawyers and merchants in the city—as well as those who rose above it into the nobility—such new Elizabethan families of achievement as the Cecils, Bacons, Russells and Cavandishes who provided the dynamic leadership of the newly emerging society.

The dissolution of the monasteries played a vital part in bringing about this new society. Suddenly, over a decade or two, almost one-fifth of the land in England came on the *market* (contract vs status) for investment and secular ownership. At first, the new land went into the hands of the secular nobility. By the beginning of the seventeenth century nearly all the peerage, many of them "new men" of the Tudor period, held monastic lands. The secularization of land ownership was "accompanied by the abolition of confession, penance and the sale of indulgences, and by the destruction of altars, windows, statues, etc. all of which reduced popular respect for the more mysterious powers of the church, its sacraments and saints."[15] Most of these changes were completed in Edward VI's reign and were supported by the Puritan leaders who came to the fore in the century between 1540 and the revolution in 1640. At the same time, from the Marian reaction through the first two Stuarts, support of the church as against the Puritan reformers gradually became the order of the day at court: "no bishops, no king, no nobility."

The destruction of the sacramental and mystical church, as well as Henry's allowing the *Bible* to be translated into English, unwittingly led to the Puritan Revolution with its highly organized and ideological army, marching into battle singing psalms after an inspiring sermon by one of the Puritan ministers. Before the Revolution broke out, however, a social and economic revolution had already taken place. Although the dissolution of the monasteries at first brought the land into the hands of a narrow group of peers, most of the properties were resold, in the course of the seventeenth century, to country gentlemen and monied men from the city, most of them supporting the Puritan and parliamentary party against the church and crown: Charles I's Secretary of State saw the inevitable irony of history when he noted that "Henry VIII committed such sacrilege by profaning so may ecclesiastical benefices in order to give their goods to those who, being so rewarded, might stand firmly for the king in the lower house; and now the king's great enemies are those who are enriched by these benefices... O the great judgements of God!"[16]

Not only had the land passed out of the hands of the Church hierarchy and into the hands of the traditional nobility, a process of the secularization of power; when it was eventually resold to members of the merchant and gentry classes, it was put not only to secular but to more rational and far more profitable uses—in more capitalist forms of agriculture, in the extractive industries, and in manufactures, especially and at first in the clothing industry. The Marian exiles had brought back manufacturing and industrial techniques from abroad, and abbeys were converted into worsted mills, glass factories and iron works.

The merchants, gentry and lawyers were usually combined in one and the same person or family. It was, for instance, the grandfather of

John Winthrop, Governor of Massachusetts, who began the family's rise into the gentry class. As a successful clothier, Adam Winthrop founded the family fortune, got the freedom of the city of London, and finally obtained a grant in the manor of Groton, part of the dissolved monastery of Bury St. Edmonds, in East Anglia. Adam's son was trained in the law and then became auditor of St.John's and Trinity colleges at Cambridge. In the third generation, John Winthrop of Massachusetts, was born in the manor at Groton and educated at Trinity as well as at the Inns of Court, after which he came back to Groton where he became a Justice of the Peace at the age of eighteen. It was in the seventeenth century that the "J.P." (in the style of the Calvinist and Puritan ideal of the "magistrate") became the symbol of the country gentleman's rule in England (whose independence and autonomy Tocqueville was later to contrast with the sycophantic, courtier class in his native France).

This pattern of gentry-legal leadership was also illustrated in the career of Edward Coke, Elizabeth's Attorney General, who was the great rival at the Inns of Court of his famous enemy, Francis Bacon. While Bacon is now famous for his rationalizations of the new scientific philosophy, Coke is remembered as the brilliant, legal mythmaker and architect of the British common law tradition. Like Winthrop, Coke was born in East Anglia, near its informal capital city of Norwich, often called the "nursery of lawyers." Like Winthrop he went away to Trinity and the Inner Temple. In the course of his highly successful career at the law and in public office, Coke also made money and spent it wisely, unlike so many of his extravagant and noble contemporaries. When he died, hated by many and loved by few, he left some sixty manors as witness to his affinity with the gentry class in the country. He had made his money in the city but, like so many country lawyers, he also handled cases involving the buying and selling of land, in this age of increasing mobility (and increasing *contract,* as the sociologists would put it). As a mark of his arrival at the top, Coke was knighted by James I, who opened the mobile and status seeking seventeenth century by knighting some 900 men including Coke within four months of his coming to the throne in 1603 (one of the greatest inflation in honors in British history).

It is important to note that both Coke and Winthrop (and Oliver Cromwell) grew up in East Anglia, the Galilee of English Puritanism which Professor Morison describes with pride of race and region as follows:

> Here is our very homeland. In an afternoon's drive of seventy or eighty miles, we may visit Framingham, Ipswich, Dedham, Braintree, Boxford, Groton, Sudbury and Haverhill, and spend the night at Cambridge. Suffolk is the heart of East Anglia, the section of England, which according to Havelock Ellis' "Study of British Genius," has produced the greatest statesmen, scientists, ecclesiastics, scholars and artists in English history, and which has always been distinguished for a profound love of liberty and independence. In East Anglia, the Puritan movement bit deepest. From East Anglia came the heaviest contingent for the planting of Massachusetts Bay; and Massachusetts as colony and commonwealth, by every known test of eminence, has produced more distinguished men and women in proportion to her population, than any other state in the Union.[17]

The Alienated Intellectuals and the Universities

After the abolition of the monasteries, the new owners of the land collected the tithes and patronized the clergy. The Puritan clergy would never have been such an influential group if it had not been for this lay patronage. And it was these Puritan preachers, the alienated and polemical intellectuals of the Stuart period, who supplied the ideological propaganda for this age of change. For the pulpit was the major means of communication during the first half of the seventeenth century. It has been estimated that some 340,000 sermons were preached—in churches, at the Inns of Court, in parliament, in meeting halls in London, at the court at Westminster, and at the universities—between 1600 and the opening of the Revolution in the 1640s.[18]

Thomas Hobbes, obsessed with society's need for authority and order in an increasingly individualistic and revolutionary age, saw that the universities—which were training clergymen as well as an ever increasing number of gentlemen who would have previously been reared as clients in some noble household—lay at the very core of the rebellion: "The universities," he wrote in *Leviathan,* "have been to this nation, as the wooden horse was to the Trojans." Hobbes clearly saw "the chief leaders were ambitious ministers and ambitious gentlemen; the ministers envying the authority of bishops, whom they thought less learned; and the gentlemen envying the privy council, whom they thought less wise than themselves....Therefore I despair of any lasting peace among ourselves, till the universities shall bend...to the teaching of absolute obedience to the laws of the King and to his public edicts under the great seal of England."[19]

Hobbes was a critic of both his own Oxford and her sister, and far more Puritan, Cambridge. While Oxford was the older of the two universities, Cambridge rapidly came to the fore during the Elizabethan and Puritan ages. While Oxford tended to be Catholic, medieval, Anglican and Royalist both Cambridge and many of the Inns of the Court were more Elizabethan and eventually Puritan in character and in architecture. Elizabeth herself had been educated by Cambridge men and her bishops were more likely to have come from the new university.

At Cambridge, though Trinity was the great college of the new age, the founding of Emmanuel in 1584, and Sidney Sussex in 1595, provided important intellectual seedbeds of the Puritan Revolution in England, as well as for the founding of Massachusetts Bay and Harvard College; John Winthrop was a product of Trinity, John Harvard went to Emmanuel, and Oliver Cromwell to Sidney Sussex. Indeed Sir Walter Raleigh's reply to Queen Elizabeth's inquiries about the possible dangerous consequences of the founding of these new colleges was rather prophetic: "Far be it for me," said Sir Walter "to countenance anything contrary to your established laws, but I have set an acorn, which when it becomes an oak, God alone knows what will be the fruit thereof."[20]

The Church was, on the whole, understaffed with poorly trained ministers when Elizabeth came to the throne. In 1564, for example, Cambridge had about a thousand students, most of them coming from the poorer classes and preparing for orders. This number was increased to three thousand by 1623, at which size it remained for some two centuries thereafter. Oxford, the older and larger university also increased in size during this period. At both universities there was such an increase in the numbers preparing for the church, especially at the Puritan colleges, that there was a definite oversupply (about 100 more than were needed were coming down from Oxford and Cambridge each year after 1600). A contemporary of Hobbes saw the dangers resulting from an oversupply of intellectuals when he said that "learning without living doth but breed traitors as common experience too well showeth."[21]

Many of the best educated and more capable and politically-oriented preachers, denied living in local parishes, were forced to obtain lectureships. Thus the widow who endowed Sidney Sussex College at Cambridge also endowed a lectureship at Westminster and the total amount of charitable contributions to support lectureships, in the four decades preceding the Rebellion, far exceeded the sums given to supplement the stipends of parish clergy. These lecturers, concentrated in London and the larger population centers, were rootless intellectuals without the balancing particularistic routine of personal contacts on the intimate face-to-face parish level which was such an absorbing part of the lives of the local clergy. Yet they were the intellectual leaders of the growing Puritan oligarchy which led the social changes taking place in England in the years before the Rebellion.

The career of the Reverend John Preston provides an excellent example of the role of the parishless preacher. Born the son of a decayed gentry family in Northamptonshire, educated at Cambridge by a wealthy uncle, and determined to get ahead in the world, he nevertheless became one of the twice-born saints when he was converted by a sermon of John Cotton's (later the "Pope" of New England Congregationalism). But his saintly career was not without great worldly influence. "In 1622," writes Christopher Hill, "Preston was appointed Preacher at Lincoln's Inn, 'where he was assured many Parliament men and others of his best acquaintance would be his hearers'... Among Preston's intimate friends were the Earls of Warwick, Lincoln, Pembroke, Bedford, Lord Saye and Sele, the second Lord Brooke, Sir Richard Knightly,Sir Henry Mildmay, Lady Vare, Gilbert Pickering, Henry Lawrence. It was a nominal roll of the Puritan opposition. Preston also had 'formed a strong party in the City', where in 1617 he had been sworn a member of the East India Company (gratis), and bought *L* 400 worth of joint stock."[22]

Preston continued his leadership role at Cambridge: "In his six years as Master of Emmanuel," writes Professor Morison, "Preston left his stamp on the college, and on New England. He had the rare combination of social, moral, and intellectual distinction that always impresses the undergraduates; no personality of old Cambridge was so often and affectionately mentioned by the founders of New England. It was during his mastership that the number of founders reached its peak. Of important laymen were Bradstreet, Denison, the younger Saltonstall, and William Perkins; of ministers many more. Samuel Stone, inseparable colleague of Hooker, was 'instructed with the light' and 'nourished with the cup' at this time by his tutor Richard Blackerby, Thomas Shepard, the greatest evangelist of early New England, was converted by a sermon of the Master's in the college chapel; and it was during Preston's mastership that John Harvard entered pensioner."[23]

Scholars and Gentlemen

While Puritan saints like Preston at Cambridge were converting poor clerical scholars into polemical preachers, both Oxford and Cambridge, as well as the Inns of Court, were gradually becoming veritable finishing schools for the some of the gentry along with more and more younger sons of the nobility.

The dissolution of the monasteries, as we have noted earlier, proved to be a great boom to the development of the two universities, especially Cambridge, where Trinity, Emmanuel and Sidney Sussex were all founded on sites of medieval friaries.

In spite of the growing importance of education under Henry and Elizabeth, however, among a majority of the gentry and the nobility, in a still traditional society of status, stability and personal patronage, higher education was not widely valued. It was said, for instance, that the 1st Earl of Pembroke, a privy councilor under Elizabeth, could not read or write. Even the famous Cambridge educator and tutor of Elizabeth, Roger Ascham, outlined the ideal gentlemanly education as follows:

> To rise comely, to run fair at the tilt or ring, to play at all weapons, to shoot fair in bow, or surely in gun, to vault lustily; to run, to leap, to wrestle, to swim, to dance comely, to sing and play of instruments cunningly; to hawk, to hunt, to play at tennis and all pastimes generally, which be joined with labour, used in open place, and in the daylight, containing some fit exercise for war, or some pleasant pastime for peace, be not only comely and decent, but also very necessary for a courtly gentleman to use.[24]

But as the technical requirements of public service in the new nation state demanded less leisurely and military, and more intellectual and organizational, talents, new leaders such as William Cecil, Chancellor of Cambridge from 1559 till his death in 1598 and, under Elizabeth, one of the greatest public servants in all British history, saw the need for producing an educated elite. From this day on, the movement of the secular elite into the universities increased steadily until, in the 1620's for the first time, the sons of the gentry and the nobility exceeded in number the commoners preparing for orders.

This was also the period when certain selected boarding schools began to educate the youthful sons of the nobility and gentry into a common elitist culture. John Wilson, the first teacher at the Boston Church and later the most vehement opponent of Anne Hutchinson, was a product of Eton and King's College, Cambridge. Though early records are scarce, Lawrence Stone notes that "we have a glimpse of Eton in the early 1630s showing two sons of the Earl of Peterborough, a son of the Earl of Dever, two sons of the Earl of Cork, four sons of the Earl of Southampton, and two sons of the Earl of Northampton sitting down to dinner at the second table with knights' sons. The picture is a familiar one: Eton has arrived."[25] The ideal of elite education had now become, for those who could afford it, a matter of private tutors, boarding school, Oxford or Cambridge, the Inns of Court and finally a Grand Tour on the Continent. In accord with this new pattern, it is important to stress the fact that Oxford and Cambridge did not measure up to their Continental counterparts in either scholarship, research or learning. For men like John Choke, of Cambridge, former Marian exile, Provost of King's, Regius Professor of Greek, tutor to Prince Edward, and brother-in-law and close friend of William Cecil, thought the production of an educated elite prepared to rule was far more important than the production of scholars. And this tradition was carried on by men like Jewett at nineteenth-century Oxford and at Harvard, at least through the regimes of Eliot and Lowell. The ideal of this educated vanguard was described by Professor Morison in his *Founding of Harvard College,* as follows:

> A new upper class was arising. Enriched by the woolens trade or overseas commerce, glutted by the spoils of the abbeys, families like the Cecils, Russells, Greshams, and Winthrops wished to educate their sons as gentlemen, and prepare them for active life. Oxford and Cambridge colleges were appropriate dwellings for such youths. They offered an opportunity, in luxurious surroundings and congenial company to read the polite literature which Erasmus told them was necessary for a gentlemen's education. It is true that the University did not admit the logic of the situation—Englishmen seldom do. All students were supposed to be clerks and behave as such.... One can hardly exaggerate the importance of this intrusion of 'young gentlemen' into the English universities, for there they remain, and to Harvard they have come. Owing to the fact that England simultaneously received the Reformation, the Renaissance, and this notion of a gentleman's education, there was brought about an unwilling compromise between gentility and learning, a rubbing of shoulders between the poor scholar and the squire's son, that has made the English and American college what it is today.... To this sixteenth century compromise, become a tradition, we owe the common figure of the English-speaking world, "a gentleman and a scholar." Such were several among the leading founders of New England, and of Harvard: both Winthrops and both Saltenstalls, Downing and Brainstreet, Bollingham, and Peter Buckley, of whom Cotton Mather wrote, "His Education,...was learned, it was Genteel, and...Pious." To Harvard they brought a new zeal for scriptural religion and the

> humanist tradition. From her opening day, Harvard has included a large proportion of young men who had no professional intentions. They have been complained of by their more serious preceptors, these three hundred years. They have committed every sort of folly and extravagance. New colleges such as Williams and Amherst have been founded in order to provide a place where poor but pious youths could be educated for the ministry, uncontaminated by the "rakeshells," "bleeds," and "sports" of Harvard—and the same class of students have flocked to the new colleges. Even after countless examples of gentlemen who have become scholars and scholars who have become gentlemen by this illogical commingling, there are some people who would admit none to our colleges but serious students, and others who would set a standard of luxury and expense impossible for poor students. As long as Harvard remains true to her early traditions, rich man's sons and poor, serious scholars and frivolous wasters, saints and sinners, puritans and papists, Jews and gentiles will meet in her Houses, her Yard, and her athletic fields, rubbing off each other's angularities, and learning from friendly contact what cannot be learned from books.[26]

One wonders, after reading this paragraph, whether Harvard and others of her peers among American universities have not replaced this tradition in recent decades by the more Continental ideal? Have they not replaced the ideal of the "scholar and gentleman" with that of the SAT genius preparing to be a technical expert, and taught by all too many faculty members who lost their faith in the Choke-Jewett ideal and replaced it by an avid zeal for advancement through technical research and financially rewarding outside consultantships? As we shall suggest below, this may be one reason why anarchy reigns and leaders no longer lead.

London Science and Medicine

As was the case with the polemical Puritan preachers, so science and medicine grew up in the London of Elizabeth, financed and supported by wealthy merchants. Gresham College became the center of the new scientific movement and the 'New Philosophy' (four of the twelve founders of the Royal Society were professors there). "Sir Thomas Gresham (1518–79), merchant and financier, the son and nephew of Lord Mayors of London," writes Christopher Hill, "built the Royal Exchange and left the revenue from shops there jointly to the City of London and the Mercers' Company to found a college. Despite pleas from Cambridge his *alma mater* that the money might more appropriately be left to the university, Gresham followed the example set by many merchants who endowed grammar schools in the sixteenth century, and was careful to put control of his college in the hands not of clerks but of merchants like himself. He endowed seven professorships: in Divinity, Law, Rhetoric, Music, Physics, Geometry, and Astronomy, with higher stipends than Henry VIII had given the Regius Professors of Divinity at Oxford and Cambridge. Gresham College, like the Bodleian Library, was founded to combat Popery. The Professor of Divinity was naturally the senior professor: he was to employ his time in sound handling of controversies, 'especially against the common adversary of the Church of Rome.'"[27]

Gresham College was mainly a teaching rather than a research institution. Though formally controlled, as Gresham wished, by merchants rather than clerics, it was Henry Briggs, an "ardent Presbyterian" and first professor of Geometry, who built up the college and was of first importance in the intellectual history of his age (he finally resigned in 1620). Like Briggs, none of the leading scientists of the early seventeenth century—Gilbert, Harvey, Bacon, Napier—held university posts. Medical men went abroad to study at Padua or Leiden. In England, Gresham college served as a center of the advancing sciences, as a kind of center of adult education and especially as a congenial meeting place for the followers of the New Philosophy.

Francis Bacon, twice related to Thomas Gresham, was the major propagator of the New Philosophy, even though most of his voluminous writings were in the fields of religion, politics and law. His *Novum Organum,* published in 1620, was the landmark book which urged the substitution of the inductive methods of science for the deductive and authoritarian model stemming from Aristotle and Aquinas. His influence on this period was shown by the fact that his *Essays* went through seventeen editions before 1639 and a large proportion of his works were published during the two years before the outbreak of the Great Rebellion (1640–1641).

The New Philosophy had a strong levelling influence on the hierarchical Elizabethan and Stuart ages. The Copernican Revolution, as Hill has shown, "democratized the universe by shattering the hierarchical structure of the heavens; Harvey 'democratized' the human body by dethroning the heart."[28] As far as Bacon was concerned, "one researcher was as good as another, and better than any mere speculative scholar." It was no wonder that Bacon's ideal was a career open to talents and the advancement of able men regardless of their degree or profession.

Robert K. Merton, in his intensive study of the lives of early members of the Royal Society, clearly demonstrated the affinity of Baconians and scientists with Puritanism.[29] Others have shown that most of the Baconians were of the parliamentary party. By the end of Elizabeth's reign, according to A. L. Rowse, Bacon himself was "one of the leading Commons Men...on innumerable committees and a speaker always heard with attention."[30]

Parliament Comes to the Fore

Beginning in the Elizabethan period and rapidly accelerating under the Stuarts, the Puritan legal gentry progenitors of the emerging rational-legal age of achievement and mobility found their political home in the House of Commons. In the first place, during the course of the sixteenth century, Commons increased in size from 296 to 462 members, Elizabeth adding 32 boroughs and 64 members. And the gentry contributed most of the members; though by law there were supposed to be 90 knights of the shire and 372 burgesses, there were actually only some 60 real burgers, and the rest of the MPs being members of gentry families, the heads usually representing the shire and minor members representing the local boroughs. A father often sat from the shire while his son represented the local town. This suited the townsmen as it relieved them of the costs of maintaining a representative at Westminster, as the gentry were usually able to support themselves. On the whole, the members of Parliament were rich and local in character; some of the richest men in England sat in commons and it has been estimated that, by 1628, their average income was three times as high as those sitting in the House of Lords; local roots are suggested by the fact that, in 1640-1641, the members included 122 local sheriffs, at least 219, and probably more, Justices of the Peace, and over 250 members of local commissions. In accord with the spirit of the age, it is interesting that the proportion of university men sitting in Commons increased from 35 percent in 1593 to 57 percent by 1640.[31]

In a paragraph from Wallace Notestein's excellent book, *The English People on the Eve of Colonization,* we are imaginatively shown how the country gentry, deeply rooted in the affairs of their local shires, gradually grew, much like Topsy, into a self-conscious, national class of parliamentarians during the early years of the seventeenth century: "When

Sir Faithful," writes Notestein, "went up from Devonshire to Westminster he learned that members from other shires, with local loyalties as intense as his, were after all men of his own kind. Some of them were cousins of his, or cousins of cousins. Sir James, whom he had met on a committee, was a Somerset man, but knew his brother-in-law. Sir John, with whom he had happened to sup at the Seven Stars off Fleet Street, and who was on the same committee, was a Glaucestershire man, but kin to Devonshire friends. Both Sir John and Sir James thought the King was going too far. They talked sensibly, and mentioned to Sir Faithful abuses in their counties which he had seen in his. The more he thought and talked about it, the more he was inclined to go along with the committee in the statement being framed to answer the King. Gradually, in committee service he was finding himself a working unit of an assembly that was dealing with the affairs of the Kingdom and he discovered, almost with surprise, that such affairs were as compelling as those of Devonshire. No loyalty is so binding as that of common service. Sir Faithful was becoming a House of Commons man."[32] And men like Sir Faithful, in contrast to the extravagant and dissolute courtiers of the day, were more than likely to be men of Puritan convictions.

From Status to Contract

"The force of revolutionary movements most truly shows itself," wrote William Haller in *The Rise of Puritanism,* "in the gradual transformation of the imaginative ideals, of the habits of thought and expression, the moral outlook and modes of behavior of whole classes of people. Puritanism was such a movement. It was, then, more than an affair of church government, more than the logomachy of church and schismatics. It was a new way of life, overrunning all the divisions which from time to time seamed its surface and threatened in each of its manifestations to disrupt the existing society. Eventually it was to subdue English civilization to an attitude of mind, a code of conduct, a physiology, a manner of expression, the vitality of which far outran the particular forms of religious life which sprang up from time to time in the course of its irresistable advance."[33] Max Weber, of course, also saw these same "transformative" qualities in Puritanism: "Cavaliers and Roundheads," he wrote in *The Protestant Ethic and the Spirit of Capitalism,* "did not appeal to each other simply as two parties, but as radically distinct species of men, and whoever looks into the problem must agree with them.... It was the power of religious influence, not alone, but more than anything else, which created the differences...."[34]

In the preceding pages, we have briefly outlined in concrete detail some of the more important ways in which the Puritan movement was related to the new way of life which was gradually emerging in Tudor and Stuart England. In the more abstract terms of classical sociology, this transformation may be conveniently summarized conceptually as a movement from a predominately *sacred* or *status* form of society to one of increasing *secularism* and *contract,* or, in Max Weber's own system of ideal types, from a *traditional* to a *rational-legal* system of order and authority.[35]

And it all began, as we have seen, when the land of England (the principle source of wealth and status at the time) was changed from a more or less sacred trust, of the Church, the family or the community in common, to a secular commodity to be bought and sold on the market. At the same time, the large extended family ideal, as for instance the noble household with its host of retainers, clients and even private armies, was gradually replaced by the Puritan ideal of the immediate family of parents and children; marriage changed from one of scared and sacramental status to one of secular and contractual legality (eventually allowing for divorce as Milton urged); the mystery and magic of the sacramental church and priestly hierarchy gradually gave way to the rational and educated minister preaching to an autonomous congregation; the ascribed parish gave way to the voluntary congregation and the pulpit replaced the altar as the sermon did the processional (Christopher Wren in rebuilding St. Paul's Cathedral, his masterpiece, recognized these changes when, even after the Restoration, he replaced former processional space with pews for families listening to sermons); from the intermittent rhythms of work and play symbolized by the irregular calendar of Saint's days to the regular and more rational rhythms of rest on Sunday brought about by the Puritan Sabbatarian movement; from work as a necessary evil to work as a positive good; from avarice as a vice to accumulation as a virtue; from poverty as Godly and inherent in the nature of things to poverty as a vice to be eradicated by moral regeneration of the poor; willfulness was replaced by discipline, being by doing, personal ornament by personal accomplishment, and the extravagant and ceremonious ideal of the court by the simple style of the country;

from aestheticism to asceticism, from breeding and heroism to learning and civility, and from the duel and personal honor to the law and individual rights; from the authority of scholasticism to the empiricism of science; from personal loyalty to public service; from the brawling, and often drunken, lord to the disciplined and sober judge; from war as the sporadic and unorganized sport of kings and noble lords to war as a highly organized crusade against anti-Christ, as witness the New model Army; and finally and most central to our thesis, from a hierarchy of *ascriptive estates* to an achievable, *functional class* system based on talent and merit.

Now it is important to emphasize the fact that these broad changes in the structure of English society, while they may be conveniently conceptualized as a movement *from* status *to* contract, were primarily a matter of changing central tendency, *more* or *less, both/and* rather than *either/or.* In other words, the English social structure, from the seventeenth century down to the present, has always been characterized by a subtle blending of the social forces of *both* status *and* contract, both inheritance and merit, lords and lawyers, (and lordly lawyers), both the sacred and the secular, both tradition and law (and the traditional law, i.e., the common law), and so forth. The point is that, in the transitory Tudor and Stuart periods, the former and traditional social forces were, for the first time, rather rapidly being challenged by the latter. Finally, of course, although such of Elizabethan culture was still maintained by John Winthrop's generation, it was primarily the latter forces of contract, the emphasis on merit and work as ends in themselves, and other values which may largely be summed up in the Calvinist concept of the *calling* and the ideal of the "Magistrate" which were brought to New England. In the 1630s for instance, when two leading Puritan peers, Lord Say and Sele and Brook, were contemplating emigration to New England, they wrote to the authorities in Massachusetts in an attempt to obtain assurance that their family claims to dignity and status would be respected. The official reply was characteristic of how the New Philosophy had been transplanted to the New World:

> Where God blesseth any branch of any noble or generous family with a spirit and gifts fit for government, it would be taking God's name in vain to put such a talent under a bushel, and a sin against the honor of magestry to neglect such in our public elections. But if God should not delight to furnish some of their posterity with gifts fit for magistracy, we should expose them rather to reproach and preju-

> dice, and the commonwealth with them, than to exalt them to honour, if we should call them forth, when God doth not, to public authority.[36]

Birth and breeding along with talent, yes; birth and breeding alone, definitely and politely, no. No wonder that Tocqueville, two centuries after the founding of New England, saw the American aristocracy as composed of a functional class of lawyers rather than a hereditary caste of lords.

The Crisis of Order and Authority

All this is another way of saying that 17th century England was passing through a crisis of authority largely because the authority of sacred traditions was being weakened by competing forms of secular authority. Perhaps when a "new philosophy calls all in doubt" and "all coherence" appears to be gone, as John Donne felt about his age, it is better to speak of a vacuum, rather than a decline, in authority; when seen in historical perspective, most periods of so-called declining authority turn out to have been due to the fact that the advocates of new forms of authority usually couch their rhetoric in terms of the need for more equality as against the evils of established authority at any given time.

Thomas Hobbes obsessed as we have been with the fear of anarchy and the need for order and authority, went to the heart of this problem in his *Leviathan,* appropriately published in 1651 in the midst of the Great Rebellion. Though its classic greatness, of course, transcended his age, it is important to see that it was taken by many of his contemporaries to be a defense of absolute monarchy, and by others, especially the great historian of the Rebellion, Clarendon, as an iniquitous defense of the authoritarian ways of Oliver Cromwell. As Hobbes was loyal to his noble patrons, the Cavendishes, who supported him in the luxury of "Chatsworth" and as he presented his thesis first to King Charles, it is probable that he himself, as well as the supporters of King and Court, thought he was writing in support of the established authority of the day. Actually Hobbes was an extreme atheist, and, when read with care and historical hindsight, his *Leviathan* was definitely on the side of the new philosophy, science, materialistic individualism, and rational, contractual associationalism. He saw the decline of the sacred chain of being and the need for a new and secular chain of command; he saw that when passive faith in the sacred cross had declined it must be replaced by the secular sword, which had, of course, always been hidden behind the cross anyway. The greatness and timelessness of his book was that it laid bare the need for any and all *de facto* establishments, in the tradition of Machiavelli, to exercise power and force if need be in the defense of order and authority as against the everpresent threat of anarchy, or a "war of every man against every man." With no faith in the sacred himself, it is no wonder that Hobbes, as well as many materialists after him, saw life as "a perpetual and restless desire for power after power, that ceaseth only in death."

It is in the work of Max Weber that we find, I think, an attempt to go further than Hobbes. Weber, like Hobbes, lived in a period of increasing disorder and what he called "the disenchantment of the world." And he was also obsessed with the problem of order and authority, as David Little has recently shown in his excellent book, *Religion, Order and Law.*[37]

In many ways, it is too bad that Weber's *Protestant Ethic,* which concentrated on the narrow problem of the relationship between Calvinism and rational capitalism, has become so famous. For it was only a small part of his enormous body of work on the sociology of world religions. In this broader work, Weber tried to show how one of the major functions of religion, in all societies, was that of legitimating order and authority: "In general," he wrote, "it should be kept clearly in mind that the basis of every system of authority, and correspondingly of every kind of willingness to obey, is a belief, a *belief* by virtue of which persons exercising authority are lent prestige."[38] What Weber was saying is that no secular institutions or systems of hierarchy and authority are ever self-justifying; rather they always depend, in the long run, on some form of religious sanctification, which is what we mean, I think, by the concept of the sacred used in a broad sense. Here Weber is going beyond Hobbes by admitting that while secular power is inevitably and ultimately backed by the sword, it must always be clothed, in an ordered society, by some form or other of sacred authority: men are willing to obey it because they believe it to be legitimate (or sacred).

Weber concentrated his discussion of religion and capitalism,in the *Protestant Ethic,* on the post-Restoration period when pure Puritanism was on the decline in both Old and New England. His broader interest in the legitimizing function of religion, and the transformative characteristics of Puritanism, are much more appropriately applied to an understanding of the period under discussion in this chapter (when dynamic Puritanism was at its height and on the offensive). Using his concepts of *traditional, charismatic* and *rational-legal* authority, Weber was convinced that the main problem facing the modern western world was how the sacred, patrimonial-traditional order of Medieval society could be replaced by a rational-legal order. And he saw that legitimation of the new order was the function of the Calvinist-Puritan ethic.

In a system of legal-rational authority, he wrote, "submission does not rest upon the belief and devotion to charismatically gifted persons, like prophets and heroes, or upon sacred traditions, or upon piety toward a personal lord and master who is defined by an ordered tradition, or upon piety toward the possible incumbents of office fiefs and office prebends who are legitimized in their own right through privilege and conferment. Rather, submission under legal authority is based upon an impersonal bond to the generally defined and functional 'duty of office.' The official duty—like the corresponding right to exercise authority: the 'jurisdictional competency'—is fixed by rationally established norms, by enactments, decrees, and regulations, in such a manner that the legitimacy of the authority becomes the legality of the general rule, which is purposely thought out, enacted and announced with formal correctness."[39]

Though he does not make the point explicitly in the above paragraph or, as far as I know, elsewhere, a sympathetic understanding of Weber's point of view would, I should think, postulate a change from the "sacredness" of status and hereditary privilege to the "sacredness" of office and law. Here Weber's concept of *charisma* becomes appropriate. Unfortunately, most of us have become accustomed to think of charisma in highly individualistic and personal terms. But Weber also used the terms *lineage-charisma* and the *charisma of office,* though these concepts were hardly as systematically worked out as was his more familiar usage which stressed its personal aspects. Furthermore, as Parsons has pointed out, Weber's use of charisma is almost identical to the concept of the sacred as used by Durkheim for whom religion was the "collective sacred".[40] In other words, the social changes issuing out of the Puritan revolution in Tudor and Stuart England were *not* a trend from tradition to reason, but rather from the *sacredness* of tradition to the *sacredness* of rational-legal objectivity, from the divine right of kings to rule their passive subjects to the divine right of magistrates to enforce the law, which active citizens obey because they consider it right and proper (sacred) to do so.

Weber's preoccupation with the sociological function of religion as the supreme institution for legitimizing authority lies at the very core of this essay. Calvinism and Puritanism, in the sixteenth and seventeenth centuries, were legitimatizing a new authority which attracted a host of sociologically successful, but masterless, men whose conversion brought them faith in their ability to transform the world. It is no wonder in our day when anarchy is once again loosed upon the world, that Yeats saw the only answer in some sort of *Second Coming.* When the sacredness of any established authority declines, perhaps new authorities are only born in either the personal charisma of a religious leader or of another caesar.

The Calling, Worldly Asceticism and the Magistrate

The idea of the calling lies in the very heart of the Protestant legitimation of authority. In contrast to the purposeful Puritan, "the normal medieval Catholic laymen," wrote Weber, "lived ethically, so to speak, from hand to mouth." His life had no rational plan or distant, this-worldly goal, but consisted largely of a series of spontaneous acts. Salvation, a matter of his following the traditional and magical rituals of his Church, was definitely not of this world but of the next. In other words, he had no vocation. In the Catholic double standard of morality, only monks followed a definite vocation, which Weber described as follows:

> Without doubt Christian asceticism, both outwardly and in its inner meaning, contains many different things. But it has had a definitely rational character in its highest Occidental forms as early as the Middle Ages, and in several forms even in antiquity. The great historical significance of Western monasticism, as contrasted with that of the Orient, is based on this fact, not in all cases, but in its general type. In the rules of St. Benedict, still more with the monks of Cluny, again with the Cistercians, and most strongly the Jesuits, it has become emancipated from planless other-worldliness and irrational self-torture. It had developed a systematic method of rational conduct with the purpose of overcoming the *status naturae,* to free man from the power of irrational impulses and his dependence on the world and on nature. It attempted to subject man to the supremacy of a purposeful will, to bring his actions under constant self-control with a careful consideration of their ethical consequences. Thus it trained the monk, objectively, as a worker in the service of the kingdom of God, and thereby further, subjectively, assured the salvation of his soul. This active self-control, which formed the end of the *exercitia* of St. Ignatius and of the rational monastic virtues everywhere, was *also the most important practical ideal of Puritanism.* In the deep contempt with which the cool

> reserve of its adherents is contrasted, in the reports of the trials of its martyrs, with the undisciplined blustering of the noble prelates and officials can be seen that respect for quiet self-control which still distinguishes the best type of English and American gentlemen today.[41]

The Catholic vocational ideal of monasticism, with its emphasis on rationally organized work and other-worldly asceticism, was, then, replaced by Protestantism with the ideal of the secular calling and this worldly asceticism. Not only monks but all men were now called by God to some particular vocation which they must fulfill in a rational and ascetic way for the Glory of God and the good of society as a whole. While central to Continental Calvinism, the idea of the calling was even more central to English Puritanism; and its theological meaning was far more systematically worked out and emphasized by the leading English casuists than was the case of Luther or even Calvin.

Williams Perkins, who wrote a lengthy treatise on vocations, was, according to Christopher Hill, "the first systematic theologian in England..., the dominant influence in Puritan thought for forty years after his death" in 1602.[42] Calvin, Beza and Perkins were often considered "the trinity of the orthodox." Perkins' many books, translated into French, Dutch, Italian and Spanish, were widely read in both Old and New England. "No books," according to Haller, "were more often to be found upon the shelves of succeeding generations of preachers, and the name of no preacher recurs more often in later Puritan literature.[43] Among his students and followers at Cambridge, in addition to the already mentioned Preston of Cambridge, the Inns of Court, and John Cotton of New England, were William Ames, the theologian of New England Congregationalism, and many future leaders in both church and society. At less than fifteen years of age, for instance, John Winthrop went up to Trinity in the year of Perkins' death. He never met Perkins and dropped out of college when he fell seriously in love and was married in 1605. After marriage, however, he studied under one of Perkins' followers, the local preacher to his wife's family, seeking, he later noted in his *Journal,* a "better assurance by the seal of the spirit" which was greatly influenced by the "reading of Mr. Perkins." Throughout his tenure of office in Massachusetts, Winthrop tried to fulfill the calling of magistrate as outlined in the work of Perkins.

Like Hobbes and Weber, Perkins was obsessed with the problem of order. In the Calvinist tradition, he saw order as imposed upon man by

God, and disorder and anarchy as the work of Satan. He propounded an ordered and fixed society held together by functionally interdependent callings. "God is the General," he wrote using military analogies in the style of Calvin. "God is the General, appointing to every man his particular calling and as it were his standing: and in that calling he assigns unto him his particular office; in performance whereof he is to live and die."[44] And each calling required reciprocal duties in the interests of society as a whole. "A vocation or calling," he wrote, "is a certain kind of life, ordained and imposed on man by God, for the common good...For example, the life of a king is to spend his time in the governing of his subjects, and that is his calling; and the life of a subject is to love in obedience to the Magistrate...A master of a family, is to lead his life in the government of his family, and that is his calling."[45]

Every Christian must fulfill his calling by giving it the best of his ability; at the same time, due to men's having differing abilities as gifts from God, society must be hierarchically arranged: "Persons are distinguished by order," Perkins wrote, "whereby God hath appointed, that in every society one person should be above or under another; not making all equal, as though the bodie should be all head and nothing else."[46]

Though hierarchally organized on the basis of gifts and importance of function, all callings were of equal importance in the eyes of God. What Perkins, and the whole Puritan movement after him, was doing was to substitute the personal pride of birth and status with the professional or craftsman's price of working to do one's best in one's particular calling; the good Christian society needed the best of kings, magistrates and citizens; above all Perkins emphasized the work ethic from Genesis: *"In the sweat of thy brows shalt thou eat thy bread."*

All good Christians must follow honorable callings; dishonorable callings, as well as leisure and time-wasting, were conclusive to disorder and the work of Satan: "As for example, such as live by usury, by carding and dicing, by maintaining houses of gaming, by plays and such like...are no callings or vocations, by a vocation from God and his ways."[47] Perkins was quite naturally strongly against the idle members of the gentry or nobility who lived "no proper calling" but spent "their time in eating, drinking, sleeping and sporting." As with the leisure class at the top, so with the poor idlers at the bottom of society: "It is a foul disorder in any commonwealth, that they should be suffered rogues, beggars, vagabonds; for such kind of persons commonly are of no civil society or corporation, nor of any particular Church; and are rotten legs, and arms, that drop from the body."[48] It is the function of the magistrate "to punish him for his idleness, and compel him to labor." Both the idle rich and poor who "choose to live in their own liberty, are in the kingdom of darkness, that is, Sinne and Satan." Though idleness was indeed a sin, Perkins did see that God "admitteth lawful recreation... because it is a meanes to refresh either bodie or minde, that wee the better see the duties which pertaine unto us." One is reminded of the over-worked American executive who plays golf on Sundays, only to keep in shape for the rigors of the work week ahead. The Sabbatarians of Perkins' generation were preparing the way for these more secular mores of a post-Protestant but still puritanical age (which "anti-squares" are now bound to demolish in favour of a new aristocratic ethic, modeled on the "lilies of the field" and "Merrie", rather than Protestant, England).

Puritanism was indeed no radical or sentimental creed but a new and demanding system of order and authority. Nor was it an order which either encouraged directly, or permitted, the unregulated and individualistic pursuit of profit which so many critics of Weber have accused him of attributing to the Protestant ethic. Perkins was very explicit on this point and emphasized an organic rather than individualistic view of social structure: "A vocation or calling," he asserts, "is a certain kind of life, ordained and imposed on man by God... *for the common good:* that is, for the benefit and good estate of mankind. In man's body there be sundry parts and members, and every one hath his several use and office, which performeth not for it self, but for the good of the whole body; as the office of the eye, is to see, of the ear to hear, and the foot to go. Now all societies of men, are bodies, a family is a body, and so is every particular Church a body, and the commonwealth also... And that common saying, "*Every man for himself, and God for us all,* is wicked, and is directly against the end of every calling or honest kind of life."[49]

For Perkins and his generation of English theologians, possibly even more than for Calvin, the office of magistrate was the highest secular calling. As Michael Walzer has written with great insight, "magistracy was a far better description of the saints' true vocation than was either capitalist acquisition or bourgeois freedom." It was this magisterial ideal, after all, which drove the English gentry, with a new zeal after their conversion, first to seek local office ("J/P") and then to go up to London to fulfill the duties of their calling as Members of Parliament; conversely, the rising city merchant or lawyer not allowed by this new ethic to remain satisfied with the mere accumulation of wealth, was led to purchase land, seek local office, and then come back to Parliament. This ideal of magistracy was, of course, not in contradiction to, but rather in accord with—and reinforced with systematic and disciplined zeal—the more leisurely, aristocratic ideal of *nobless oblige,* a concept implying the duties of one's advantageous, inherited estate. One must bear in mind that the Puritan ethic, especially in the generations of Perkins down through John Winthrop and Oliver Cromwell, was a conservative and rigidly hierarchical one which, in this sense, did not run counter to the traditional, aristocratic ethic; rather it took hierarchy, and even ascription, for granted but, as the same time, placed far more emphasis on the rational carrying out of the duties of office, as against the spontaneous fulfillment of the duties of birth alone. As suggested above, Winthrop was greatly influenced by Perkins, especially his writings on the role of magistrate. And it was the Elizabethan Puritan ideals which Winthrop and the founders of New England brought to the New World. Edmond S. Morgan has nicely described them as follows:

> Winthrop was not relying simply on his own notions of what a governor should be. A governor was a magistrate and sixteenth-century Puritan mentors like William Perkins had described the calling of a magistrate with some care. Throughout his tenure of office in Massachusetts Winthrop sought to practice the virtues described in Perkins' treatise on Christian equity. A magistrate was supposed to enforce the laws, but this did not mean an unbending application of the same punishment in every case. This much any fool could do. The calling of the magistrate demanded special talents to fit the punishment to the crime, to bend the law to the particular circumstance. Winthrop earned a good deal of criticism for his 'leniency,' but he was always ready to defend his practices as proper to his calling. The social and political implications of the idea of the calling were conservative. It had been common in the Middle Ages to think of society as composed of different "estates" into which men were born and lived out their lives... The idea of estate lingered on in Puritan times, helping a man to discern his calling; and the two conceptions easily merged in the often repeated Puritan warning that every man, for the good of society, must remain in the place to which God had called him. Winthrop could remind the emigrants to Massachusetts that God had so ordered the condition of mankind that 'in all times some must be rich and some poore, some highe, and eminent in power and dignity; others mean and in subjection,' and he was properly shocked when a servant suggested to a master who was unable to pay him that they change places.[50]

Though the callings of the magistrate and the minister stood at the apex of the Puritan pyramid of authority, Perkin's generation of theologians were by no means against "*wealth per se.* "Men are honored for their riches," wrote Perkins (and has been so quoted out of full context by those who accuse Calvinism of sanctifying pure acquisitiveness) and then carefully qualified himself: "I mean not riches simple but the use of riches; namely as they are made instruments to uphold and maintain virtue." In order words, not riches alone but riches rightly used for the benefit of society as a whole lay at the heart of the Puritan ethic.

Wealth-seeking, status-striving and conspicuous consumption, which Veblen found so characteristic of late nineteenth century capitalism, were post-Puritan and materialistic, as well as aristocratic, courtly and pre-Puritan vices. As we have seen, Perkins postulated, not a status-striving and mobile, but an ordered and fixed hierarchy of callings ordained by God. He was explicitly against conspicuous consumption which was, in his day, but especially under the Stuarts, all too characteristic of the "worldly" society at Court. On the contrary, one must, according to Perkins, "honor God with thy riches" and live ascetically: "in daily attire, the noblest are the plainest," he warned those who consumed beyond their means or proper station in life.

The Puritan emphasis on worldly-asceticism and the right use of riches led to the tradition of private philanthropy which has been characteristic of both this country and England even down to our own day (witness the endowing of private schools and universities, from Oxford and Cambridge to Harvard and Yale, in contrast to government support of education on the Continent). W. K. Jordan, in his *Philanthropy in England, 1480–1660,* has shown how this tradition was grounded in the ethic of the merchants and Puritan gentry rather than in that of the peerage. For example, whereas the merchants and tradesmen contributed 71.65 percent, and the gentry 15.46 percent of all funds donated in the period 1601–1640, the nobility contributed only 5.17 percent. Puritan philanthropy made possible the independent lecturers, but it also endowed and founded new schools, scholarships and corrected the abuses of poverty. As Christopher Hill observes in the following comment on the implications of Professor Jordan's studies of philanthropy:

> Merchants and Puritan gentry, by endowing schools, scholarships, assistance for apprentices and other charities studied by Professor Jordan, were building up a society in which careers were much more open to the talents than in the traditional hierarchical society which crown and Laudian clergy wished to reserve. (It is significant that the peerage played a far smaller part than the merchants in these endowments.) 'Power,' Professor Jordan concludes, 'as history has so often demonstrated, flows inevitably to those unafraid to assume the burdens of respon-

sibility.' The instrument of the transmission of power in the Civil War was the New Model Army, an army of the careers open to the talents.[51]

And Sir William Petty, physician to Cromwell's army, political economist and a pioneer in the science of statistics, applied this New Philosophy to education when he said that none should be "excluded by reason of the poverty and inability of their parents: for hereby it hath come to pass that many are now holding the plough that might have been made fit to steer the state."[52]

Charity, in the Catholic and aristocratic ethic, involved a spontaneous, stop-gap, and Christian response to the always visible and suffering poor, in a world where poverty was accepted and even cherished. Philanthropy, on the other hand, was an infinitely Puritan and rational response to social conditions which as Perkins as well as the scientist, William Petty, saw, were dysfunctional to the best use of talent in promoting an efficient division of labor, or hierarchy of callings. In contrast to charity, there was nothing sentimental about the systematic philanthropy of the Puritans; it transformed society and, inadvertently, brought power and authority to the participants in the new emerging world of careers open to talent.

It is no wonder that most Americans have worshiped work rather than their ancestors. For, from the very beginning, the ideal of the calling has played a major role in forming our dominant cultural traditions. Although, for example, Williams Perkins, the Elizabethan, would hardly have understood Benjamin Franklin, the archetypical mobile American, nor his substitution of Perkins' God as General for God as Mechanic, he would, one feels certain, have sympathized with the concept of the calling as implied by Franklin in the following advice given to perspective immigrants to Pennsylvania: "The Americans," said Franklin, "do not inquire of a stranger, '*What is he?*' but, '*What can he do?*' If he has any useful art, he is welcome; and if he exercises it, and behaves, well, he will be respected by all that know him; but a mere Man of Quality, who, on that account, wants to live upon the Public, by some office or salary, will be despised and disregarded. The Husbandman is in honor there, and even the Mechanic, because their employment is useful. The people have a saying, that God Almighty is himself a Mechanic, the greatest in the Universe; and he is respected and admired more for the variety, ingenuity, and utility of his homework, than the antiquity of his family."[53]

Exodus and Revolution

A good case can be made for the argument that revolutions are the products rather than the producers of social change. Just as Tocqueville saw that the seeds of the French Revolution were sown in the centralizing measures of Louis XIV, so the English Revolution of the sixteen-forties and fifties was a product of the social changes in Tudor and Stuart England which we have attempted to describe and analyze in this chapter. Great social changes, unfortunately, are almost always accompanied by gradually accumulating reactionary sentiments which eventually come to the fore in concrete events and personalities, often leading to violence and revolution. Thus the immediate cause of both the English Revolution and the Puritan migration to Massachusetts Bay was the coming to power, in the sixteen twenties, of Charles I and his famous (or infamous) ally, Archbishop Laud.

It is indeed interesting that two of the greatest monarchs in English history were women; both were parsimonious and pragmatic and possessed the usual feminine disregard for ideology; both commanded tremendous loyalty and admiration from their close political associates; both reigned in periods of transition, when one age was dying and a new one trying to be born; and both were filled to the brim with their own unique and curious attributes of personal *charisma* (some said that Elizabeth maintained her virginity partly to enhance her love affair with the whole British public). Just as the seeds of our violent twentieth century were sown in the relatively ordered age of Victoria, so the seeds of the violent seventeenth century were sown during the reign of Elizabeth (both died at the opening of the two centuries). Just as Darwin, Marx and Freud were all essentially Victorians, so men like Perkins, Coke, Gresham, Bacon, Harvey, Winthrop and Cromwell were all essentially Elizabethans.

Elizabeth had, as in many ways had her father, been able to brilliantly (and charismatically) blend the old with the new, and she died in bed. But the Stuart were an entirely different story, and Charles I died on the scaffold. In contrast to the parsimonious and judicious virgin Queen, James I was an indolent, extravagant and fearful monarch (he went around his court in loosely flowing robes which hid a coat of armor underneath). He feared, not only the plotting intrigues of his sycophantic court, but also parliament and the Puritans (whom he alienated almost immediately after coming to power, at the Hampton Court Conference).

Unfortunately, Robert Cecil, who continued the Tudor competence of royal administration in spite of James' nepotism and cronyism, died in 1612. He was eventually replaced by George Villiers, parvenu founder of a family line which steadily produced brilliant leaders down through British history to Winston Churchill, who was made Earl and finally Duke of Buckingham by James. After 1618, Buckingham controlled the royal patronage and, as with many founders of the best families, to his own enormous profit. James arrogantly tried to place himself above both parliament and the law. During the decade following 1611, there was only one brief and sterile parliament, in 1614. James finally dismissed Coke from the Chief Justiceship, in 1616, and continually thereafter threatened the independence of the judiciary.

Charles I came to the throne in 1625. Of a far more serious turn of mind than his father, Charles had, nevertheless, neither the talent nor the will to rule. He remained under the sway of Buckingham who was finally, to the relief of many Englishmen, assassinated in 1628, the same year William Laud was made Bishop of London. Laud, a sincere and self-righteous High Church Anglo-Catholic, soon was elevated to the Archbishop of Canterbury where he proceeded to attack the Puritan party with great puritanical zeal. Determined to oust the last vestiges of Calvinism from the Church, he restored much of the traditional ritual, including the doctrine of the "real presence" at Mass, confession, and clerical celibacy (no wonder he was suspected of Popery).

In response to the Laudian reaction, there seemed to be only two alternatives open to the Puritan opposition—escape or revolution. The last parliament before the revolution in 1640 was dissolved by James in 1629; at its final meeting violence reigned and the speaker had to be held down, weeping violently, in his chair. In the meantime, many Puritans began planning to leave England to establish a new England overseas.

In March, 1629, a group of East Anglians secured a royal charter from the king and formed the Massachusetts Bay Company, which granted large powers of government within the territory covered by the charter. There next occurred a very characteristic, if surprising, move by a group of leading stockholders who themselves expected to come to America. In late July, John Winthrop, Isaac Johnson, son-in-law of the Earl of Lincoln, Thomas Dudley, the Earl's steward, and several others met together at the Earl's residence in Sempringham. Here it was agreed that those stockholders who planned to go to the New World were to secretly buy up the shares of all those who planned to remain in England. Even though those who remained at home might be good Puritans and sympathetic to the ideals of the New Zion, things might change; any way, the move was symbolic of the New England ideal, which was not democracy, equality or even freedom, but *self-government*. The leaders were taking no chances with absentee control. As Cotton Mather later put it: "We came hither because we would have our posterity settled under the pure and full dispensations of the gospel, defended by *rulers which should be ourselves.*"

Some four months later, on August 26, 1629, twelve men met in secret at Cambridge (possibly at Emmanuel) and finally decided to emigrate, "provided that the government of the colony, together with the patent, be first transferred to us." The general court of the company so voted a few days later and elected Winthrop governor of both the company and the colony. Word was spread among families and friends of stockholders and the following March sixteen vessels led by the *Arabella* sailed for the New World. By the end of the year, some nine-hundred passengers had landed on the shores of Massachusetts Bay and settled at one of the five towns along the shores of Boston harbor. Conditions were severe and the colony just managed to hold its own until 1633 when Laud became Archbishop of Canterbury and the prosecution of Puritans was intensified. The great migration then began, and a floodtide of Englishmen departed for the shores of Massachusetts Bay in the decade preceding the outbreak of the Puritan Revolution.

Notes

This previously unpublished chapter was written in 1970.

1. Charles H. Cooley, "Genius, Fame and the Comparison of Races," *Annals of The American Academy of Political and Social Science* (May 1897): 317–58.
2. Samuel Eliot Morison, *The Founding of Harvard College* (Cambridge, MA: Harvard University Press, 1935), 87.
3. For a thorough discussion of the exiles under Mary, see Christina Garrett, *The Marion Exiles* (Cambridge: Cambridge University Press, 1938), and H. C. Porter, *Reformation and Reaction in Tudor Cambridge* (Cambridge: Cambridge University Press, 1958), chap. 4.
4. Roland H. Bainton, *The Reformation of the Sixteenth Century* (Boston, MA: Harvard University Press, 1952), 201.
5. Michael Walzer, *The Revolution of the Saints* (Cambridge, MA: Harvard University Press, 1965), 64.

6. Lawrence Stone, *The Crisis of the Aristocracy 1558–1641* (Oxford: Oxford University Press 1967), 101.
7. Ibid., 113.
8. Max Weber, *The Protestant Ethic and the Spirit of Capitalism* (New York: Scribners, 1958), 119.
9. Stone, *The Crisis of the Aristocracy,* 109.
10. Ibid., 312.
11. E. W. Ives, "Social Change and the Law," in *The English Revolution 1600–1660,* ed. E. W. Ives (New York: Barnes and Noble, N. Y., 1968), 120.
12. R. H. Tawney, "The Rise of the Gentry," *Economic History Review* (1941): 21.
13. E. W. Ives, "Social Change," 116.
14. A. L. Rowse, *The England of Elizabeth* (New York: The Macmillan Company, 1951), 235.
15. Christopher Hill, *Puritanism and Revolution* (London: Secher & Warburg, 1965), 38.
16. Ibid., 39.
17. Samuel Eliot Morison, *Builders of the Bay Colony* (Boston: Houghton Mifflin Company, 1958), 52-53.
18. Walzer, *Revolution of the Saints,* 325.
19. From Thomas Hobbes, *Behemoth,* as quoted in Mark H. Curtis, "The Alienated Intellectuals of Early Stuart England," *Past and Present,* 23 (1962).
20. While this quote has been attributed to Raleigh by several authors, Morison is probably correct in attributing it to Sir Walter Mildmay, Elizabeth's chancellor of the exchequer. See *Builders of the Bay Colony,* 107.
21. See Mark H. Curtis, "Alienated Intellectuals."
22. Hill, *Puritanism and Revolution,* 240.
23. Morison, *The Founding of Harvard College,* 103.
24. Quoted by A. L. Rowse, *England of Elizabeth,* 531.
25. Stone, *Crisis of the Aristocracy,* 310.
26. Morison, *The Founding of Harvard College,* 54-57.
27. Christopher Hill, *Intellectual Origins of the English Revolution* (Oxford: The Clarendon Press, 1965), 34.
28. Ibid., 112.
29. R. K. Merton, "Science, Technology and Society in 17th Century England," *Osiris* 4.
30. Rowse, *England of Elizabeth,* 307.
31. For the sources of figures and other information in the above paragraph, see Rowse, *England of Elizabeth,* 304 ff., Stone *Crisis of the Aristocracy,* chap. 12.
32. Wallace Notestein, *The English People on the Eve of Colonization* (New York: Harper *Torchbook* 1967), 196.
33. William Haller, *The Rise of Puritanism* (New York: Harper, 1957), 18.
34. Weber, *Protestant Ethic,* 88-89.
35. See H. S. Maine, *Ancient Law* (London, 1861), H. H. Gerth and C. Wright Mills, *From Max Weber: Essays in Sociology* (New York: Oxford University Press, 1946); A. M. Henderson and Talcott Parsons, *Max Weber: The Theory of Social and Economic Organization* (New York: Oxford University Press, 1947), chap. 3.
36. Stone, *Crisis of the Aristocracy,* 348.
37. David Little, *Religion, Order and Law: A Study of Pre-Revolutionary England* (New York: Harper *Torchbooks,* 1969).

38. Quoted in ibid., 7.
39. Ibid., 9.
40. Talcott Parsons, *Sociological Theory and Modern Society* (New York: The Free Press, 1967), 50.
41. Weber, *Protestant Ethic,* 118.
42. Christopher Hill, *Puritanism and Revolution,* 215.
43. Haller, *Rise of Puritanism,* 64–65.
44. Quoted from Edmund S. Morgan, ed. *Puritan Political Ideas 1558–1794* (New York: Bobbs-Merrill Company, Inc. 1965), 37.
45. Ibid., 36.
46. Ibid., 51.
47. Ibid., 37.
48. Ibid., 52.
49. Ibid., 39.
50. Ibid., xvii.
51. Christopher Hill, *The Century of Revolution 1603–1714* (New York, W. W. Norton & Company, Inc. 1961), 103.
52. Ibid., 181.
53. Quoted by Morgan, *Puritan Political Ideals,* xxxviii.

Index